Legal Science in the Early Republic

Legal Science in the Early Republic

The Origins of American Legal Thought and Education

Steven J. Macias

LEXINGTON BOOKS
Lanham • Boulder • New York • London

Published by Lexington Books
An imprint of The Rowman & Littlefield Publishing Group, Inc.
4501 Forbes Boulevard, Suite 200, Lanham, Maryland 20706
www.rowman.com

Unit A, Whitacre Mews, 26-34 Stannary Street, London SE11 4AB

British Library Cataloguing in Publication Information Available

Library of Congress Cataloging-in-Publication Data

Names: Macias, Steven J., 1977- author.
Title: Legal science in the early republic : the origins of American legal thought and education / by Steven J. Macias.
Description: Lanham : Lexington Books, 2016. | Includes bibliographical references and index.
Identifiers: LCCN 2016010687 (print) | LCCN 2016011127 (ebook) | ISBN 9781498519465 (cloth : alkaline paper) | ISBN 9781498519472 (electronic)
Subjects: LCSH: Jurisprudence—United States—History—19th century.
Classification: LCC KF380 .M33 2016 (print) | LCC KF380 (ebook) | DDC 340.1092/273—dc23 LC record available at http://lccn.loc.gov/2016010687

∞™ The paper used in this publication meets the minimum requirements of American National Standard for Information Sciences Permanence of Paper for Printed Library Materials, ANSI/NISO Z39.48-1992.

Printed in the United States of America

Contents

Acknowledgments

Many thanks are in order. First, the SIU School of Law has been a supportive environment for a new scholar, allowing me time to complete the research and writing of this book as well as supporting conference presentations of the same. Library Director Doug Lind has gone out of his way to make sure that I had access to everything I needed to complete this work. Praise is also due to the two other institutions where I briefly spent time, also in supportive environments: California Western School of Law and the University of Oregon School of Law.

The idea of a career as a legal historian was sparked when I took Jack Rakove's courses on race and the Constitution and the history of constitutional interpretation as a senior at Stanford University. I was then encouraged and supported at UC Berkeley to a degree far undeserved by the late Tom Barnes whose courses on English legal history and Tudor-Stuart Britain broadened my horizons to new possibilities in Anglo-American legal history. The intellectual fires were further stoked by studying with Harry Scheiber and David Lieberman. The structure and the fundamental ideas of this work owe much to my discussions with David of early drafts of various chapters and for that I will always be grateful. Paula Fass also contributed in ways that she could never imagine. Finally, with respect to the Berkeley crowd, I thank Barbara Shapiro for reading the manuscript and giving it her stamp of approval.

Much of this work is the direct result of my intellectual experiences at the Bentham Project at University College London under the direction of Phillip Schofield. Not only did I find in Jeremy Bentham an agreeable thinker whose ideas still have resonance some two-hundred years on, I became convinced that early-nineteenth century US intellectuals found him agreeable as well. I could not imagine a better steward of the Bentham legacy than Phillip Schofield to whose patient mentorship I am forever indebted.

Finally, I would like to thank those responsible for the production of this book, especially Kate Tafelski, Ashleigh Cooke, other members of the editorial team at Lexington Books, and Robert Swanson of Arc Indexing, Inc. Their patience with me was greatly undeserved. Thanks also to Professor Michael Ariens for his close reading of the manuscript and his suggestions for improvement, which I am certain made it a better work.

The introductory chapter is a revised version of an essay that first appeared as "Legal Thought from Blackstone to Kent and Story," in *A Companion to American Legal History*, eds. Sally E. Hadden and Alfred L. Brophy (Malden, MA: Wiley-Blackwell, 2013), 484–505.

An Introduction to the History of Law in the Early Republic

Speaking at century's end, Oliver Wendell Holmes, then chief justice of the Massachusetts Supreme Judicial Court, explained in an 1899 bar association address that lawyers ought to embrace "an ultimate dependence upon science because it is finally for science to determine, so far as it can, the relative worth of our different social ends."[1] But Holmes was not the first to articulate the value of science as the ultimate arbiter of social struggle to the American jurisprudential tradition. Nearly a century earlier, a loosely connected group of legal intellectuals began critiquing the American legal system and developing a consciously conceived "legal science" as a means of bolstering the reputation of the legal profession among the learned disciplines and as a means of raising the new nation's cultural prominence in the international arena.

The early American republic was alive with ideas, and lawyers were major participants in the intellectual debates concerning the young nation's future. Thoughtful lawyers grappled with questions such as, Would America follow the common law of England, or would the country work to develop a native jurisprudence based less upon precedent and more upon utility? To what extent was law similar to the natural sciences, thus requiring a liberal education in order to discover its fundamental axioms, as opposed to the specialized training necessary to master the artificial reasoning that characterized existing English law? What was at stake in these questions was more than simply professional speculation about how to attract more business. The answers to these questions were no less important than determining whether the revolution would continue beyond the political realm, through the legal spectrum, and down to the intellectual and metaphysical outlook of intelligent American society. In other words, within these discussions about the nature of early American law, we can detect that certain lawyers were affected by much more than what modern legal historians call the socioeconomic context of the times. Instead, there existed a vibrant intellectual climate in which elite lawyers engaged in deliberate efforts to philosophize about the human condition in a heretofore untried and untested state of social organization. What follows is an intellectual history of law informed by a pragmatic understanding that ideas have mattered to the concept of law in the past, just as much as they should matter to the practice of law in the present.[2]

LAWYERS IN THE EARLY REPUBLIC: THE LARGER HISTORICAL DEBATE

When one immerses oneself in the early nineteenth century literary and legal periodicals, it is impossible not to appreciate the extensive effort by legal elites to create a new system of American law in the first half of the nineteenth century. By "legal elites," I mean prominent lawyers and judges who wrote extensively for the public and the profession in periodicals and treatises. Members of this set of elites frequently knew each other, or at least knew of each other from their widely circulated writings. Members of this group varied in degrees of influence and productivity and were by no means geographically exclusive. The most remarkable finding is the general tone of agreement on the need for improvement of the English common law and the need to consciously set out a uniquely American position.

One might think that William Nelson had already discovered the "Americanization" of the common law and that Morton Horwitz had described the "transformation" of the same.[3] Yet, there is another historiographical tradition, led in part by Michael Hoeflich, who argues that little attention has been paid to "high legal culture."[4] If there is one thing this group of "legal elites" was insistent about, it was the need to rebuild American law from as eclectic a mass of source material as possible. This frequently included foreign law, especially from contemporary European civil law nations, as well as Roman law. But perhaps more surprisingly, these men looked to non-traditional legal sources with which to craft the new "legal science."[5] There is a suggestion of a heavy influence of European natural law philosophy, especially in the development of American notions of equity. There is also constant fascination with the progress of the natural sciences, which gave to many the hope that law could be advanced in a similarly rigorous fashion. Hence, we frequently hear how law needs to be given a more solid foundation from which sounder deductions can take place. Finally, a number of legal scholars emphasized the role of the "science of political economy" in the development of American law. Three of the leading American political economy texts were written by practicing lawyers: Daniel Raymond (1820),[6] Thomas Cooper (1826),[7] and Willard Phillips (1828).[8] By all accounts these texts were successful, but with far less unanimity as to the doctrines of political economy. The most successful, and most controversial, that of Daniel Raymond, was, by its fourth edition in 1840, entitled *The Elements of Constitutional Law and Political Economy*, the "constitutional law" part being an addition to the new edition.[9] Again, we see a strong faith in the "science" of political economy permeating the thinking of this group of legal elites.

This work challenges some of the older historiography exemplified by Lawrence Friedman—the "greatest of American social-legal historians," according to Robert Gordon.[10] Friedman critiqued Perry Miller's classic work on the "Legal Mentality" in antebellum America, claiming that Miller's search for systematic legal thought was in vain because of the "lack of a great jurisprudential school in the early days of the republic." Friedman backed up his assertion by noting that unlike civil law systems, common law systems were not dependent upon "scholars" to serve as authoritative guides; rather, "cases and enactments" made the law in early America. "Therefore there was no *need* for a system of jurisprudence, and none sprang up. The common law countries were weak in philosophy of law."[11] Nearly forty years later, Friedman reiterated his belief that Miller's work was "not very enlightening," but he now acknowledged that "the literature on legal literature and legal thought is not entirely satisfactory," thus implying that such a literature is at least worth having.[12] Although Friedman is correct that the historiographical output on early American legal thought over the past half-century is far from ideal, one also wonders whether the early critiques by socio-legal historians stunted the growth of this field of historical inquiry.

This work is written in the spirit of Miller, although I have extended my research to "technical legal material [such] as case reports and statutes," which Friedman criticized Miller for ignoring.[13] The cases support the findings from the works of "formal jurisprudence." Further, a number of the "treatises of important lawyers" were explicitly undertaken as a critique of actual cases decided and real arguments made in court and their authors felt no need to "hide the fact" as Friedman had hypothesized.[14] Moreover, citation to Roman and civilian authorities and political economists by lawyers and judges was not out of the ordinary. Nor was it unusual for these same lawyers to be interested in the "science of legislation," thus affecting the development of statute law, not to mention the fact that a number of these legal elites were legislators themselves at both the state and congressional levels. However, part of my argument is that there was a deliberate attempt to increase the power of the judicial branch, sometimes at the expense of the legislative branch, as there lingered, to varying degrees, a suspicion of democracy among the vast majority of these legal elites.

SITUATING THE EARLY REPUBLIC

The legal scholars of the early republic did not arise in a vacuum, but instead were preceded by a colonial and revolutionary bar that has its own complex history and historiography. The general consensus among historians is that the late eighteenth century bar was theoretically unsophisticated. One of the realities facing colonial lawyers was that they had to wear multiple hats, unlike their more specialized English counterparts. Thus John Adams noted in 1758 that the American lawyer "must do the duty of a counsellor, a lawyer, an attorney, a solicitor, and even of a scrivener."[15] Combined with the fact that many colonial judges were laymen untrained in the law, American lawyers enjoyed neither the time nor incentive to develop a learned jurisprudence. "Needless to say," explains Daniel Boorstin, "colonial America produced no great legal systems or encyclopaedias. What it did produce were the varied, dispersed, and miscellaneous efforts of hundreds of laymen, semi-lawyers, pseudo-lawyers, and of a few men of solid legal training."[16] William Nelson, in emphasizing the overarching importance of precedent, explains the low level of intellectual effort: "Americans of the prerevolutionary period expected their judges to be automatons who mechanically applied immutable rules of law to the facts of each case."[17]

Nevertheless, the political struggles that the colonists experienced with Parliament forced the revolutionary leaders to think systematically about the nature of law. Whether colonial legal thinkers ever adhered to a true natural law paradigm, as Nelson suggests, by the time the pre-revolutionary struggles began, there existed "a basic ambiguity in the American mind about the nature of law that was carried into the Revolution." Gordon Wood explains that the Americans "were firmly committed to the modern notion of statute law based on legislative enactment—a commitment implicit in their resort to fundamental law and written charters."[18] Contrary to Boorstin, "colonial adjudication was not simply a matter of applying some kind of crude, untechnical law to achieve common-sense 'frontier' justice." For Wood, "by the middle of the eighteenth century, in Massachusetts and New York at least, colonial jurisprudence approached very closely that of the English."[19]

Wood's thesis is supported by a number of shorter studies on pre-revolutionary lawyers. Daniel Coquillette discusses John Adams's self-conscious attempt to distinguish himself at the bar by studying Roman law. Adams, along with other practicing lawyers, would meet in a formal reading group in 1765 to discuss the civilian natural law writers.[20] Likewise, John Jay, while a practitioner in New York's colonial courts, would gather with fellow lawyers to moot points of law.[21] Interestingly, both Adams's and Jay's groups contained individuals who would later take up the loyalist cause, perhaps indicating that legal and constitutional thought could remain distinct only for so long.

In a sense, this work picks up where Wood left off, arguing that the early republican bar carried forth the modernization efforts even more so than Adams's and Jay's cohorts. But the important point to emphasize is that the subsequent efforts of the legal elites were on par with the intellectually focused efforts of Adams and Jay. To the extent the law was used instrumentally, it was primarily for creating a moral society via the jurisprudence of legal science.

THE CULTURAL HISTORY OF LAW

As previously mentioned, a key starting point for post-revolutionary jurisprudence is Perry Miller's Pulitzer Prize-winning *The Life of the Mind in America: From the Revolution to the Civil War*, published posthumously in 1965, in which he proclaimed, "the great issue of the nineteenth century" was "the never-ending case of Heart versus Head."[22] Several years before he composed the relevant chapters of *Life of the Mind*, Miller became interested in what he called, "the legal mind." Miller was fascinated by the debates in the 1820s and 1830s over codification of the common law. At the time he was writing, in the late-1950s and early-1960s, the standard explanation for any sharp division in public life was political (just as it would later be economic). Hence, labeling the codifiers as Jacksonian Democrats and the anti-codifiers as conservative Whigs satisfied many historians about why lawyers would divide on such a question—but not Miller. In fact Miller said that to accept the political motivation "as the full explanation is to settle for a shallow comprehension of the American mind."[23] Instead, Miller discovered beneath the surface of this legal debate, "a basic problem for American culture"—how far did the revolution extend? What did it mean to be a civilized nation? What was the meaning of the frontier? Like the novelists Miller had previously studied, the lawyers were concerned about something "which transcended the particular forms or the language," they were concerned "to ascertain the meaning of America."[24]

Nearly twenty years after Miller's *Life of the Mind* appeared in print, Robert Ferguson noted, "little has been added to Miller's insistence that lawyers and legal thought were crucial to literary development in the antebellum period." In *Law and Letters*, Ferguson chose to emphasize how "the struggle for a collective identity imposed aesthetic and intellectual boundaries" that were particularly legal in character and uniquely understood through the medium of the lawyer-writer's literary output.[25] Ferguson's main insight was that in the antebellum era, "the bond between knowledge, general literature, and law remained paramount, and the epistemological implications involved would shape the meanings Americans attached to all three concepts."[26]

In explaining the sources of legal knowledge, Ferguson latched on to American legal scholars' frequent praises of Blackstone as revelatory of "the lawyer's epistemological self-confidence." What the Americans were really praising was Blackstone's organization and eloquence—his true accomplishment. Because there was a dearth of native statutory and case law, early American lawyers looked to mastery of "more generic proficiencies," such as philosophy, history, and rhetoric, in determining professional competence. What Blackstone did was to "convert general knowledge into design and then into power in places where others found only confusion."[27]

Few historians who studied Blackstone's own thought or early American legal thought would disagree with Ferguson. Daniel Boorstin viewed the *Commentaries* as the product of Enlightenment views of history, science, religion, and moral philosophy. He concluded that Blackstone's work was a product of its time, exhibiting then-existing tensions in English culture between logic and mystery.[28] Michael Lobban, although agreeing that eighteenth-century lawyers found law in more general bodies of knowledge, concluded that Blackstone's effort was actually a challenge to this epistemological eclecticism. English lawyers challenged the *Commentaries* as too superficial.[29]

It makes sense that American and English lawyers would view Blackstone's efforts differently. If Blackstone was indeed a challenge to legal orthodoxy, as Lobban believes, then it is understandable why the English bar would view Blackstone's apparent simplification of their profession as an affront. However, for that very reason, Americans found Blackstone's endeavors to be a blessing. The simpler it imposed order on a new nation's laws, the better.

The search for order, of course, is not a theme unique to the historiography of the early republic, but it nevertheless is an enduring one. Central to that search for order is the role of law. Historians explaining the common law's resilience in the United States (despite overt attacks upon it) have turned to the stability it provides in an otherwise volatile culture. This very question motivated Miller in the first place.

Miller began "The Legal Mentality" by retelling James Fenimore Cooper's story of frontiersman Natty Bumppo. In Cooper's Leatherstocking Tales, Miller found explanatory binaries that illuminated the cultural struggles in the new nation. On Bumppo's side was the heart and its associated elements: nature, wilderness, common justice, instinct, and feelings. The Jeffersonians advocated this side, preferring cultural, if uncultivated, independence through native means to dependence on more sophisticated English ways. These democratic republicans also had a Protestant preference for popularizing specialized knowledge, which, for law, meant putting law books into people's hands. Bumppo was interesting to Miller because Cooper's character is eventually subdued and civilized by none other than one Judge Temple, the law incarnate.

The other side—and, in the early republic, the victorious one—was dominated not by the heart, but by the head. The head was associated with society, the intellect, formal law, and artificial restraints on conduct. Politically, Federalists (also identified as aristocrats and monarchists by their enemies) and then Whigs dominated this side of the spectrum. Rather than natural, instinctual justice, these conservatives relied on the common law for the rules of society. The head side had a preference for Blackstone and, it seemed, other English standards of excellence.

Recent cultural historians basically confirm Miller's thesis that support for the idea of the common law had more to do with abstractions than with concrete economics or political affiliation. Marshall Foletta's story of second-generation "young Federalists" in *Coming to Terms with Democracy* focuses much more on their patriotic hopes and visions than on their partisan intrigues. Foletta explains their support of the common law, not as a means of maintaining a Federalist stronghold on the judiciary, but as a means of maintaining a cultural aristocracy impervious to the uncouth designs of the Democrats. "Young Federalists" created institutions such as common schools, universities, civic and philanthropic organizations, and literary journals, all designed to reinforce an idealized cultural hegemony.[30] The common law, especially as taught in the emerging law lectures of the 1820s and 1830s, kept at bay those less qualified to practice this "real science." It was not that the young Federalists naively resisted the rising democratic tide sweeping across the country—they wanted to find ways to channel it into an orderly framework. As Foletta explains, "Holding this framework together was a web of law that required scientific and professional execution," one that could provide society "a more unified and authoritative set of moral, religious, and legal truths."[31]

SOUTHERN LAWYERS

American intellectuals' cultural interaction with the law was not limited to Foletta's New England-based young Federalists. Michael Hoeflich presents a history of the "high culture" of law in his work explaining the legacy of Roman and civil law upon American jurisprudence. One of the most interesting and unique features of Hoeflich's analysis is his focus on southern thinkers. "In the first half of the nineteenth century," Hoeflich tells us, "there flourished a brilliant and distinctive legal culture in the southern United States." He contrasts northern lawyers, with their focus on "the more technical aspects of law," with southern lawyers, who were "also men of broad culture." Hoeflich raises a historiographical challenge that has yet to be met by legal historians: "it is particularly unfortunate that as the antebellum southern tradition died out and the historiography of the period became obsessed with analyzing the influence of slavery, the full vitality and breadth of this tradition have been utterly forgotten."[32]

Michael O'Brien's multi-volume work on antebellum southern thought is a welcome addition to intellectual history, doing in essence for the South what Perry Miller had done for the New England Puritans.[33] He shows that sincere thinkers existed, even among social groups popularly presumed to be reactionary, who grappled with the persistent questions of social ordering. Even though O'Brien divides his second volume into sections on discrete disciplines such as history, literature, government, economics, philosophy, and theology, one notices the omission of law. Law's absence is especially noticeable because O'Brien's previous work included a biography of native South Carolinian Hugh S. Legaré, United States Attorney General under President John Tyler and widely recognized to be the most intellectual of practicing lawyers.[34] No less than Progressive historian Vernon Parrington included a chapter on Legaré in his monumental *Main Currents in American Thought* as a representative of the conservative legal mind.[35]

The only other intellectual historian of the South who attempted to capture law as a field of thought interdependent on the more general intellectual milieu was Richard Beale Davis. For Davis, O'Brien, and Hoeflich, Legaré played a prominent role in explaining what jurisprudence meant for southern thinkers. What Davis wanted to explain was why southerners of Legaré's generation, who, in another age might have been poets, novelists, or critics, clung steadfastly if conflictedly to the legal profession.[36] Even though Davis wrote before Ferguson, another way to consider Davis's concern is to ask why all of Ferguson's lawyers-turned-writers were northern. Davis explained how law and oratory went hand-in-hand in Jeffersonian Virginia and how subsequent generations learned that Jefferson, Marshall, and Madison were the figures one should strive to emulate.[37] In other words, the social pressures (and opportunities) were stronger in the South for channeling one's creativity into the legal profession.

Hoeflich includes Legaré among three South Carolinians, the other two being Francis Lieber and James Walker, who employed continental legal scholarship in their work on the American common law. Lieber, the German émigré who eventually made his way to New York and Columbia University, was a close friend of Joseph Story and published many of the Justice's writings on legal topics in his Encyclopedia Americana. Moreover, Lieber's 1838 *Legal and Political Hermeneutics*, dedicated to Chancellor Kent, demonstrated not only his "extensive knowledge of Roman and civilian sources but also his ability to employ principles contained in these systems to analyze Anglo-American law."[38] It was Legaré, however, whose library contained more works on the civil law than the Library of Congress. And it was Legaré who began a literary journal, the *Southern Review*, designed to rival the young Federalists' *North American Review*, especially with its inclusion of legal articles. Hoeflich points to the wide circulation of Lieber's books and Legaré's journal articles, as well as Legaré's performance as attorney general, to conclude that civil law made some headway into antebellum American jurisprudence. Chapter 5 is dedicated to examining Legaré's understanding of legal science.

In a very recent essay, Alfred Brophy set out a challenge to legal historians of the intellectual and cultural bent—try "seeing antebellum southerners as intellectuals or as serious thinkers."[39] While acknowledging O'Brien's work, Brophy cautioned that too few intellectual histories of the South focus on legal intellectuals and too many focus on "those who cut against the grain of southern ideas," that is, those southern intellectuals who were antislavery. His fear is that these outliers "may lead us to mistake the central character of southern society." Instead, Brophy suggests that the bulk of southern thinkers "emphasized experience, order, and utility" in justifying slavery over and above a sort of natural law moralism espoused by antislavery advocates. Lawyers and judges in particular "looked to the context rather than to universal truths" when dealing with real life cases. Hence, Brophy concludes that "one of the great problems of intellectual history"—"connect[ing] ideas to action"—might be greatly advanced by studying the work product of legal intellectuals. The result might yield new information such as the impact of "moral philosophy" on judicial opinions, but, Brophy opines, a moral philosophy based even more strongly on utility than previously realized.[40] The chapters herein that focus on Cooper and Legaré respond to and confirm many of Brophy's suggestions.

THE USUAL CAST OF CHARACTERS

More than southern jurists helped spread civilian notions of law to American lawyers.[41] Hoeflich counts Joseph Story as the most prominent American jurist to actively rely on Roman and civil law concepts. In order to appreciate Hoeflich's claims about Story, we need a better picture of the historiographical narrative of the leading lights of American jurisprudence, namely reflexive admirers Story and New York's James Kent. Both Kent and Story, as part of their legacies, left American law libraries with volumes to rival Blackstone. Even before Kent and Story wrote their *Commentaries*, however, several other leading jurists made an impact on American jurisprudence either through lectures, published works, or both. Most notable among those earlier jurisprudents was James Wilson.

A native of Scotland, James Wilson came to America in 1766 and settled in the Philadelphia region. Reared on doctrines of the Scottish Enlightenment, Wilson read law soon after his arrival in Pennsylvania. He became the first professor of law at the College of Philadelphia in 1790 and there delivered a widely regarded series of law lectures that many contemporaries considered to have rivaled Blackstone's lectures. Such an occasion was Wilson's first lecture at which none other than President Washington was in attendance. However, Wilson's lectures were not published until after his death in 1804 by his son. Given that Wilson was one of the first appointees to the new Supreme Court in 1789, one might expect to find an incisive exposition of early American jurisprudence in the lectures. The only recent work devoted exclusively to Wilson's ideas is Mark Hall's *The Political and Legal Philosophy of James Wilson*. Hall criticizes previous scholars for not recognizing Wilson's "traditional Christian conception of natural law."[42] He further contends that Wilson's moral aims posed a stark contrast to the materialism of many British thinkers.

English historian Michael Lobban concluded that Wilson, along with Kent and Story, presented a "more scholarly view" of the early American vision of law.[43] However, Lobban found little coherence when he examined their writings in depth. Lobban makes much of the anti-lawyer and anti-British hostility against which these legal scholars were writing in order to explain their defense of law as a customary system. On the whole, the Americans appeared to be more in keeping with Lockean consent theorists than Blackstonian command theorists. This is because their sources of law so often appear to be metaphysical, such as God's will for Wilson in particular, and otherwise natural law based. Lobban describes what he calls Wilson's Baconianism, also shared by Story. This legal philosophy held that natural law was universal, but that its application was subject to local and historical variations, and that its principles could be inductively sought. These tenets amounted to what contemporary jurisprudents would call legal science.[44]

James Kent's lesser popularity as compared to Joseph Story is probably linked to the fact that Kent never sat on the United States Supreme Court. As a result, Kent has had no sustained book-length treatment in over seventy years. Daniel Hulsebosch has begun to turn the tide, publishing several recent articles on Kent.[45] Of all early American legal scholars, only Kent matched Blackstone in publishing a four-volume original work that purported to be a comprehensive analysis of American law. Although no major recent biography exists, Kent has drawn the attention of several prominent legal historians.[46]

One dominant feature of this historiography is a general concurrence that Kent and Story triumphed in their jurisprudential endeavors. Perry Miller was one of the few who thought Kent and Story's greater reputations among historians were responsible for the slighting of University of Maryland's first law professor, David Hoffman.[47] A more common judgment is that of G. Edward White, who thought, "The most influential legal historians of the late eighteenth and early nineteenth centuries, when American jurisprudence took its distinctive character, were James Kent and Joseph Story."[48] Although it is sometimes difficult to glean any differences between the two in the histories of early American law, Kent's uniqueness comes through most clearly, not in his political attitudes, but in his jurisprudential outlook.

David Raack set out to prove that "Kent's legal thought does in fact merit serious attention." Overlooked by historians White, Friedman, and

Horwitz, and overshadowed by contemporaries Marshall, Story, and Shaw, the New York chancellor was a worthy legal thinker whose ideas, when they have been considered, have been frequently mischaracterized. "Kent was neither closed-minded nor reactionary: he was an intellectual, interested in new ideas and opinions. He was not the inveterate conservative that he is often portrayed."[49] Kent's image as a conservative was cemented with a 1939 biography, *James Kent: A Study in Conservatism.*[50] Likewise, Kent's counterpart, Joseph Story, was similarly stuck with a conservative label by his biographer, Kent Newmyer, who subtitled the work, "Statesman of the Old Republic," suggesting that the Justice was somehow passed by in time, and frequently spoke of his "New England conservatism."[51]

There are several reasons Kent loomed large among his contemporaries. First, as a member of the state supreme court and then as chancellor of New York, he wrote many opinions at a time when few published law reporters existed anywhere in the nation. As a result, the New York reports had the ability to influence more than just the development of New York law. After the state's mandatory retirement age forced him off the bench at age sixty, Kent then reassumed the post of law professor at Columbia University, which he had previously held prior to his judicial appointments, and proceeded to write and publish his *Commentaries on American Law* between 1826 and 1830.

Kent's *Commentaries* have not fared as well under historical evaluation as Blackstone's. According to Lobban, "Kent's theoretical discussions of the foundations of the common law were not profound, and in some areas, seemed inconsistent."[52] Perhaps that sort of frank judgment can only come from a working English historian, but it was certainly not unheard of in Kent's own time. One hopes that some work in the near future will capture a fuller contemporaneous evaluation of Kent.

John Langbein has examined Kent's *Commentaries* in the context of the history of legal literature, concluding that "it is instructive to see Kent's Commentaries not so much as an early treatise, but as a late institutionalist."[53] Coming from the European civil law tradition, legal institutes attempted a comprehensive description of an entire legal system and were primarily didactic in nature, oriented towards the neophyte in training. While European institutes were intended to reconcile the national law with the Roman law, Kent was interested in reconciling American law with the English common law.

Substantively, Kent's endeavors have been labeled "nationalistic" by numerous historians. Most recently, Hulsebosch has applied the metaphor of "empire" to Kent's efforts, explaining that Federalist jurists like Kent applied a "transjurisdictional conception of law" to promote "an empire of law in which law was conceived as a set of legal principles that should operate everywhere in the union."[54] Hulsebosch wants to go even further, however, in arguing that English legal culture exerted an imperial reign in America well after the Revolution. Judging by the works that Kent read and used in his writings, "American law became more Anglicized than ever."[55] In a sense, the imperialism of English law was mediated by Kent and like-minded jurists who were transmitting this Anglo legal culture through their treatises and judicial opinions.

Historians of Kent's thought have highlighted his original and frequent use of foreign authority.[56] However, in considering Kent's use of the civil law, he apparently fared worse than the jurists examined by Hoeflich. According to Alan Watson's study, Kent's Roman and civil law citations, both in his judicial opinions and in his *Commentaries,* served largely as "mere window dressing."[57] In fact, Watson found that Kent continued to cite post-revolutionary English law, seemingly reinforcing Hulsebosch's claim that English law continued, perhaps even increased, its authority in America. Thus, whenever Kent actually employed a foreign citation, there was almost always ample Anglo-American authority to back up the underlying proposition. What was Kent's purpose, then, citing works like Pothier, Emerigon, and Valin? Was it to infer a large body of knowledge because, as Ferguson argued, the contemporary culture measured a lawyer's worth by his mastery of breadth?

Kent himself offered an explanation for his foreign citations within his personal correspondence. Recalling his time riding circuit with Jeffersonian judges, Kent observed, "The judges were Republican and very kindly disposed to everything that was French, and this enabled me, without exciting any alarm or jealousy, to make free use of such authorities and thereby enrich our commercial law."[58] The explicit focus of Kent, Story, and others on commercial law has created a legal history industry dedicated to explaining this so-called "transformation in American law"—a shift from personalized justice toward the impersonal, commercial focus it retains in our capitalist world. Jurisprudentially speaking, however—focusing on the intellectual motivation behind the commercial emphasis—historians have found mixed motives.

For Miller, the evolution of American common law represented a shift from "a philosophy of law which was primarily contractual in character to one that was conscious of history."[59] Thus, the explicit renunciation of static English common law principles was symbolic of more than a desire to foster commerce; it recognized that an ideal national law could never be considered ahistorically. Calls for a native American jurisprudence, therefore, were not a rejection of commerce, but of England's commercial laws. Instead, American jurists urged lawyers and legislators to recognize that the United States represented something new in history and therefore required a new jurisprudence to meet its needs. According to Miller, what Kent, Story et al. were attempting was getting the lawyers' minds "out of the eighteenth century and into the nineteenth."[60]

Well after I began this work, a new work by Ellen Holmes Pearson appeared, which studies a similar cohort of legal intellectuals in the early republic.[61] Pearson makes the case that early republican legal scholars—those writing to *circa* 1830—were central to defining national identity and to creating an American culture. Pearson's term for the subjects of her study is "legists"—a term she borrows from the Roman law tradition to describe the teachers of the civil law. Her terminology would be quite at home in this study as well and captures much of what I intend to convey in the terms "legal elites" and "legal scientists." However, I have decided to forego employing Pearson's term out of a concern that it does not explicitly allude to the social and cultural position of this group of lawyers, which was important to their own conceptions of their work product. Nevertheless, this work comfortably engages Pearson's monograph and complements much of it, although our ultimate focuses are different.

Pearson focuses on the legists' endeavors to Americanize the common law and constitutionalism by emphasizing the concepts of custom and consent. In looking at the specific fields of land law (including western expansion), property distribution and inheritance, and the law of slavery, Pearson shows how the legists explained American alterations in their substantive content by reference to a rationally informed morality.

My focus is on the very method of legal reasoning rather than any particular field of law. Legal methodology worried legal elites because the new Enlightenment interest in science undermined their preexisting epistemological foundations. As Pearson hints at, many of them found a new morality in universal notions of justice located in natural and Roman law. Moreover, they found that turn-of-the-century rationality and utility provided the means by which the law could attain just solutions to complicated social problems. Natural law and utility are frequently thought of as antagonistic modes of proceeding. However, early republican legal scholars borrowed freely from both traditions, not in some post hoc fashion, but in a serious endeavor to give grounding to American legal science. Chapter 2 focuses on the rationality provided by English utilitarianism primarily because that prong of philosophical influence has been much neglected in the literature.

In what follows, I show that legal scientists like Verplanck, Cooper, Legaré, and Story were concerned with the big questions Miller studied. In part, this is intended to be the sort of "intellectual history" described by Richard Rorty, which "consists of descriptions of what the intellectuals were up to at a given time, and of their interaction with the rest of society."[62] The goal is that one will come away with "a sense of the differences between the options open to an intellectual at different times and places,"[63] or, more specifically, a sense of the differences between the options open to a legal intellectual in the early American republic and a modern legal intellectual. "The main reason we want historical knowledge of what unre-educated primitives, or dead philosophers and scientists," and I will add, dead lawyers, "would have said to each other is that it helps us to recognize that there have been different forms of intellectual life than ours."[64] As Rorty notes in calling Quentin Skinner to his aid, a main point of all humanistic studies is self-awareness. "'The indispensable value of studying the history of ideas' is to learn 'the distinction between what is necessary and what is the product merely of our own contingent arrangements.'"[65] Studying these legal scientists should open our eyes to what the lawyers in society were once able to do, what they thought they were able to do, what they failed to do, and what they probably should not have done. In order to realize this simple but ambitious goal, it is necessary to historically reconstruct their intellectual lives. This means paying particular attention to their conscious intent to affect a legal system.

The four legal scientists who are the focus of part II are themselves less important as individuals than are their methods of legal analyses, although their personal backgrounds often shed light on the nuances of their individual brands of legal science. By examining the texts they left behind—including theoretical, political, and judicial writings—we get a sense of a very different conception of law than exists today. What we find, is that law was not valuable primarily as a means to maintain state power, and certainly not because it redistributed wealth in any particular direction, nor because it could open up free markets. Instead, law was worthy of study and attention because it was a means of enforcing a natural moral order, which in turn promoted public utility. Certain forms of government and economy indeed made the law's task of promoting morality easier, but they too were merely the means to the end that was the moral end of public happiness.

THE LEGAL SCIENTISTS

The legal scientist herein selected for extended discussion represent a range of backgrounds, temperaments, and politics, yet they all shared a similar devotion to bettering the substance of their chosen profession. Gulian Verplanck, Thomas Cooper, Hugh Legaré, and Joseph Story were all self-acknowledged devotees of legal science, but they were also recognized by men of letters to be among the nation's most learned of American authors. The 1855 *Cyclopædia of American Literature*, edited principally by Evert Duyckinck, gave prominent entries to all four men.[66] The inclusion of these prominent lawyers helps us understand the importance that legal scientists played in literary culture more generally and their importance to those whose self-appointed task was to fret over the international status of American letters.

As one historian has noted, Duyckinck was "one of the most important taste-shapers of the nineteenth century."[67] He joined forces with John O'Sullivan, leading the intellectual wing of the New York-based Young America movement. Their goal was to revitalize American culture in a highly nationalistic fashion. As Duyckinck noted in the preface to the *Cyclopædia,* his purpose in editing the two volumes was "to exhibit and illustrate the products of the pen on American soil." But the most characteristically Young-America aspect of the work was its conscious attempt to unite the nation across regions and hence, there was deliberate inclusion of southerners and westerners. Duyckinck emphasized that "mental activity has been uniformly developed" throughout the country; the North, and especially New England, held no position of cultural superiority. Moreover, the encyclopedia included "foreign scholars and writers who have visited us and lived among us" out of a recognition that "the higher interests of letters" is "to associate all nations in intellectual amity and progress."[68] Verplanck (a New Yorker), Cooper (a foreign immigrant), Legaré (a South Carolinian), and Story (a New Englander) reflect the diversity that a contemporary like Duyckinck thought representative of the best of American letters.

Each of the legal scientists on whom I focus has had a biography written of him within the past century. Joseph Story has easily garnered the most academic attention, almost always with respect to his legal ideas.[69] I am primarily interested in Story to show how a familiar character within the historiography can be differently appreciated when viewed in light of those legal scientists not usually discussed, hence, the inclusion of Verplanck, Cooper, and Legaré. Story comes to be seen as just another contributor to the legal-science conversation, rather than a leader. In fact, Story's views on legislation and codification, upon which chapter 6 focuses, tend to be responsive to others' ideas then in vogue.

Verplanck, Cooper, and Legaré have received far less attention from historians in general, and almost no specific attention from legal historians. The oldest relevant work is Dumas Malone's 1926 work on Thomas Cooper.[70] What Malone wrote nearly ninety years ago holds true today: "I find it difficult to explain the long neglect of him." Malone's work was very much a political biography in which he explicitly omitted discussion of "the more technical philosophical, scientific, and legal treatises" that Cooper composed.[71] More recently, a British press has published a set of Cooper's philosophical writings in three volumes, however no analytical work on Cooper's thought in general, much less his legal thought, has been written since Malone's biography.[72]

Verplanck's biography was published in 1951, while Legaré's 1985 biography is the most recent.[73] Similar to Malone's political biography of Cooper, Robert July's work on Verplanck is very much a contextualization of his subject within the realm of New York politics. O'Brien's volume on Legaré is more of an intellectual biography, but one that explicitly disclaims being the biography of a lawyer.

Given the relative lack of attention to these figures' jurisprudence, my goal has been to examine the specifically legal writings of Cooper, Verplanck, and Legaré. Along with Story, these four productive individuals reveal unique insights into legal science in its incipient phase. Verplanck, Cooper, Legaré, and Story were all either classroom lecturers or authors of educational and scholarly volumes. The next two chapters set the stage for the individualized consideration of these four legal scientists. They provide a lay of the intellectual landscape by considering the work of the initial law professors and the philosophical motivations of the scholarly writers.

NOTES

1. Oliver Wendell Holmes, "Law in Science and Science in Law," in *The Collected Legal Papers* (New York: Harcourt, Brace, & Co., 1920), 242.
2. James Kloppenberg described an excellent example of this sort of application of intellectual history to law. Kloppenberg advocated what he termed "pragmatic hermeneutics" to the study of legal history. Pragmatic hermeneutics negotiates between the deconstructionists and the contextualists—or, as he calls them, the "de" and the "re" people—who dominate modern intellectual history. As he explained: By pragmatic hermeneutics, I mean a critical method attuned to the complex and elusive interplay between texts and contexts, alert to the instability of meanings, and concerned equally with the range of meanings available in the past and with the particular perspectives that critics bring to their interpretations as a result of their own positions in the present. James T. Kloppenberg, "The Theory and Practice of American Legal History," *Harvard Law Review* 106 (1993): 1332, 1335–36.
3. William E. Nelson, *Americanization of the Common Law: The Impact of Legal Change on Massachusetts Society, 1760–1830* (Cambridge, MA: Harvard University Press, 1975); Morton J. Horwitz, *The Transformation of American Law, 1780-1860* (Cambridge, MA: Harvard University Press, 1977).
4. M. H. Hoeflich, "Roman Law in American Legal Culture," *Tulane Law Review* 66 (1992): 1723.
5. In this context, I mean "non-traditional" from the point of view of contemporary legal practice. Michael Lobban has argued that eclecticism of source material was the rule, not the exception, in England prior to Blackstone. Michael Lobban, *The Common Law and English Jurisprudence, 1760–1850* (Oxford: Oxford University Press, 1991).
6. Daniel Raymond, *Thoughts on Political Economy* (Baltimore: Fielding Lucas, Jun'r, 1820).
7. Thomas Cooper, *Lectures on the Elements of Political Economy*, 2nd ed. (Columbia, SC: M'Morris & Wilson, 1829; repr., New York: Augustus M. Kelley Publishers, 1971).
8. Willard Phillips, *A Manual of Political Economy, with Particular Reference to the Institutions, Resources, and Condition of the United States* (Boston, 1828; repr., New York: Augustus M. Kelley Publishers, 1968).
9. Daniel Raymond, *The Elements of Constitutional Law and of Political Economy* 4th ed. (Baltimore: Cushing & Brother, 1840).
10. Robert Gordon, "Friedman, Lawrence M.," in Roger K. Newman, ed., *The Yale Biographical Dictionary of American Law* (New Haven, CT: Yale Univ. Press 2009), 207.
11. Lawrence M. Friedman, "Heart Against Head: Perry Miller and the Legal Mind," *Yale Law Journal* 77 (1968): 1254.
12. Lawrence M. Friedman, *A History of American Law*, 3rd ed. (New York: Simon & Schuster, 2005), 589.
13. Friedman, "Heart Against Head," 1244–45.
14. Ibid., 1254. For example, Gulian Verplanck undertook his work on contracts, discussed in chapter 3, as an overt criticism of Chief Justice John Marshall's understanding of legal doctrine.

15. Daniel J. Boorstin, *The Americans: The Colonial Experience* (New York: Vintage Books 1958), 195 (quoting Adams).
16. Ibid., 201.
17. Nelson, *Americanization of the Common Law*, 19.
18. Gordon S. Wood, *The Creation of the American Republic, 1775–1787* (Chapel Hill: University of North Carolina Press 1969), 295.
19. Ibid., 297.
20. Daniel R. Coquillette, "Justinian in Braintree: John Adams, Civilian Learning, and Legal Elitism, 1758–1775," in *The History of Legal Education in the United States: Commentaries and Primary Sources*, ed. Steve Sheppard (Pasadena, CA: Salem Press 1999), 1:82.
21. Herbert Alan Johnson, "John Jay: Lawyer in a Time of Transition, 1764–1775," *University of Pennsylvania Law Review* 124, no. 5 (1976): 1282.
22. Perry Miller, *Life of the Mind in America from the Revolution to the Civil War* (New York: Harcourt, Brace & World, Inc., 1965), 100.
23. Perry Miller, "The Common Law and Codification in Jacksonian America," *Proceedings of the American Philosophical Society* 103 (1959): 463, 466.
24. Ibid., 468.
25. Robert A. Ferguson, *Law and Letters in American Culture* (Cambridge, MA: Harvard University Press, 1984), 5–9.
26. Ibid., 28.
27. Ibid., 31.
28. Daniel J. Boorstin, *The Mysterious Science of the Law: An Essay on Blackstone's* Commentaries (1941; repr., Chicago, IL: University of Chicago Press, 1996).
29. Lobban, *The Common Law*.
30. Marshall Foletta, *Coming to Terms with Democracy: Federalist Intellectuals and the Shaping of an American Culture* (Charlottesville: University of Virginia Press, 2001), 136.
31. Ibid., 172.
32. M. H. Hoeflich, *Roman and Civil Law and the Development of Anglo-American Jurisprudence in the Nineteenth Century* (Athens: Univ. of Georgia Press, 1997), 50–51.
33. Michael O'Brien, *Conjectures of Order: Intellectual Life and the American South, 1810–1860*, 2 vols. (Chapel Hill: University of North Carolina Press, 2004).
34. Michael O'Brien, *A Character of Hugh Legaré* (Knoxville: University of Tennessee Press, 1985).
35. Vernon L. Parrington, *Main Currents in American Thought: An Interpretation of American Literature from the Beginning to 1920* (New York: Harcourt, Brace & Co., 1927).
36. Richard Beale Davis, "The Early American Lawyer and the Profession of Letters," *Huntington Library Quarterly* 12, no. 2 (1949).
37. Richard Beale Davis, *Intellectual Life in Jefferson's Virginia, 1790–1830* (Knoxville: University of Tennessee Press, 1964).
38. Hoeflich, *Roman and Civil Law*, 58.
39. Alfred L. Brophy, "The World Made by Laws and the Laws Made by the World of the Old South," in *Signposts: New Directions in Southern Legal History*, ed. Sally E. Hadden and Patricia Hagler Minter (Athens: University of Georgia Press, 2013), 219.
40. Ibid., 221–29.
41. Peter Stein, "The Attraction of the Civil Law in Post-Revolutionary America," *Virginia Law Review* 52 (1966).
42. Mark David Hall, *The Political and Legal Philosophy of James Wilson, 1742–1798* (Columbia: University of Missouri Press, 1997), 37.
43. Michael Lobban, "The Age of the Federalists," in *A History of the Philosophy of Law in the Common Law World, 1600–1900* (Dordrecht: Springer, 2007).
44. Howard Schweber, "The 'Science' of Legal Science: The Model of the Natural Sciences in Nineteenth-Century American Legal Education," *Law and History Review* 17, no. 3 (1999): 421–66; M. H. Hoeflich, "Law and Geometry: Legal Science from Leibniz to Langdell," *American Journal of Legal History* 30 (1986): 95–121.

45. Daniel J. Hulsebosch, "Debating the Transformation of American Law: James Kent, Joseph Story, and the Legacy of the Revolution," in *Transformations in American Legal History: Essays in Honor of Professor Morton J. Horwitz*, ed. Daniel Hamilton and Alfred L. Brophy (Cambridge, MA: Harvard Univ. Press, 2009); Daniel J. Hulsebosch, "An Empire of Law: Chancellor Kent and the Revolution in Books in the Early Republic," *Alabama Law Review* 60, no. 2 (2009): 377–424.

46. John H. Langbein, "Chancellor Kent and the History of Legal Literature," *Columbia Law Review* 93, no. 3 (1993): 547–94; Alan Watson, "Chancellor Kent's Use of Foreign Law," in *The Reception of Continental Ideas in the Common Law World, 1820–1920*, ed. Reimann (Berlin: Duncker & Humbolt, 1993), 45–62; G. Edward White, "The Chancellor's Ghost," *Chicago-Kent Law Review* 74, no. 1 (1998): 229–62.

47. Miller, *The Life of the Mind*, 118.

48. G. Edward White, "The Path of American Jurisprudence," *University of Pennsylvania Law Review* 124, no. 5 (1976): 1250.

49. David W. Raack, "'To Preserve the Best Fruits': The Legal Thought of Chancellor James Kent," *American Journal of Legal History* 33, no. 4 (1989): 325.

50. John Theodore Horton, *James Kent: A Study in Conservatism, 1763–1847* (New York: D. Appleton-Century Co., 1939).

51. R. Kent Newmyer, *Supreme Court Justice Joseph Story: Statesman of the Old Republic* (Chapel Hill: Univ. of North Carolina Press, 1985), 173, 182, 226, 238.

52. Lobban, "The Age of the Federalists," 147.

53. Langbein, "Chancellor Kent and the History of Legal Literature," 586.

54. Hulsebosch, "An Empire of Law," 378.

55. Ibid., 379.

56. White, "The Chancellor's Ghost," 247.

57. Watson, "Chancellor Kent's Use of Foreign Law," 49, 61–62.

58. Ibid., 48.

59. Miller, *The Life of the Mind*, 127.

60. Ibid.

61. Ellen Holmes Pearson, *Remaking Custom: Law and Identity in the Early American Republic* (Charlottesville: University of Virginia Press, 2011).

62. Richard Rorty, "The Historiography of Philosophy: Four Genres," in *Philosophy in History: Essays on the Historiography of Philosophy*, ed. Richard Rorty et al. (Cambridge: Cambridge University Press, 1984), 49, 68.

63. Ibid., 69.

64. Ibid., 51.

65. Ibid.

66. Evert A. Duycknick and George L. Duyckinck, ed., *Cyclopædia of American Literature*, 2 vols. (New York: Charles Scribner, 1855).

67. Edward L. Widmer, *Young America: The Flowering of Democracy in New York City* (New York: Oxford University Press, 1999), 94. Duyckinck also formed the basis for Miller's work on early American literary culture. As Melville's literary editor, Miller used Duyckinck as the leading representative of the democratic tendency in American literature, in contrast to the more conservative Knickerbocker group. Perry Miller, *The Raven and the Whale: Poe, Melville, and the New York Literary Scene* (New York: Harcourt, Brace, & World, 1956).

68. Duyckinck, *Cyclopædia*, 1:v–vii.

69. The most recent and complete legal biography of Story is Newmyer, *Supreme Court Justice Joseph Story*.

70. Dumas Malone, *The Public Life of Thomas Cooper* (New Haven, CT: Yale University Press, 1926; repr. Columbia: University of South Carolina Press, 1961).

71. Ibid., xii.

72. *Philosophical Writings of Thomas Cooper*, ed. Udo Thiel, 3 vols. (Bristol: Thoemmes Press, 2001).

73. Robert W. July, *The Essential New Yorker: Gulian Crommelin Verplanck* (Durham, NC: Duke University Press, 1951); Michael O'Brien, *A Character of Hugh Legaré* (Knoxville: University of Tennessee Press, 1985).

Part I

Legal Science

ONE

Expounding Legal Science

Early Republican Law Lectures

I recommend the study of Law, to thousands in our country, who are far removed from the necessity of practising it.

—William Littell, Law Lecture, 1818[1]

Ours being emphatically a government of laws . . . there is no country on earth where a thorough, extensive, and general knowledge of the elements of jurisprudence may be so useful, or can be so indispensable to the welfare of men, and the stability and authority of just and equal institutions.

—George Robertson, Law Lecture, 1835[2]

I have considered law and government as branches of human learning, peculiarly fit and proper in every country, but especially in a free one to form a part of the general education, both useful to the man and ornamental to the general scholar.

—Lucas Powell Thompson, Law Lecture, 1839[3]

Surprisingly little has been said about the existence of, much less the ideas disseminated by, the first generation of American law professors. In 1911, Charles Warren largely dismissed these initial efforts because, as he put it, "none of these professorships attempted to afford a complete or practical education for law students."[4] Over one hundred years later, Warren's work remains the most authoritative source on the American bar in the early republic. However, the American bar imagined itself as much more than a guild, solely concerned with the practicalities of maintaining the standards of a trade. Instead, the leaders of the American bar thought of themselves as a moral and intellectual aristocracy. Preservation of this elite class meant conducting legal education in such a way that the lessons learned reinforced this natural leadership role.

The attempt of early legal academics to raise the law to a respectable field of study is important for several reasons. Primarily, it serves to remind us that entrance into the legal profession did not solely consist of "reading the law" in the office of a practitioner as some images of legal education presume, not even in the late-eighteenth century. Instead, a steadily increasing number of professors established themselves in universities across the country, emphasizing the necessity of legal knowledge for responsible republican citizenship. But more than civic training grounds, the law lectures also served to acquaint future lawyers with the science of law, since scientifically trained lawyers were the hope of the future of the profession.

This chapter's focus on antebellum law lectures allows us to understand how legal scientists attempted to pass on their learning to a new generation, and allows us to examine the extent to which legal-scientific thinking transcended regional and political differences. If legal science succeeded as an objective study, then we might expect to find law lectures given in South Carolina or Virginia comparing favorably with lectures from Massachusetts and New York. Likewise, one might not expect to find, or at least detect from their lectures, partisan leanings of the professors of legal science. For the most part, this is indeed the case. Although there were clear disagreements over the meaning of constitutional law, the methodological approaches and the professional goals of the law lecturers were, to a great extent, uniform.

SOME GENERAL OBSERVATION ON THE ANTEBELLUM LAW LECTURE

The published law lecture was somewhat of a novelty in the early-American republic. Law lectures in American universities began as early as the first decade of the republic when James Wilson delivered his famous series of lectures at the University of Pennsylvania in the early 1790s. Even before Wilson, George Wythe had been appointed to teach law at the College of William and Mary in 1779; unfortunately none of his materials survive. In 1793 James Kent was appointed as the first professor of law at Columbia, and we still have his first 1794 lecture. But lack of student interest and intervening political appointments soon distracted him from that calling. Wythe's successor at William and Mary, St. George Tucker, was perhaps the most influential in laying the groundwork for what a university-based law curriculum would look like.[5] Tucker's legacy is best preserved in his five-volume Americanized version of Blackstone's *Commentaries*.[6] The editorial additions lengthening the original four-volume work consist mainly of his lecture notes explaining to his students when and how American law differed from English law.[7] However, it is really not until the third and fourth decades of the nineteenth century that law takes its place among its sister sciences in the university setting.

The most common type of published law lecture was the so-called "introductory lecture." Most were printed as stand-alone pamphlets, and usually at the request of the student audience then in attendance. Prefixed to such lectures were the written requests to the lecturer along with his humble acquiescence and a statement that he never expected or deserved such an honor. More prominent lectures appeared in general-interest periodicals and law journals. Although formulaic in appearance, the lectures were not all of one voice. They did, however, sound common notes on fundamental themes and thus form the heart of legal science. As one might expect, all lecturers thought academic law training was a good idea, and most lectures were an attempt to turn this thought into public currency. But their specific ideas about law as a discipline and their evaluations of the state of the profession are what most capture our attention.

LEGAL EDUCATION AND REPUBLICAN IDEOLOGY

Regardless of the current historiographical status of the "republican thesis" in revolutionary and early-republic studies, its value for the analysis of legal change in the early-nineteenth century is quite apparent.[8] Lawyers constantly worried whether or not the path American law was traversing was in keeping with republican sensibilities. The realm of legal education was particularly relevant to republican-minded lawyers because it was upon the students whom they could impress the importance of civic and professional responsibility.

The mastery of law was so fundamental to the success of the new nation because law itself was concerned with nothing less than the study of man in society. If the republican experiment had any hope of longevity, it was only through a careful understanding of the conditions necessary to maintain the delicate balance between liberty and society. Law was the great, omnipresent arbiter, preserving both individual freedom and social cohesion. Nor did the law's pervasiveness know state or regional boundaries. As Thomas Grimké of South Carolina observed, "Law, indeed, it is obvious, pervades in its operations, all society."[9] While Massachusetts's Simon Greenleaf thought, "the law constitutes the very element of our social existence."[10] In the same way that religion serviced our morality, and medicine our frailty, law serviced the social aspect of our being, Timothy Walker explained in his introductory law lecture delivered in Cincinnati, Ohio.[11] The necessity of legal knowledge to both individual and social well-being had particular implications for the development of higher education in the early republic.

The law's social ubiquity was reason enough to recommend it as a part of every learned American's general education. Thus, James Kent thought that the "efficacy and eminent value of legal learning" was obvious, especially to "that part of the rising generation, who are destined by their education and genius to act a distinguished part on the theatre of public action."[12] In 1827, Grimké, in arguing for codification of South Carolina's law, cited as one of his reasons the ease with which a code would allow every man to know the law. He argued, "it is the only science and the only art, of which it is the interest and duty of every man, as far as his education and opportunities permit, to know, at least, the elements."[13] Commentators also recognized the social engineering aspects of legal systems, and urged that legal knowledge was essential to verify that legal rules produced their intended results. Because of the law's "intimate connexion with human happiness, and its tendency to mould the characters of men," Americans had to keep a watchful eye on the resulting moral order.[14] Education provided an advantage in this regard because it enabled Americans to judge "with more accuracy and intelligence, how the proposed maxims of our adopted ethics, and our legal code, will produce the effect intended."[15] Thomas Cooper went even further in suggesting that legal systems were simply more successful "in proportion to the quantum of knowledge, experience, and civilization, prevalent in the community," by the very fact that more-enlightened individuals were more conscientious in appreciating the moral imperative of social organization.[16]

Another line of argument in urging law "as a branch of general education" was to focus, not on the social aspect of the balance beam, but on the individualistic rights side. Constitutional law was especially important in this regard. Thus Timothy Walker warned: "He can but poorly appreciate the freedom he enjoys, who does not understand the great charter which secures it. I was about to go further, and say, that he does not deserve to be free, who will not inform himself in what his freedom consists."[17] Beverley Tucker concurred in Walker's appraisal that every man "owes it to his country to acquire a certain proficiency in constitutional law."[18] Revolutionary lore was never far out of mind when discussing liberty, and thus Tucker called forth that great friend of American freedom, Edmund Burke, in describing "the study of law, as a school of political rights."[19] Even Kent, that self-described "zealous Federalist,"[20] in one of his earliest pronouncements, acknowledged that "the elementary learning of our law" promoted "a keen sense of right, and a warm love of freedom."[21] However, if the republican experiment was to succeed, far more than a selfish knowledge of individual rights was necessary. What was needed was the recognition that America was different from all other nations because legal knowledge was not a mere gentlemanly adornment, but rather a civic duty.

As early as 1794, James Kent was teaching that "the nature of their government" put "the people of this country under singular obligations." These obligations arose from the democratic aspects of the republic. The fact that any citizen might be called upon to assume public office, act as a juror, or perform some other civic function of social importance was both exciting and frightening—exciting because the experiment was new, frightening because of the enormous interdependency upon individuals' active engagement with the body politic. Knowledge of both law and the "science of civil government" was necessary for all, even those who remained in private life.[22] By virtue of one's citizenship and corresponding "social duties," each individual should be interested in such knowledge.[23] This theme was repeated, not only in law lectures, but also in justifications for authoring legal treatises, or in John Reed's case, revising Blackstone. Reed noted, "All citizens, besides their immediate duties as men, and as mere members of the community, are liable to be called on as jurors, magistrates, arbitrators, or to some of the long list of highly important and responsible county or township offices."[24] But even if one never accepted the call of active civic duty, another reason why "the study of the general principles of jurisprudence" was more in demand in the United States than in any other country was that "public opinion is here omnipotent."[25] In a civilized republic, this public opinion was "regularly expressed through the medium of law."[26] However, even a democrat like Beverley Tucker reminded his law students, "power does not imply wisdom or justice." Moreover, Tucker realized that there were no means of securing wisdom and justice when opposed by "constitutional authority and physical force." Hence, "the enlightened sense of justice and right in the constituent body" must be nourished by constant attention to the study of law so that the wrong majoritarian sentiment never took hold in the public mind.[27]

Most legal educators also took notice of the fact that in the United States lawyers were particularly likely to be chosen by the people as public functionaries, and thus, they were especially in need of formal legal education.[28] John Anthon thought that "with us," "every lawyer is necessarily a statesman, and consequently the moulding of proper national sentiments is at every step of his career an important duty."[29] Simon Greenleaf of Harvard argued that professional character was best formed in the classroom. He added, "in a government of laws, the formation of this character, by such a discipline, is a subject of public interest."[30] Law professors saw themselves as performing a public service in preparing future lawmakers to carry out their public trusts honorably. Kent believed that university education was the best way to preserve "our political fabrics and systems of jurisprudence" from "the insidious operations of faction."[31] Forty years later, Beverley Tucker warned students at William and Mary that public functionaries were more likely to abuse their positions in a republic than in a monarchy because of the temptation to follow a temporary, localized majority contrary to the best interest of the nation. He thought study of constitutional law principles would counter this tendency to abuse. In 1835, Daniel Mayes of the Transylvania University in Lexington, Kentucky, rationalized his endeavors as follows: "Hundreds of our pretended statesmen enter the halls of legislation, without having, in their whole lives, devoted one single hour to the study of the form, structure, constitution, and laws that govern that body politic for whose diseases they are about to prescribe."[32] In his second time around as law professor at Columbia, Kent said, "no one can presume to be an accomplished statesman," without knowledge of the law of nations, which concerned itself with peace and war.[33] What America's first law professors were saying was that for the new governmental form to succeed, it would need to be staffed with men who were educated in its founding principles, had a familiarity with foreign governments, and had the moral sense to resist factionalized public opinion in favor of working towards the common good.

Besides convincing the public that formalized legal study was a requisite part of every citizen's general education, and particularly necessary for members of the legal profession, the content of that course of study had to be set out in order to explain how the doctrines taught would further a republican character. In his first set of lectures at Columbia in 1794, Kent explained that legal education should rest upon America's own native history. "We shall by this means imbibe the principles of republican government from pure fountains; and prevent any improper impressions being received from the artificial distinctions, the oppressive establishments, or the wild innovations which at present distinguish the Trans-Atlantic World."[34] In order to assure that American law students gained "a correct acquaintance with genuine republican maxims," they had to be taught "to distinguish between the principles of one government, and the genius which presides in the other."[35] The problem facing both law professors and law students was that there existed few native American textbooks out of which one could successfully study the law in a genuine republican fashion. As late as 1831, John Reed thought Pennsylvania students were "better acquainted with the forms and technicalities of the king's bench, and high court of chancery in England, than with those of the various courts of this commonwealth."[36] Reed was one of the handful of early-American revisers of Blackstone. These revisers saw their undertaking as necessary to prevent American students from relying too heavily upon the un-American principles espoused by the "learned commentator." As Reed noted, "in their original shape" Blackstone's *Commentaries* were "an unsafe guide," and were "calculated rather to mislead, than instruct an American student."[37] The year after Reed's *Pennsylvania Blackstone* came out, the second edition of John Anthon's *Analytical Abridgement of the Commentaries* was published. Anthon cautioned the American student "in relation to the political principles contained in these volumes."[38] "Keeping in view the political principles of the American lawyer," Anthon "strongly recommended" Chancellor Kent's *Commentaries on American Law* as a good alternative.[39]

Kent's *Commentaries* (1826–1830) arose out of his second attempt as the sole law professor at Columbia University, at a point in time when the place of the law teacher was still being debated in the American legal profession.[40] Although not the first American law lecturer at a university, Kent's appointment in 1793 was "the first instance in the annals of this seat of learning, that the science of our municipal laws has thus been admitted into friendship with her sister arts, and been invited to lend her aid to complete a course of public education."[41] But it was not until the 1830s that university law lectureships were gaining in number. Thomas Cooper thought it was because "the want of elementary instruction has been so deeply felt in our own country, that Law Lectureships have been widely introduced." "This could not have been the case," Cooper explained, "if the necessity of a Law School, and of Lectures on the elements of Legal knowledge, had not been deeply felt by the public, in the cities where such lectures have been established."[42] Whether it was due to popular demand as Cooper thought, or from some other common source, universities began to take seriously the field of law as a co-equal intellectual undertaking. It was during this decade that new professorships were established, or prominent professors appointed, at New York University, Harvard, South Carolina College, the University of Virginia, William and Mary, Transylvania University, and Cincinnati College.

THE PROMISE OF A MORE EDUCATED PROFESSION

The status quo against which legal intellectuals were working consisted of law-office study, or legal clerkships. Legal educators widely agreed, "Instruction in law offices is necessarily quite imperfect." The problem was that students failed to get the attention they needed from busy lawyers, and as a result, they were turned out to the public "very ill qualified for the duties of their profession."[43] Law schools, on the other hand, offered an advantage to the student over the traditional law-office education.

The legal profession was slower than the medical profession to realize the value of theory as a worthy counterpart to mere practical skills. Physicians had come to prefer "the halls of science" to "the offices of private practitioners," observed Daniel Mayes in 1835. Even though Mayes predicted that law schools would eventually overtake law-office placements, other lawyers saw the profession's bias toward practical education as a major obstacle. At Harvard, Simon Greenleaf vowed that he would not "confine the education of a lawyer to the technical learning of his profession, or to the code of his particular state."[44] Students in Beverley Tucker's course at William and Mary were reminded that "this is not a mere school of professional education," and thus it was his duty "to present views more important to the statesman, than to the practitioner."[45] The

American Jurist in 1832 reviewed John Park's introductory law lecture at King's College London and took solace in the fact that England was facing similar difficulties in advancing legal education.[46] The article noted that a correspondent of Park's had described to him the "Herculean task" of eradicating the belief "that no knowledge is worth walking and paying for, however cheaply, which is not practical;—and that practical knowledge can only be acquired in an office."[47]

Aside from a solid grounding in theory and legal science, formalized education held out the promise of improving the reputation of the legal profession. Scholars have previously examined the anti-lawyer sentiment in the early republic.[48] Whether or not the critics were accurate, what is important here is the extent to which legal pedagogues thought they could improve the standing of the profession in the public's eye. "I am well aware that there are prejudices against the profession," wrote Timothy Walker in 1837. However, Walker was alone among law professors in casting all the blame on the public. "If there were no dishonest or knavish clients," Walker explained, "there would be no dishonest or knavish lawyers."[49] Walker's chauvinism also extended to a celebration of "those difficulties of acquisition, which render our profession so arduous, so exclusive, so indispensable, and, therefore, so respectable." He even warned of the consequences of codification, namely, that it would make the law simpler and thus "would tend to diminish the importance which at present attaches to this profession."[50]

Simplification of the law, however, was a worthy lesson most instructors were willing to give. In South Carolina, Thomas Grimké thought codification would improve the public favor of the law and thus of the legal profession.[51] Thomas Cooper agreed with his fellow statesman that complication was an evil in need of a remedy. Thus he taught his class, "so it is, in Divinity, in Medicine, and in Law, where Mystery stalks forward in front, we have cause to suspect that fraud and oppression follow in the rear."[52] One way to remove the mystery of the law, and thus the appearance of collusive fraud, was to teach general principles over technical forms. Kent argued that the law chair at Columbia should "effect in elevating the attention of some of our youth from the narrow and selfish objects of the profession, to the nobler study of the general principles of our government, and the policy of our laws . . . and thereby produce a more general interest in their support."[53] As historian Michael Hoeflich has shown, this new focus of the American law professors was taken notice of in England during the parliamentary investigation into legal education in 1846. Andrew Amos, professor of English Law at London University, testified that the Americans "are not so much fettered by our technical rules, and they study jurisprudence in a more general way than we do here," thus indicating "the existence of a better legal education there than in England."[54]

Another way to improve the public reputation of the legal profession was to instill in its newest members a strong sense of republican ethics, a field to which scholars have devoted less attention than it merits.[55] "Knowledge alone is not sufficient for pure and lasting fame," Kent explained to his students in 1824. "It is mischievous, and even dangerous, unless it be regulated by moral principle."[56] Although "wisdom is as much the offspring of the heart as of the head," the "zeal for justice" had to be "inculcated by precept and practice"—hence the role of the law professor and the law school. A successful law school experience would produce a graduate who understood that "No reproach is keener or more just, than that of a client who has been decoyed into expensive litigation by the rapacity of the disingenuous, or the blunders of the unskilful."[57] A lawyer was to understand that his first duty was to his community, not to himself or to his client. As such, he should not stir up needless controversy or feed upon "the petty strifes of the country"[58] in order to turn a profit; he should be "a peacemaker,"[59] even if it meant the loss of business.

Being a good republican lawyer meant more than just counseling peace; it sometimes meant telling a client that one's duties as a citizen trumped any obligation to represent a morally dubious position in court. In his inaugural lecture, Simon Greenleaf passionately told his audience:

> I look with pity on the man, who regards himself a mere machine of the law;—whose conceptions of moral and social duty are all absorbed in the sense of supposed obligation to his client, and this of so low a nature as to render him a very tool and slave, to serve the worst passions of men;—who yields himself a passive instrument of legal inflictions, to be moved at the pleasure of every hirer;—and who, beholding the ruin and havoc made by a lawsuit, which "two scruples of honesty" in his counsel might have prevented, can calmly pocket his fee with the reflection, that he has done his duty to his client, alike regardless of the duty to his neighbour and his God.[60]

Greenleaf would see to it that no Harvard lawyer would forget that "our clients are not always the best judges of their own interests," especially when they have forgotten that they are not merely "solitary individuals," but "men connected with society by enduring ties."[61] David Hoffman agreed that to avoid being "mischievous to society," lawyers had to counsel clients against cases "founded on bad, if not the worst of passions."[62] For Hoffman, the ethical lawyer could not even plead the statute of limitation "based on the *mere efflux of time*." According to Resolution XII of his standards of professional deportment, which he advised students to read "twice every year" while in practice, "if my client is conscious he owes the debt; and has no other defence than the *legal bar*, he shall never make me a partner in his knavery."[63] This sort of morally based instruction was designed to be "conducive to the interests of the community, and to the honor and usefulness of the profession."[64]

THE ELEVATION OF LAW TO A SCIENCE

If there was one premise upon which every legal intellectual in the early republic agreed, it was that law was a science. An article in the *American Jurist* in 1833 summed up the reigning belief in a rhetorical question: "Is law a science, or is it something less dignified?"[65] To suggest that law was anything but a science, in an age when the natural sciences were proving themselves so useful, was to cast an aspersion upon an entire profession. But more than an insult, to view the law something other than a science was to tacitly approve of uncertainty in the subjects with which law dealt—society, the nature of man, and so forth. In an era when the first generation of non-revolutionary leaders was coming to the fore, the search for certainty and stability in governmental and social organization was crucial to their sense of accomplishment, as well as to satisfy the new leaders' sense of obligation to the past generation's heroic deeds. A naturalistic understanding of law as a science promised both mastery and absolution—a sense of control over society with the excuse of an uncontrollable nature always at hand to explain the failures.

Howard Schweber has illuminated this area by focusing on the natural science aspects of legal science. Schweber found that beginning in the 1820s, a new strand of American legal science began to appear. "This was naturalistic legal science," as distinguished from "law as an element of the moral sciences." The line Schweber draws between the natural and moral sciences seems a bit too distinct for early-republic legal thinkers. But his more significant point, describing the "Protestant Baconianism" of legal elites as a combination of four features—natural theology, bounded inductivism, grand synthesis, and professional improvement—is quite sound.[66]

The scientific, or naturalistic, understanding of law is perhaps the most difficult idea to comprehend by twenty-first century minds that only partially retain eighteenth-century notions of natural science. Thus most of us would agree with Jesse Bledsoe, who told his law students in 1827 that blood circulated in the human body prior to William Harvey's discovery of that fact in the same way that electricity existed prior to Benjamin Franklin's kite experiment. Harvey and Franklin were merely describing phenomena of nature. However, we would have more difficulty with Bledsoe's next assertion that laws governing mankind and social organization similarly exist in nature, like blood flow and electrical flow, regardless of whether or not man correctly described them.[67]

The study of history was particularly useful to the scientifically oriented lawyer. For him, recorded human history was like the collected observations of an astronomer's celestial gazing: it provided raw data from which he could induce the natural laws responsible for producing the recorded facts. History was "the great mirror" of nature.[68] Yet, rather than revealing the laws of planetary motion, the study of history revealed the laws of human nature and the laws of politics and government. A student could better understand the common law from a historical perspective, keeping in mind the social circumstances a particular law was designed to address. But just because the common law might have arisen in a haphazard manner, it did not mean that there was no reason underlying any particular rule. What the slow development of the common law did mean for the new legal scientists was that a lot of work had to be done to distill the rules down to their fundamental principles.

Besides history, comparative studies were equally useful to gather information on different social experiments from which one could gain knowledge of legal science. As Simon Greenleaf explained, "In this science, as in the comparative anatomy of a sister profession, we best understand our own system of laws by comparing it with those of other nations."[69] The value of comparative studies was similar to the value of history in that both exposed "the great truth," that with conditions constant, "the laws necessary for this government, are essentially the same"[70]—the same, that is, as in all other nations, at all other times.

The consequences of the existence of legal science were profound. If municipal law was a science—a product of nature, not of man—then a correct description of the law was not bounded by time or space. Blood and electricity did not flow differently in other eras or in other countries, and neither did fairness or justice operate differently. Other countries and other times may have been cruel and unjust, just as they had been ignorant of, and unlearned in, biology and physics. "Reason and justice, are of no particular country; and every community, governed by laws, experiences the necessity of adapting them to its condition."[71]

If law was an objective science, in search of answers far more profound and important to mankind than the intricacies of blood and electrical flow, its professors needed to seriously reform the law curriculum away from the case method and reorient the profession to view itself as more than a trade. The case method was problematic because it focused the lawyer's attention too much on the idiosyncrasies of any given case, usually to the exclusion of the principles underlying the decision. This would be like studying electricity with excessive attention to the peripheral details of Franklin's experiment—his clothes, the time of day, his mood, the number of other observers, and so forth. While any of those details might affect the recorded observations, none of them mattered to the laws governing electrical current. The heart of any scientific study had to be the already verified natural laws. The student of science first had to be taught how to correctly deduce results from known laws before he could engage in experimentation and induce, that is, discover, new laws of nature. The number of legal-scientific experiments (reported cases) was vast enough that legal scholars should have been able to extract from them numerous principles of natural law governing social organization. According to Thomas Cooper:

> These cases serve, like the experiments in Chemistry; they are multiplied, till, by careful analysis and comparison of each with the others, we discover the general law that pervades and explains them all. When this is done with due diligence and caution, the principle deduced, renders unnecessary a thousand experiments in Chemistry, and decides at one, a crowd of perplexing doubts and difficulties in Law.[72]

These general principles should then have been laid out in a simple format with which students could practice mastering these timeless truths of human government. Hence, rulebooks, not casebooks, were the antebellum ideal in legal texts.

The study of cases was highly misleading to budding legal scientists because it tended to lead them astray into memorizing outcomes rather than grasping scientific principles. The *American Jurist* warned the novice that he "will find it utterly impossible to become an eminent or successful lawyer, who relies upon his memory in the exigencies of practice, to furnish him with decided cases for the resolution of his doubts."[73] John Anthon preferred to teach law out of an institutional treatise like Blackstone rather than a mass of case law because clashing cases contained "unconnected matter," loose and unsettled principles that "tend much to unhinge and unsettle the mind."[74] Cooper reminded his students that jurisprudence was "not a science of decisions, constituting a load upon the memory, but of principles deducible by laborious but logical inferences from those decisions."[75] Jesse Bledsoe went even further in explaining the professional consequences of falling under the sway of case law:

> One great reason, among others, why there are so few eminent lawyers, is, that they are too apt to learn law, as a parrot does language: by rote. Cases, are read with a view, to their particular circumstances only; while the principles upon which the decision is based, are overlooked or not understood. A mere case lawyer, can never be a great one.[76]

Bledsoe was not alone in explaining to his law students the professional indignities resulting from non-scientific training.

One of Bledsoe's successors at Transylvania, Daniel Mayes, was especially critical of the practices of "mere case lawyers." Mayes's lectures in the remote regions of Kentucky made their way to Boston and greatly impressed the editors of the *American Jurist*, which positively reviewed an 1832 introductory address. Mayes thought that most difficulties faced by lawyers in practice resulted from "following cases, instead of principles." "How often have the ablest ministers of justice been compelled to smother the cries of conscience, and sacrifice the rights of a party upon the altar of the idol, *stare decisis*!"[77] Mayes explained that poorly educated lawyers were ill equipped to deal with novel questions. Whenever a new case did come along, the unscientific lawyer was likely to try to fit it into an already decided line of cases based upon superficial appearances, not upon the principle or justice of the case.

> If a question is proposed of a case they have not seen, they are at a stand for want of a rule by which to test the case. This must ever be our condition, so long as we memorize cases, instead of studying principles. Cases are useful; but their greatest use is, that they serve to illustrate principles. If they are read and not resolved into elementary principles, the profit of the reading is not worth the time it occupies. He who is only able to say *ita lex scripta est*, has not commenced making himself a lawyer, in any proper sense of the term, even if able to repeat every reported case from the Year Books down to the present day.[78]

Mayes had a way with analogies, and described to his students how scientific knowledge was as essential to a lawyer as it was to a chef, and hence, how the lawyer stood "in the same relation to law, that the cook does to chemistry."[79] What Mayes most wanted his students to understand was that certain "relations, connexions, and dependencies" existed between the science of law and the art of law, even if the average lawyer was ignorant of the science and only emulated the art of others. For example, the average cook was probably unaware of "the existence of certain chemical laws, uniform in their action, and universal in their application, which are upon investigation not only discoverable, but easy of comprehension," and which are responsible for his wonderful culinary creations. Rather, he likely follows the combinations and methods he "has always seen"; in other words, he follows someone else's recipe. Unscientific lawyers acted the same way: "Wholly unable to assign a reason for any thing they do, but acting as the preceptor acted before them, because he so acted, they acquire the art, whilst wholly ignorant of the science of jurisprudence."[80]

NOTES

1. William Littell, *A Lecture, delivered at Frankfort, Ky. January 15th, 1818, by William Littell, Esq. L.L. D. On the Necessity of Establishing Law Colleges in the United States* (Frankfort, KY: Bledsoe & Farnham, 1818), 5.
2. George Robertson, "Introductory Lecture, Delivered in the Chapel of Morrison College, on the 7th of November, 1835," in *Scrap Book on Law and Politics, Men and Times* (Lexington, KY: A. W. Elder, 1855), 183.
3. Lucas Powell Thompson, "Introductory Lecture Delivered by Judge Lucas P. Thompson before His Law School in Staunton, December 3, 1839," in *Essays on Legal Education in Nineteenth Century Virginia*, ed. W. Hamilton Bryson (Buffalo, NY: William S. Hein & Co., 1998), 121–22.
4. Charles Warren, *A History of the American Bar* (1911; repr., Washington, DC: Beard Books, 1999), 357.
5. See Craig Evan Klafter, "St. George Tucker: The First Modern American Law Professor," *Journal of the Historical Society* 6, no. 1 (2006): 133–50.

6. St. George Tucker, *Blackstone's Commentaries: with Notes of Reference to the Constitution and Laws, of the Federal Government of the United States, and of the Commonwealth of Virginia: with an Appendix to Each Volume, Containing Short Tracts upon Such Subjects as Appeared Necessary to Form a Connected View of the Laws of Virginia as a Member of the Federal Union*, 5 vols. (Philadelphia: William Young Birch and Abraham Small, 1803).

7. Tucker's primary notes to Blackstone were reprinted as, St. George Tucker, *View of the Constitution of the United States with Selected Writings* (Indianapolis, IN: Liberty Fund, Inc., 1999).

8. For critiques of the historiographical category of republicanism, see Robert E. Shallope, "Republican and Early American Historiography," *William and Mary Quarterly* 39 (1982): 334–56; Joyce Appleby, "Republicanism in Old and New Contexts," *Williams and Mary Quarterly* 43 (1986): 20–34; Daniel T. Rodgers, "Republicanism: The Career of a Concept," *Journal of American History* 79 (1992): 11–38.

9. Thomas S. Grimké, *An Oration on the Practicability and Expediency of Reducing the Whole Body of the Law to the Simplicity and Order of a Code* (Charleston: A. E. Miller, 1827), 30.

10. Simon Greenleaf, *A Discourse Pronounced at the Inauguration of the Author as Royall Professor of Law in Harvard University* (Cambridge, MA: James Munroe and Company, 1834), 5.

11. Timothy Walker, *Introductory Lecture on the Dignity of the Law as a Profession* (Cincinnati: Daily Gazette Office, 1837), 3.

12. James Kent, *A Lecture, Introductory to a Course of Law Lectures in Columbia College* (New York: Clayton & Van Norden, 1824), 6–7.

13. Grimké, *An Oration*, 29–30.

14. Greenleaf, *A Discourse*, 4.

15. Thomas Cooper, *Introductory Lecture to a Course of Law* (Columbia, SC: Telescope Office, 1834), 7.

16. Ibid., 9.

17. Walker, *Introductory Lecture*, 11.

18. Beverley Tucker, "Law Lecture at William and Mary," *Southern Literary Messenger* 1 (1834): 148.

19. Ibid., 152.

20. James Kent to Thomas Washington, New York, Oct. 6, 1828, reprinted as "An Unpublished Letter of Chancellor James Kent," *Green Bag* 9 (1897): 208.

21. James Kent, "An Introductory Lecture to Course of Law Lectures" (1794), reprinted in *Columbia Law Review* 3 (1909): 332.

22. For example, Beverly Tucker argued that "even in private life, as soon as he puts on manhood, [the citizen] assumes a 'place in the common wealth.'" Tucker, "Law Lecture at William and Mary," 151.

23. Kent, "An Introductory Lecture," 331.

24. John Reed, *Pennsylvania Blackstone: Being a Modification of the Commentaries of Sir William Blackstone, with Numerous Alterations and Additions, Designed to Present an Elementary Exposition of the Entire Laws of Pennsylvania*, 3 vols. (Carlisle, PA: George Fleming, 1831) 1:9.

25. Ibid., 8.

26. Greenleaf, *A Discourse*, 7.

27. B. Tucker, "Law Lecture at William and Mary," 151.

28. See Reed, *Pennsylvania Blackstone*, 1:7.

29. John Anthon, "An Essay on the Study of Law," in *An Analytical Abridgment of the Commentaries of Sir William Blackstone*, 2nd ed. (Philadelphia: P. H. Nicklin & T. Johnson, 1832), 37.

30. Greenleaf, *A Discourse*, 12.

31. Kent, "An Introductory Lecture," 332.

32. Daniel Mayes, *An Address to the Students of Law in Transylvania University, Delivered at the Beginning of the Session for 1835* (Lexington, KY: J. Clarke & Co., 1835), 24.

33. Kent, *A Lecture*, 14-15.

34. Kent, "An Introductory Lecture," 333.
35. Ibid., 334.
36. Reed, *Pennsylvania Blackstone,* 1:iii.
37. Ibid., iv.
38. Anthon, "An Essay on the Study of Law," 39–40.
39. Ibid., 41.
40. James Kent, *Commentaries on American Law,* 4 vols. (New York: O. Halsted, 1826–1830).
41. Kent, "An Introductory Lecture," 330.
42. Cooper, *Introductory Lecture,* 20, 22.
43. Benjamin F. Butler, *Plan for the Organization of a Law Faculty and for a System of Instruction in Legal Science, in the University of the City of New-York* (New York: University Press, 1835), 6–7, n.*.
44. Greenleaf, *A Discourse,* 14.
45. B. Tucker, "Law Lecture at William and Mary," 150.
46. For more on the early professors of law in London, see Raymond Cocks, *Foundations of the Modern Bar* (London: Sweet & Maxwell, 1983), 40–51. Cocks describes "ideas about education" as presenting "the most persistent challenge" to the legal establishment.
47. "Legal Education," *American Jurist and Law Magazine* 8 (1832): 259 (review of J. J. Park, "An Introductory Lecture, delivered at King's College, London, November 1, 1831"). See also Josiah Quincy, *An Address Delivered at the Dedication of Dane Law College in Harvard University, October 23, 1832* (Cambridge, MA: E. W. Metcalf & Co., 1832), 16 (quoting Park).
48. See, e.g., Maxwell Bloomfield, *American Lawyers in a Changing Society, 1776–1876* (Cambridge, MA: Harvard University Press, 1976), esp. ch. 2, "Antilawyer Sentiment in the Early Republic"; Gerard W. Gawalt, *The Promise of Power: The Legal Profession in Massachusetts, 1760–1840* (Westport, CT: Greenwood Press, 1979).
49. Walker, *Introductory Lecture,* 23, 24.
50. Ibid.,13.
51. Grimké, *An Oration,* 28.
52. Cooper, *Introductory Lecture,* 23.
53. Kent, "An Introductory Lecture," 343. Kent argued much the same during his second time around as a Columbia professor in 1824. Kent, *A Lecture,* 11.
54. M. H. Hoeflich, "The Americanization of British Legal Education in the Nineteenth Century," *Journal of Legal History* 8, no. 3 (1987): 253–54 (quoting Amos).
55. See M. H. Hoeflich, "Legal Ethics in the Nineteenth Century: The 'Other Tradition,'" *Kansas Law Review* 47 (1999): 793–817; Norman W. Spaulding, "The Myth of Civic Republicanism: Interrogating the Ideology of Antebellum Legal Ethics," *Fordham Law Review* 71 (2003): 1397–1459.
56. Kent, *A Lecture,* 8–9.
57. Beverley Tucker, "Professor Beverley Tucker's Valedictory Address to His Class," *Southern Literary Messenger* 1 (1835): 599.
58. Reed, *Pennsylvania Blackstone,* 1:4.
59. Greenleaf, *A Discourse,* 16. Reed also argued that lawyers should avoid being "destructive to the country's peace." Reed, *Pennsylvania Blackstone,* 1:4.
60. Greenleaf, *A Discourse,* 17.
61. Ibid.
62. David Hoffman, *A Course of Legal Study, Addressed to Students and the Profession Generally,* 2nd ed. (Baltimore: Joseph Neal, 1836; repr., New York: Arno Press, 1972), 745, 751.
63. The same went for a plea of infancy to avoid a debt. Ibid., 754, 775. In addition to the public morality that is suggested by Hoffman and others' refusal to be merely handmaidens of their clients, Michael Ariens suggests that a private morality grounded in the "concept of honor" also undergirded the sentiments expressed in this paragraph. This is a very tenable conclusion given the honor culture that existed at the

time, especially among southerners. Michael Ariens, "Lost and Found: David Hoffman and the History of American Legal Ethics," *Arkansas Law Review* 67 (2014): 600.

64. Butler, *Plan for the Organization of a Law Faculty*, 23.

65. "Whether Law Is a Science?," *American Jurist and Law Magazine* 9 (1833): 349 (reviewing Daniel Mayes, *An Introductory Lecture, Delivered to the Law Class of Transylvania University, on the 5th of November, 1832* [Lexington, KY: H. Savary & Co., 1832]). The *American Jurist* misprinted the title of the lecture as being delivered on the "8th" of November, but the published lecture is correctly cited in the parenthetical.

66. Howard Schweber, "The 'Science' of Legal Science: The Model of the Natural Sciences in Nineteenth-Century American Legal Education," *Law and History Review* 17, no. 3 (1999): 421–66. Schweber, like a number of others who have written about the same period, finds Scottish Common Sense philosophy to be particularly influential in countering the epistemological skepticism of Locke. I am skeptical about this claim for two reasons: 1) the moralizing of the legal elites can usually be traced to materialistic or objective claims based in history, custom, or comparative studies, not intuition; 2) the writings of Hugh Legaré, a legal elite who actually studied law and moral philosophy at Edinburgh and openly embraced Dugald Stewart, hardly resemble the work product of his intellectual cohort. For others who discuss Common Sense, see Craig Evan Klafter, *Reason over Precedents: Origins of American Legal Thought* (Westport, CT: Greenwood Press, 1993) 60–61. For others who discuss the relationship between law and science, see M. H. Hoeflich, "Law and Geometry: Legal Science from Leibniz to Langdell," *American Journal of Legal History* 30 (1986): 95–121. Barbara Shapiro has done the same for English law in the early modern period: Barbara J. Shapiro, "Law and Science in Seventeenth-Century England," *Stanford Law Review* 21 (1969): 727–66. This issue forms the basis of chapter 3.

67. Jesse Bledsoe, *Introductory Lecture on Law* (Nashville: Republican & Gazette, 1827) 4.

68. Ibid., 7. Others who noted the value of history include: Anthon, "An Essay on the Study of Law," 36; William Barry, *An Introductory Lecture on the Study of Law, Delivered in the Chapel of Transylvania University, on Monday, October 1, 1821* (Lexington, KY: W. G. Hunt, 1821), 14-15; Jesse Bledsoe, *An Introductory Lecture, Preparatory to a Course of Instruction on Common and Statute Law, Delivered in the Chapel of Transylvania University, on Monday, November 3d, 1823* (Lexington, KY: William Tanner, 1823), 18; Littell, *A Lecture*, 19; Daniel Mayes, *An Address Delivered before the Trustees and Faculty of Transylvania University at the Opening of the Session of the Law Department, on the 7th Nov. 1831* (Lexington, KY: Finnell & J. F. Herndon,1831), 14; Mayes, *An Address to the Students of Law in Transylvania University*, 16; Isaac Parker, "Inaugural Address Delivered in the Chapel of Harvard University, by the Hon. Isaac Parker, Chief Justice of Massachusetts, and Royal Professor of Law," *North American Review* 11 (1816): 24; Robertson, "Introductory Lecture," 181. One contrasting voice is that of Lucas Powell Thompson, who warns students to keep other disciplines, including history, subordinate to law. Thompson, "Introductory Lecture," 124.

69. Greenleaf, *A Disourse*, 14.

70. Ibid.

71. Bledsoe, *Introductory Lecture on Law*, 11.

72. Cooper, *Introductory Lecture*, 24.

73. "Whether Law Is a Science?", *American Jurist*, 352.

74. Anthon, "An Essay on the Study of Law," 56.

75. Cooper, *Introductory Lecture*, 12, 24.

76. Bledsoe, *Introductory Lecture on Law*, 9

77. "Whether Law Is a Science?", 355.

78. Ibid., 369.

79. Mayes, *An Address to the Students of Law*, 3.

80. Ibid., 5.

TWO

The Philosophy of Legal Science

If the educational efforts, exemplified by the law lectures, were the primary means of spreading the knowledge of legal science, then the Enlightenment invigoration of utility emerging from Britain provided a new means of justifying the reform efforts of the legal scientists. The role of utility as part of a coherent philosophy of utilitarianism has been underexplored in the existing legal historiography. As noted in the introduction, Alfred Brophy has recently begun to take notice of utility as the basis for southern judicial opinions. The chapters that follow partly examine how legal scientists responded to the utilitarianism of William Paley and Jeremy Bentham. Although the judgment was not uniform among the legal scientists as to the correctness of the underlying philosophies, many of the justifications for legal reforms urged by the legal scientists sounded in utilitarian terms.

In *Utilitarian Jurisprudence in America*, Peter King traced the influence of Benthamic utilitarianism on the nineteenth-century American legal profession. He held up Thomas Cooper, David Hoffman, and Richard Hildreth, as those early American legal thinkers most notably influenced by Bentham.[1] For King, Hildreth represented "the first real fruition of Benthamism in America," whereas Cooper's use of Bentham was subservient to his Southern ideology, and Hoffman's use was mainly to "reinforce" a utilitarianism otherwise "derived from Paley."[2] Hildreth is, indeed, a complex figure whose wide-ranging writings extend past the early republic and focused to a great extent on slavery and the Civil War. A re-evaluation of Cooper within the broader context of early republican jurisprudence is what follows in chapter 5. Because Cooper became an advocate of southern secession late in life, too many historians have dismissed his life's work, which consisted of serious intellectual undertakings in law and philosophy, as well as medicine and chemistry. Hoffman is partly discussed in this chapter in order to provide additional examples of the utilitarian influence on American legal scientists. Unfortunately, Hoffman has become a man for all seasons among legal historians. His seven-year course of legal study contained such a vast and eclectic array of titles, that one can superficially paint Hoffman as advocating just about anything. As of late, Hoffman has been discussed as a leading American exponent of Scottish Common Sense philosophy, second only to the St. Andrews-educated James Wilson a generation earlier.[3] This tension between Hoffman-the-utilitarian and Hoffman-the-Scot requires a new examination. A fresh look at the utilitarian influence on American jurisprudence also requires that we acknowledge the influence of William Paley, a figure far more at home in early American colleges than Bentham.[4]

The goal of this chapter is not to argue that American jurists hewed closely to philosophical utilitarianism and faithfully applied it in every case. Rather, the hope is to add to the literature that has focused solely on the legal implications of common sense, or moral intuitionism. Further, the chapter seeks to demonstrate that legal arguments based on utility were not devoid of considerations of feelings or sentiments, and thus did not fit neatly into the "head" side of the "heart versus head" distinction articulated by Miller and others.[5] Instead, the best legal policies were frequently premised on a respect for human sentiment, which, in turn, provided for predictable and reasonable legal outcomes.

By examining the commonalities of these self-described legal scientists, the influence of utilitarianism as a political and legal philosophy on legal science is more readily apparent. Most displayed a strong preference for reason over instinct or intuition when coming to a conclusion about the morality of a legal outcome. All either engaged directly with the thought of Paley and/or Bentham, or at least formulated their own utilitarian standard of moral judgment. These legal scientists criticized the existing profession for ignoring the consequences of the precedent-based system. The Roman-based civil law frequently provided a ready example as a preferable system whose method of analysis was worthy of emulation. Finally, as we partly saw in the previous chapter, legal scientists viewed the academic world as the answer to the majority of their criticisms. Within the emerging legal academy, students would learn law methodically, and usually by reading the publications of this same group of utilitarian critics.

THE CENTRALITY OF REASON

When legal scientists composed didactic works of jurisprudence or elementary treatises they almost always began with the moral foundations of obedience to the law. It is in these introductory remarks that we most clearly see the legal scientists' philosophical commitments to one school of thought or another. Among early republican legal scientists, their commitment to a rationally calculated utility as the basis for moral judgment is quite apparent. Also common among them is their skepticism toward moral systems that would rest their judgments upon some non-rational basis, like instinct, intuition, or a purely religious rationale. Frequently, the legal scholars would bracket religious, natural law, justifications, explaining that even if obedience to a particular law was a requirement of natural law, man's understanding of those godly requirements was itself the product of reason. Thus, duty to God was often folded into duty to the state and to one's fellow citizens, that is, duty to the civil law.[6]

One of the earliest relevant works is that of Thomas Cooper (1759–1839), Pennsylvania judge turned South Carolina law professor and statute compiler. Originally of Westminster, Cooper was no latecomer to the doctrine of utility. Quite the contrary, Cooper left good documentary evidence that he, not Paley, originated a new moral theory in the 1780s. While still living in England, Cooper was an active member of the Manchester Society, where he read a number of philosophical papers he eventually published in 1787 under the title, *Tracts, Ethical, Theological and Political*. "On Moral Obligation" was the first tract contained in the collection. Cooper felt compelled to drop a footnote to its listing in the table of contents indicating that the paper was originally read on 29 September 1784. He mentioned this information "chiefly because Dr. Paley's book on Morals, which was published sometime after, and which I never saw till lately, states the question somewhat in the same way I do."[7] In seeking the true source of moral obligation, Cooper proceeded to examine ten answers frequently given by moral philosophers. Two answers he found more compelling than the others: 1) "It is conducive to general utility" and 2) "It is conducive to the *bene esse*, to your own greatest good upon the whole."[8] Cooper emphasized that virtue and prudence were synonymous.[9] He thought, "private happiness is the only ultimate motive of action, where there is any apparent motive at all."[10]

Before arriving at his favored reasons for moral obligation, Cooper exerted some effort in disposing of the Scots' arguments. Cooper associated Hutcheson and Kaimes with "moral sense" and Herbert, Reid, Beattie and Oswald with "common sense," neither of which was very dissimilar from the other. Hutcheson's "*instinctive* approbation common to all men" was incredibly "unphilosophical."[11] Had there been anything to it, then "there ought to be no difference of opinion on the subject of morals." As empirical proof that "moral sense" was nonsense, Cooper pointed to "the codes of laws ancient and modern": "The difference is so great as to be the sole foundation [of those who] with some plausibility assert that nothing is just or unjust, but what is determined so to be by the laws of each state."[12] Cooper then ridiculed the notion of conscience as espoused by the common-sense crowd by showing its uselessness at distinguishing virtue from vice. He recalled a number of famous historical assassinations and massacres whose agents claimed they were motivated to take action solely by their consciences. For Cooper this was enough proof to refute those who turned their backs on the role of reason in morality. He thought his heavy-handed examples would not have been necessary but for the "arrogance of the authors themselves, and by their contemptuous manner of treating those who have *reasoned* upon the same subjects, and whose knowledge was so far superior."[13]

If Cooper's 1784 discussion was not clear enough, he made his views on "the vague and wordy discussions of the Scotch school" crystal clear in his 1831 translation of F. J. V. Broussais's *On Irritation and Insanity*.[14] Cooper intended the publication of the work to further his materialist view that the soul was non-existent. He appended one of his own pamphlets to the work in which he decried "the numberless brood of the Scotch metaphysicians." He explained,

> I cannot and will not condescend to reply to the dreadful nonsense on this subject assumed as true by Dr. Reid and Dr. Beattie, or to the shallow sophisms of Dr. Gregory, or the prolix pages of inanity of Dr. Dugald Stewart, or the ignorant hardihood of assertion of Dr. Barclay in his late inquiry.

By way of contrast, Cooper approved of Locke's demonstration that "we have no innate ideas."[15]

David Hoffman (1784–1854), the original law professor at the University of Maryland, treated appeals to unreasoned instinct as similarly unconvincing and held the same negative view of what he thought was an anti-intellectual strain to advocates of Common Sense. Hoffman was most recently singled out by Susanna Blumenthal as an example of an elite lawyer who "specially commended [the Common Sense] school of thought to those who aspired to join their ranks."[16] Blumenthal's evidence for Hoffman's Scottish leanings was his listing of the works of Beattie and Reid under the first title of his *Course of Legal Study*. Charles Barzun, in an earlier law review note,[17] also latched onto the same paragraph, in which Hoffman says, "The essays of Reid, Locke, and Stewart, are inestimable to the student, who . . . is ambitious to add the talents of profound and severe investigation, of just reasoning, and happy illustration."[18] It is unlikely, however, that Hoffman was making the case for a morality founded on intuitive notions of common sense. In placing Locke alongside Reid and Stewart, Hoffman was likely making a pedagogical point, namely, that the aspiring lawyer should be well read in competing theories of metaphysics. Hoffman regularly listed and discussed authors with whom he disagreed, most notably, Adam Smith, whose theory of sympathy Hoffman found "obnoxious to many powerful objections."[19]

Hoffman did his best to present his *Course* as a liberal studies program, offering his students instruction on all sides of philosophical and political debates. We can, however, detect Hoffman's own leanings by taking a broad view of the *Course*, noting which works he dwelled upon in the expository notes and by consulting his other writings, including those of a non-legal character. The *Course* was first published in 1817, with a second edition appearing in 1836. The "General Syllabus" of the *Course* contained thirteen titles, under which were listed numerous readings corresponding to the various subjects. There was also a listing of nine "Auxiliary Subjects," which greatly expanded the student's study. Close adherence to the *Course* would require six or seven years of full-time reading. While most of the major titles concerned traditional areas of legal study, such as equity, crimes, and constitutional law, they were sandwiched between "Moral and Political Philosophy" and "Political Economy"—the first and last titles respectively. Perhaps it was just coincidence that Hoffman entitled his first substantive section using the same name as Paley's famous volume, but perhaps not.[20]

A most notable difference between the first and second editions of the *Course* is Hoffman's significant expansion of his "note" on Paley.[21] What motivated the extended discussion of Paley were the critical reviews of Hoffman's subsequent legal writings. This is how Hoffman began his new response to the critics: "The utility of moral philosophy, as a substantive branch of scientific study, has been questioned by some, under the objection that it has generated vain and subtle theories of moral obligation, and that natural reason, and moral sense are the surest and safest guides!"[22] Hoffman never mentions these critics by name, nor does he indicate where the criticisms appeared. Later on in the note he recalls "American critics" of his intervening *Legal Outlines*, who found fault because he had "intimately connected law, not only with ethics and the physical sciences, but with the higher branches of metaphysics, and the esoteric philosophy of politics, and of legislation."[23] *Legal Outlines* was a series of written lectures based in large part on works contained in the *Course* syllabus, focusing particularly on the first title of "Moral and Political Philosophy."[24]

Although not an enthusiastic devotee of Bentham like Cooper, David Hoffman demonstrated his admiration in his educational materials. In *Legal Outlines*, Hoffman devoted six pages to an intellectual biography of Bentham, mostly excerpting an essay by William Hazlitt to paint this personal portrait.[25] The result was a legal philosopher both quixotic and sincere. Bentham was also listed as one of Hoffman's thirteen modern thinkers "who have contributed largely to the improvement of political science."[26] Not surprisingly, no Common Sense advocate was among the honored. Although Hoffman said of Bentham's utility, "we have some faith in it, but think it has not been clearly and dispassionately set forth,"[27] he agreed entirely with legal reforms that resulted from that philosophical program. American law students and lawyers should be exposed to works that "are freely censorial, pointing out what the law of evidence, in many instances, *ought* to be, rather than what it really is."[28] They should also understand the "philosophy of criminal legislation" as set out by Bentham.[29] Americans should also welcome, not fear, codification.

Of all of the reviews of the first edition of the *Course*, I have found none that could be considered, on the whole, negative. With regard to *Legal Outlines*, one review does fit Hoffman's response—a critique that appeared in 1829 in the *Southern Review* written by Hugh S. Legaré.[30] Hoffman's enthusiasm for both Paley's and Bentham's theories and reform efforts was too much for Hugh Legaré, a South Carolinian who had studied law in Scotland before returning to the United States. Legaré began his review of *Legal Outlines* by calling Hoffman's work an "enormous mass of irrelevant matter which has been huddled together."[31] He thought, "two thirds at least of the volume before us is liable to a mixed charge of irrelevancy and triteness."[32] Demonstrating his penchant for sarcasm, while criticizing the diversity of topics, Legaré wrote: "As far as utility—we use the word in its most comprehensive acceptation—is concerned, it would puzzle Jeremy Bentham himself to settle their comparative pretensions."[33] Legaré's "*beau idéal* of an elementary treatise in jurisprudence," which balanced theory and practice, was Bell's *Commentaries on the Laws of Scotland*.[34] Unlike Hoffman, Legaré, a classicist by training, had actually studied law and philosophy at the University of Edinburgh, and openly embraced the work of Dugald Stewart. His critique of Bentham in the *Southern Review*—the same pages in which Cooper had praised Bentham's *Evidence*—reveals the disparate treatment of utility by a true Stewart (common sense) partisan. Nevertheless, as we will see in chapter 6, Legaré shared a number of the other legal scientists' goals and concerns in spite of his alternative morality largely because he exempted law from moral analysis altogether.

A central theme of Bentham's critique of the English legal system was that of the single-minded self-interest of "Judge & Co." In Bentham's view, the legal profession's own interests were not restrained by considerations of public utility, and therefore required serious reform.[35] American critics similarly engaged in self-critique, invoking Bentham's notions of reform all the while.

Unlike David Hoffman's critics who questioned "the utility of moral philosophy," Hoffman himself thought that theory was essential to good legal practice. He observed that in the United States "law is both *studied* and *practised*, far more liberally and scientifically than it is in England. It is there, as well as in France, much more an art—a trade—a mere profession, and a narrow vocation, than it is in our country."[36] In offering a British edition of his *Legal Outlines*, Hoffman hoped to appeal to British students by telling his potential readers that they would find more attention paid to what "is embraced under the head of universal jurisprudence, than seems to be the case in England."[37] Elsewhere, Hoffman contrasted law with medicine—the more inferior profession—and noted that "if the history of medicine be looked into, it will be found that scarce any theory, any remedy, any prophylactic given to the world, was ever, in the first instance, fairly, and dispassionately examined by the profession."[38] The problem was that physicians "read too little, after they have obtained a goodly share of practice!"[39] Because of the centrality of intellectualism and liberal study to the profession of law, the rise of the utilitarians caused Hoffman some pause.

For Hoffman, a utilitarian was the opposite of a schoolman, most notably epitomized by Aquinas. The problem was this: "We know that learning, without judgment, characterized the schoolmen; and we apprehend that common sense, without learning, will very soon characterize the utilitarians—and both are extremes, equally to be avoided."[40] Although Hoffman appreciated the utilitarian distaste for "idle knowledge, and the influence of mere *authority*,"[41] he feared that utilitarianism was moving too far in the opposite direction. The compression and democratization of knowledge that resulted from the intense "seeking after *practicalness*," was becoming "a too visible feature in the researches of our utilitarians."[42] All of Hoffman's efforts in legal pedagogy aimed at preventing law from becoming both too esoteric and too practical. It was in this effort that Hoffman thought Bentham could prove useful.

While still justifying the value of Paley's *Moral Philosophy* to law students, Hoffman observed: "[H]ow much mistaken is the idea entertained by many in this country, that the lawyer (whose province is reasoning,) can attain to eminence, though he restricts his inquiries within the visible boundaries of his peculiar science, chiefly as it is found in the treatises of municipal law."[43] Hoffman viewed his *Legal Outlines* as a corrective to this "narrow view" of legal science. It is within the pages of this work that Hoffman most forcefully expresses his admiration for Bentham, to whom he referred as an "extraordinary man."[44] Hoffman admired many of Bentham's works, singling out his *Evidence, Théorie des Peines et des Récompenses*, and his essays on codification. He thought, "How much the world is really indebted to the labours of this conscript father of legal reforms, is even yet but little known."[45]

Nathaniel Chipman, chief justice of Vermont and law professor at Middlebury College beginning in 1816, provides an example of someone who, on the face of things, wanted to split the difference between utility and traditional natural law. In his 1833 government treatise, which he composed primarily for his students, he too began by inquiring into the foundations of moral obligation. His answer: "it arises from the moral relations existing . . . and the design and end of that system—the interest and happiness of the subject."[46] Inquiring further, he considered the traditional answer, namely, that God accounts for such moral obligation and he expressed some sympathy with this response: "This mode of accounting for the efficient of moral obligation supports the dignity of the law, and with energy brings it home to the mind." He explicitly contrasted the religious answer with that of "others" who "have found the obligation in utility only."[47] But Chipman's solution was a sort of middle ground that would have fit comfortably within Paley's philosophy.

Chipman made it clear that he sided with the utilitarians. "We may here repeat, that the utility of any class of actions, that is, their general tendency to promote human happiness is a sure, I may say, the only sure test, that the rule requiring them is a genuine law of nature." He acknowledged, "that general utility, the general happiness of the whole human race is an object too vast for the limited faculties of man; that if it be considered as a general rule, the rule is of too general a nature to be applied to immediate action in any case." But Chipman thought that municipal laws guided by the principle of utility would habituate individuals generally to do good. As he explained in more technical language, "the general rule, superinduced upon the specific and immediate rules of conduct, by affecting the disposition of the agent, qualifies his actions, and unites private with the general interest."[48] In other words, it was properly grounded law that turned individuals into good, moral citizens, rather than some *a priori* commitment to God or some innate sense of right and wrong.

Finally, it worth considering the explicit philosophy coming out of Transylvania University in Lexington, Kentucky, in the 1820s and 1830s. Not much has been written of this western institution.[49] The university modeled itself after William and Mary and then adopted Jefferson's practice at the University of Virginia in making politics a part of the curriculum. According to one scholar, the founder of the law department at Transylvania was "not only an intense Anti-Federalist or Democrat but was recognized as a leader in the political polemics of his time."[50] However, that was in the late-eighteenth century, when the Adams-Jefferson rivalry was at its height. By the 1820s, the law department, led by William T. Barry, had become a well-recognized institution of legal study throughout the nation. Joined by Professor Jesse Bledsoe, the department had its first graduation in 1823, conferring Bachelor of Laws degrees upon seventeen students.[51] By 1834, the Transylvania law department had three professors, including George Robertson and Daniel Mayes, making it the "largest law faculty in America."[52] Barry, Bledsoe, Mayes, and Robertson were all prominent attorneys or judges whose published lectures give us an insight into their jurisprudential motivations, which were remarkably consistent.

In one of his first lectures in 1821, Barry explained why "moral philosophy" was important to the law. Primarily, its study habituated the student of law "to the cultivation of science," which allowed for the comprehension of abstract principles with an ease and rapidity that would otherwise be absent. In this way, law is "placed on the basis of reason and is elevated by philosophy among the sciences."[53] It was Barry's contemporary, Bledsoe, who more explicitly articulated the substance of that moral philosophy.

Bledsoe concurred that law "is undoubtedly a science, and one too which yields in importance to no other." In explaining the goal of law, Bledsoe contended that it was "the best means of attaining happiness in this terrestrial state of being." Because law needed to address itself to intelligent beings, lawyers needed to understand how humans operated. "The desire of pleasure and the wish to avoid pain, is the first lesson we learn on our entrance into the world. . . . It is our animal propensity." For Bledsoe, nature was the ultimate legislator, whereas reason served to guide man's interpretation of what the municipal law should be. Applying reason, which came from revelation through material experience (primarily from studying history), we come to "the only proper test of all human laws": "*Quid utile quid non.*" Because "man is every where and at all times essentially the same," this test of utility was universal in its application, the substance of local law varying only because circumstances differed from location to location.[54] Bledsoe often repeated, "Utility may be said to be the foundation of right and wrong." The conclusion was that "nothing can be truly useful that is not truly right, so also in society its regulations are not right if they are not useful."[55]

The second cohort of Transylvania professors delivered the same message the following decade. Thus, Daniel Mayes began a lecture in 1831 by proclaiming, "The great object and end of all human action is happiness. Man is so constituted, that happiness is only attainable in a state of society."[56] Because of the "indissoluble connection" between law and human happiness, the "incontrovertible axiom" followed, "that the only legitimate end of law and of Government is the good of man." Hence, "government is best, which secures to the governed the greatest quantum of good."[57] For the lawyer and lawmaker, this meant that he had to understand the nature of man's constitution "with an eye to his happiness or welfare." "The subject of all law is man—its object, the promotion of his happiness."[58]

George Robertson, chief justice of Kentucky's highest court, who led Transylvania's law department the longest, through its 1858 closure, explained to students, "the greatest attainable good of the greatest number is the ultimate object of political association." The universality of this principle was reiterated as well. "Rational law prevails, to some extent, among all civilized men, and is the same every where."[59] Robertson further taught, "The fundamental principle of ethics is that human happiness, temporal and eternal, is the ultimate end of human existence, and should be the object of all human actions and pursuits."[60] Scientifically trained lawyers would recognize that the only natural law was rational law, and that the rationality of any law was judged by it ability to promote human happiness in the "greatest number" possible. Otherwise, "A lawyer is a pettifogger, as a doctor is a quack, unless he understands the science of his profession."[61]

The practical consequences of all this discussion of utility and human happiness are examined in detail in the following chapters. Each legal scientist had particular ways of executing the philosophy of legal science. Their goals, however—which varied from arguments for particular outcomes in individual cases, to doctrinal change through scholarly critique, to functional change in the judicial branch through political maneuvering—are better understood as stemming from a common source if this basis of legal science is kept in mind. Whether acting as a lawyer, a law professor, or an elected official, the legal scientists constantly returned to their shared commitments when explaining why their reform efforts should prevail.

One major consequence of the philosophy of legal science was the codification movement—the desire to reduce the common law to written form. Because its broad justifications were so closely tied to the goals of utility, I consider some of the common arguments in a section of this chapter below. The more unique insights into specific codification plans, like those of South Carolina and Massachusetts are reserved for the relevant chapters on the individuals who were intimately involved in those debates.

In order to appreciate more fully the jurisprudential atmosphere in which the codification efforts arose, it will help to consider the role Bentham played in directly attempting to influence the direction of American law. The extent to which Bentham reached out to American lawyers and politicians has been underappreciated in the literature, likewise the extent to which American legal scientists openly engaged with Bentham's ideas. To the extent historians have mentioned Bentham's apparent influence, it has usually been written off as a matter of political expediency on the part of the American lawyers. However, because Bentham himself was so adamant about getting his writings into American hands, it should not be surprising that legal scientists substantively engaged with the proposals he offered.

WOULD-BE LEGISLATOR OF THE UNITED STATES

Jeremy Bentham's interest in the United States began before the war for independence was complete. In 1780 Bentham drafted a letter to Benjamin Franklin, which was to accompany a copy of his most recent work, *An Introduction to the Principles of Morals and Legislation*, in which he urged Franklin to use the ideas to bring prosperity to the new country.[62] Fifteen years later, Bentham sent a letter to John Jay, the first chief justice of the United States, asking Jay to make use of another work of his, this one on the judiciary. Bentham "could not resist the opportunity of putting it into the hands of the most competent Judges America can afford." He also indicated in his short message to Jay that had he not exhausted his stock of *Tactics of Political Assemblies,* he would have sent that as well.[63] It is clear, however, that Bentham considered America in 1795 a fit polity to receive and make good use of his work. He went so far as to ask Jay if he thought some American booksellers might be interested in having copies of his works, for which purpose he was willing to have more printed.[64] Since we know this letter actually made its way to Jay, we can trace Bentham's serious interest in influencing the United States to at least the late-eighteenth century. However, it was not until the second decade of the nineteenth century that Bentham devoted his full energies to persuading Americans to accept his codification efforts.

In October 1811, Bentham wrote a lengthy letter to the president, James Madison. The correspondence contained an official offer from Bentham to draw up "*a compleat body* of proposed law, in the form of Statute law: say, in one word, a *Pannomion.*" The purpose of the proposed code was to supersede "that mass of foreign law, the yoke of which, in the *wordless,* as well as boundless, and shapeless shape of *common,* alias *unwritten* law." Although Bentham claimed that the offer was submitted for consideration "not to the person but to the Office" of president, internal evidence suggests that Bentham knew well his intended addressee.[65]

Bentham began by laying out the form his code would take, then discussing the advantages promised the recipient country, and then he turned to pre-empting several objections with lengthy rebuttals. The details of Bentham's Pannomion are well set out elsewhere,[66] and it should come as no surprise that his plan was not unique to the United States; since *A Fragment on Government* he had been making the claim, "That which *is* Law, is, in different countries, widely different: while that which *ought to be,* is in all countries to a great degree the same."[67] What was unique in his 1811 letter to Madison was his mode of argument, including his set of answers to presumed objections, which he presumably thought would resonate with an American audience, and Madison in particular.

The first objection Bentham answered concerned a very Madisonian preoccupation, "*Disturbance to property, and other existing rights.*" "So far as the objection confines itself to the law of *private rights,*" Bentham responded, "when these and any other number of declamatory generalities in the same strain have been expended, the only real mischief which they hold up to view, is, that which is reducible to this one expression—*to existing expectations, disappointment, productive of the painful sense of loss.*"[68] This answer was utilitarian to be sure, and emphasized how protecting expectations and preventing disappointment was conducive to happiness. We see Bentham employing the disappointment prevention principle as the basis for private property protections. He further detailed how unwritten law could only lead to uncertainty and thus did more to harm private rights than was realized. The point here, however, is that

Bentham was focusing on a very explicit concern of Madison's, which he expressed rather strongly in *Federalist 10*—the unequal distribution of property as the "insuperable obstacle to a uniformity of interests" among citizens.[69]

The second objection Bentham predicted was this: "*Foreign Yoke.—It was to free ourselves from the yoke of foreign law, that we took up arms against the Monarch of England; and shall an obscure subject of the same nation fasten another such yoke upon our necks?*"[70] Bentham's answer to this objection was in part that a foreigner could provide the objectivity and rational distance necessary to successfully undertake such a project. However, Bentham raised the specter of "local, as well as personal, enmities and partialities," that is, factions, as otherwise hampering acceptance of a code composed by any American. "Discussions of this sort do not, it must be confessed, shed any very brilliant lustre upon human nature," Bentham lamented, "but so it is, that we are constituted: and, being thus constituted, it is impossible for us to act either prudently or beneficially, any further than as we know ourselves for what we *are*." On the other hand, Bentham acknowledged that falling in with a faction "depends not altogether upon [a man's] will," rather it might be the result of what passes before his eyes, in other words, something that misleads his understanding. If this scientific description of human nature was not Madisonian enough, Bentham then remarked on two specific factions faced by the United States: the divisions between "*northern* and *southern*" and "*democrat* and *federalist*." Were a member of one of these sides to author such a code of laws, the opposing side would repel it based, not on utility or the universal interest, but on the factional interest, or in sympathy with the faction. Bentham tried to assure Madison that this was not a criticism of the United States, but merely a recognition of the case "wherever there have been *parties*:—wherever there has been either *liberty*, or the appearance of it. If to this rule the land of the United States afford an exception, it is a land—not of men, but angels."[71] It is difficult to know what to say of these sections of Bentham's letter to Madison, which not so subtly echo *Federalist 51*.[72] It might be that Bentham was attempting to use Madison's language to show his admiration for his thought and to show their common foundational beliefs. However, it also sounds as though there is a slight mocking of the author of the *Federalist*, using the arguments found there to confine its author into acceptance of Bentham's arguments. Because it is unlikely that Bentham would have been deliberately trying to affront the very person on whose help he was depending, the latter interpretation is unlikely. However, it does show that Bentham's sense of self-assuredness did not always translate the way he might have liked. If indeed this was a case where he had read the *Federalist* and correctly attributed it to Madison, then the roundabout way of arguing was not well suited to gaining acceptance. It seems a straightforward recognition of and agreement with Madison's works would have served him better, at least rhetorically.[73]

In the same letter to Madison, Bentham noted that he had already made many advances on several codes, including penal, civil, judicial, procedural, evidence, but not yet a constitutional code. Bentham only raised the issue of constitutional law "to shew that it has not been overlooked." However, he was satisfied that "no demand for alteration has presented itself to my view, nor should I myself be disposed to look out for any." It would seem that Bentham wanted to show his admiration and respect for the US Constitution as it stood. Thus in his Pannomion it would be "transcribed without the alteration of an iota."[74] When Bentham wrote a series of letters to the American public six years later in 1817 urging on them the same Pannomion, he also praised the Constitution: "To the values of this *Constitutional* Law of yours, you are none of you insensible. You hug it to your hearts, as the main source of, and security for, whatsoever you enjoy."[75] Well then, Bentham thought, the same affection could be shown for statute law and Americans would be none the more insensible for it.

One of the reasons Bentham wrote the series of letters to "the Citizens of the several American United States" in 1817, was because Madison had responded the previous year in a less than encouraging way. Nearly five years after Bentham had written to the president, Madison wrote back in May 1816. The delay is partially explained by the intervening War of 1812 between the United States and Great Britain, which was not concluded until 1814–1815. Madison's letter was rather terse and amounted to a "thanks, but no thanks" response. He praised Bentham's scheme, admired the idea of a digest of American laws, but ultimately doubted that the entirety of the nation's laws could really be reduced to a written code. Moreover, Madison reminded Bentham that much of the common law's jurisdiction was essentially the concern of the states and not the federal government.[76] However, this was precisely the type of response that provoked Bentham into a hyper-rationalist mode as exhibited by his response.

Bentham responded to Madison over a year later when Madison was no longer president. Thus it seems that this letter can be read in no other way than as a personal response to James Madison and not just to a former occupant of the White House. It did not take Bentham long to begin quoting Madison's letter back to him, explaining why he had misjudged Bentham's proposal, specifying each sentence that he felt Madison had wrong. Along with the 1817 response, Bentham sent to Madison copies of favorable responses he had received in the intervening years from various state governors, apparently to prove to Madison that at least some Americans believed in him.[77]

Never short on ambition, even at age eighty-two, Bentham wrote to another American president in 1830, Andrew Jackson. After listing his credentials concerning his relations with past American officials, Bentham noted that he enclosed his codification proposal and then summarized some of his suggestions he thought might be favored by Jackson based upon his reading of Jackson's inaugural address. Unfortunately, Bentham made a number of errors in his final attempt at getting American attention, and these miscalculations had nothing to do with a lack of understanding of the constitutional system; rather Bentham proved his ignorance of partisan politics. He began by telling Jackson of his "acquaintance which ripened into an intimacy" with his predecessor John Quincy Adams. He then expressed his disappointment upon "learning of his [Adams's] failing to receive the customary additions to his term of service." Writing these words to a man who thought Adams had stolen the presidency from him four years earlier was unwise to say the least.[78] What must have been downright scandalous for Jackson to read was this: "upon reading your Presidential Message, I found that, upon the whole, your sentiments were not only in accordance with mine as his [Adams's] had been . . . but that they were so, and I trust remain so, in a still more extensive degree, embracing several topics which, between him and me, had never been touched upon."[79] One wonders what Jackson thought upon reading an Englishman telling him he and his enemy, John Quincy Adams, had similar thoughts in politics and legislation. If that were not enough to sour Jackson, who had begun his political career as a US Senator from Tennessee, Bentham went on to explain why the Senate was "much worse than useless."[80] So ended Bentham's formal attempts at legislating for the "Anglo-American United States."

That Bentham made an impression on American legal scientists cannot be doubted. As the subject of codification came to occupy the attention of American lawyers, the scholarly publications recognized the debt owed to Bentham in making the issue salient. As David Hoffman noted in his *Course of Legal Study*, "the existing controversy respecting [the object of codes] . . . may be said to have originated with Mr. Bentham." Moreover, "Bentham's Works" were placed near the top of the suggested reading list of sources on codification.[81] Another student text, Walker's *Introduction to American Law*, also listed "Bentham on Legislation" as appropriate reading on the topic of codification.[82]

THE HISTORIOGRAPHY OF CODIFICATION

Perry Miller closed "The Legal Mentality" with a section on codification, explaining how awkwardly it fit into legal thought of the time. There was something odd about the rejection of codification during the overlapping periods of Enlightenment rationality and suspicion of English forms of governance. One might have thought that scientific reformers would have seized upon the opportunity to create a legal system from scratch, the way the Framers created a constitution from first principles. One might further think that in breaking away from England, the American legal profession would have welcomed the chance to leave the old system behind in favor of a native code of laws. Instead, what Miller found was a "perverse glorification of the Common Law" as the perfection of reason that had only failed in its clarity because of the ignorance of the pettifoggers who peddled it.[83]

In the 1820s, codes were discussed in a civil, if less than enthusiastic, manner. Or, as Miller explains, "For a short, happy period codification was a professional problem."[84] To the extent codification gained traction at this time, it was on the heels of England's law reform efforts in 1828 and part of the more general trend of simplifying, ordering, and arranging branches of human knowledge. It appears, however, as if some of the friends of codification proved to be its worst enemies. Vocal codification proponents like Robert Rantoul and William Sampson had close ties to the immigrant and labor underclasses and thus, their efforts became associated with the pettifoggers against whom legal elites were working.[85]

Scholars of codification agree that something happened in the 1830s to turn the issue from a mere professional disagreement into something more consequential. Charles Cook, who has written the sole monograph on the codification movement, argues that the codification debate became ideological with conservative forces stronger than their competitors.[86] More insightfully, Miller suggests that the real issue was "a division between two opposing ideas of America . . . a dispute over the identity of the nation." Amid "the noisy debate," Miller concludes, "was basically a contest between nationalism and cosmopolitanism."[87] More curiously, disagreement reigns over what to make of David Dudley Field's endeavors in the 1840s, resulting in New York's adoption of the Field Code of Civil Procedure in 1846. Were they the successful culmination of a movement that had begun a generation earlier, or were they the final death throes of a basically failed movement?

Craig Klafter nicely sets out the varying explanations in his work on American legal thought. Whereas Cook saw the decline of the codification movement in the strength of its opponents, Klafter argues that "the movement's decline was a product of its own limited success . . . once it had been accomplished with regard to key subject areas there was little need to continue it."[88] But it is only Miller and Edward Widmer who convincingly place Field's efforts into a larger cultural context.

Field was part of the Young America movement, a group of literary and political figures who were critical of Americans' continued emulation of English writers. While the more famous Young Americans included Melville, Hawthorne, and Holmes, Field shared their "national particularism." For Field and his allies, the essential point was "the establishment of an identity for the nation."[89] Widmer picks up where Miller left off, suggesting an even stronger connection between the legal and literary movements of the time.

In *Young America*, Widmer tells us that the legal debate over codification "resembled nothing so much as an exegetical quarrel among literary critics."[90] Field and other Young Americans rejected looking abroad for standards of excellence in all things legal and literary. Inspired by New York state senator Gulian Verplanck's speech on law reform in 1839 (discussed in the next chapter), Field wrote to Verplanck, thus beginning his career as codification champion.[91] Widmer concludes, "the call for codification was a cry for a curb on the romantic imagination, and for a heightened realism related to an improved understanding of modern America."[92]

Although nationalists themselves, prominent jurists like Kent and Story remained "within the context of an international culture" where standards of civilization were fundamentally European.[93] By contrast, Field and the Young Americans, although learned in European literature and law, sought to set standards of international culture for America. Widmer brings the generations together even more clearly: "worshipping the Revolution, as the codifiers did, allowed them to express generational disaffection and worship their elitist grandparents at the same time, to be both radical and conservative."[94]

My own interpretation of codification is squarely within the intellectual framework of legal science. To the extent it became politicized from the 1820s to the 1830s, it is not at all apparent in the substance of the arguments. Moreover, I tend to think that a majority of the historiography overstates the failure of the movement. Looking at the arguments of the legal scientists, and recognizing that codification was part of a larger jurisprudential reform effort, Craig Klafter probably has the better argument that the movement was a victim of its own limited success. However, codification is one of those ideas that had a lifespan beyond this contingent of legal scientists themselves. Thus, a full exploration of the topic would require investigation into the second-half of the nineteenth century when the driving force might have been some other set of ideas altogether.

UTILITARIAN CODIFICATION

Understanding the motivations behind the codification movement requires an appreciation of the criticism of the common law. In the previous chapter, we saw the law professors warning their students against resting their legal arguments on cases alone. Instead, the professors wanted reasoned legal arguments. The legal scientists' desire for reasoned law also led many to call for written codes as opposed to unwritten, or at least unorganized, case law. Also embedded in the calls for codification was a desire to bring to the legal system the democratic element necessary to secure the public happiness.

Thomas Cooper, whose codification efforts in South Carolina are discussed in chapter 4, expressed his frustration with the common law when speaking of the federal judiciary in his essay on the Constitution in 1826. Cooper's ultimate frustration was that by the 1820s the federal judiciary was turning out to be practically untouchable in the political realm. Cooper thought that Congress was not exercising its constitutional oversight powers to reign in the federal judges when they issued unreasoned opinions. He hoped, not that the House would impeach more judges, but that they would entertain petitions from a disgruntled public complaining about specific instances of unconstitutional judicial overreach. But it is Cooper's worst-case scenario that is most telling.

Cooper hypothesized the following:

> Suppose what has not yet happened, *but which will happen,* that the nondescript thing called the *Common Law* should be adopted by the Supreme Court. There has long been an awful squinting that way. Then may the Legislature of the Union go to rest. "Othello's occupation's gone!" With the Common Law comes in all the vague ambulatory Judge-made Law of the old Country, which having assignable parentage, or which to serve temporary purposes has been introduced by force or by stealth, has been from time to time basely and fraudulently filiated on the Common Law, as innocent of the offence, (Heaven knows!) as a child unborn![95]

Cooper was writing in 1826, sixteen years before his premonition would come to pass at the hand of none other than Joseph Story.[96] To counter the tendency toward such an occurrence, Cooper suggested a "council of censers," whose job it would be to meet periodically, every ten years or so, to revise the federal statutes and to annul those that were unconstitutional. Such a system was tried in Pennsylvania under a previous state constitution and one could find no respectable statesman "who did not speak in terms of high respect of the integrity and manifest utility of that body." What, then was responsible for its demise? According to Cooper, "the influence of the legal profession."[97]

It was bad enough that unscientific, self-interested, lawyers manipulated the common law at the state level. It now seemed to Cooper that the House of Representatives was content to "permit the plain meaning of the Constitution to be quibbled away by the verbal distinctions of Lawyers, and discard common sense from interfering in the determination of a constitutional question—putting off their character as statesmen, and submitting to the infallibility of the law."[98] The codification movement, for Cooper and like-minded reformers, was about demystifying the common law, recognizing that it was far from infallible, and replacing it with a reasoned code that was not solely, or even primarily, the product of the legal profession, but rather the product of legal science.

We can see the basic justifications for codification in the student-oriented works of David Hoffman and Timothy Walker. Walker provided a short entry on codification near the beginning of his textbook, *Introduction to American Law*, when setting out the sources of law. Walker first worked to answer potential objections to any codification project. "Is this practicable?" he asked. To see why the answer was plainly, "yes," he thought it "sufficient to refer to two experiments," that is, the codes of Justinian and Napoleon. "But we need not go abroad for examples," he continued, "Codes justly renowned have already been framed in Louisiana." The only way one could have thought such a project impractical is if one was operating under "a misconception of what is actually proposed." No one imaged a code that would account for "all future cases" that might arise in the courts. "Nothing more is sought than to incorporate into a code, existing principles."[99] Those existing principles, I suggest, are the ones set out in so many introductory sections of lecture and treatises, namely, that public utility was the end of all law.

Some of Bentham's more general principles and justifications from his American letters are present in Walker's own explanations. For example, Walker addressed the objection that a large legislative body would never be able to agree upon a comprehensive code of laws. Although he did not adopt Bentham's suggestion of using a single foreign author, he did suggest that a small committee should draft the code, with similarly small committees appointed to oversee the code from year to year to address any problems that might arise. But Walker's most utilitarian explanations come in his recitation of the five advantages that would arise from codification. First, "our laws would be better adapted to our condition than they now are." Second, "our laws would be more generally known." Third, the laws "would be more simple." Fourth, "our laws would be more certain." Finally, "our laws would be conformable to the theory of our government," meaning that they would be the product of a democratic body rather than an undemocratic judiciary.[100] Publicity, simplicity, and notoriety of the laws, were all means to the end of public happiness.[101]

Maryland law professor David Hoffman did not mince words in expressing his thoughts on codification:

> We believe consolidation—partial codefication—general codefication, and finally, an entire remodeling of the existing scheme of jurisprudence, entirely practicable; and in this country, we are aware of no reasons of policy that should occlude the attempt, if not of all at one time, yet of parts, gradually.[102]

Hoffman's rationale was indisputably indebted to Bentham's writings. He explained the object of codification as primarily the arrangement of law, which in turn would make the law more explicit. But most interestingly, he thought that a code should contain "the *motives*" of the laws, which would help the judiciary and the legislature better perform their functions. By "motives," Hoffman meant, "a course of philosophical and censorial reasoning, based on a well arranged development of principles, and relative facts."[103] This feature closely tracks Bentham's notion of "justifiedness," which he had written about extensively in his letters to the United States.[104] Thus, Bentham thought that any code of laws must be "furnished with a correspondent *body of reasons*, for its accompaniment and support."[105]

Hoffman's discussion of codification also contained a good deal of criticism of the common law. "We desire to avoid the narrow views of mere common lawyers," he noted. Two primary points followed from this criticism. First, a board of censors should be in place to keep the code in order. Similar to Thomas Cooper's suggestion, such a board would resonate more with a democratic society than the present system where judges maintained control of the common law. Second, instead of relying solely on the common law model, civil law systems should be freely consulted. Thus, law reform efforts "should be entrusted to scholars in the law,—to experienced practitioners; to those who have mastered the subject of codefication in all countries; to those who have been disciples of Justinian as well as of Coke; and to those, finally, who come to the task with all requisite wisdom, learning, zeal, and industry."[106]

Hoffman's affinity for Bentham was critiqued in a review of his *Legal Outlines*, where the reviewer observed, "Mr. Hoffman touches upon the subject of codification and the works of Jeremy Bentham, whom he treats with some respect." The anonymous reviewer also spoke of Bentham's general reputation within American legal circles in noting that he had "survived the ridicule and contempt of which he was formerly the subject." It is clear that the reviewer was not as keen on Bentham as Hoffman, but nevertheless he praised Bentham's writings on codification:

> there is no doubt that his writings have had a powerful and very salutary effect upon contemporary legislation, not merely by pointing out improvements, but more perhaps in consequence of the merciless satire and irresistible force of illustration, with which he has exposed some of the absurd maxims and senseless prejudices, which masked many hoary abuses and venerable follies.[107]

Even those, like the reviewer, who thought that Bentham was not "a safe guide, or good authority," had to acknowledge his relevance and influence on American legal science.

NOTES

1. Peter J. King, *Utilitarian Jurisprudence in America: The Influence of Bentham and Austin on American Legal Thought in the Nineteenth Century* (New York: Garland Publishing, 1986), 139–218.

2. Ibid., 180, 168.

3. On Wilson's moral epistemology, see Mark David Hall, *The Political and Legal Philosophy of James Wilson, 1742–1798* (Columbia: University of Missouri Press, 1997), 63–89. Hall emphasises the influence of Hutcheson and Reid on the development of Wilson's thought, and notes that "reason was not of primary importance for Wilson's moral theory," although neither was it "wholly unimportant." Ibid., 77. It is the argument herein that "reason" was of supreme importance to men like Cooper and Hoffman.

4. According to one writer, "more American students before 1850 read Paley than any other 'moral philosopher,' not excluding even Butler, Dugald Stewart, and Locke." Wendell Glick, "Bishop Paley in America," *New England Quarterly* 27 (1954): 347. See also Wilson Smith, "William Paley's Theological Utilitarianism in America," *William and Mary Quarterly* 11 (1954): 402, 410–11. Smith asserted, "It was . . . Paleyan utility, not Benthamic utilitarianism, which was composed within a framework of ideas that young Americans could comprehend."

5. Brophy has nicely explained the "heart versus head" argument. Alfred L. Brophy, "Reason and Sentiment: The Moral Worlds and Modes of Reasoning of Antebellum Jurists," *Boston University Law Review* 79 (1999): 1161.

6. For a discussion of natural law in early American legal education, see R. H. Helmholz, *Natural Law in Court: A History of Legal Theory in Practice* (Cambridge, MA: Harvard Univ. Press, 2015), ch. 5.

7. Thomas Cooper, "On Moral Obligation," in *Tracts, Ethical, Theological and Political* (Warrington: W. Eyres, 1787; repr. Bristol, UK: Thoemmes Press, 2001), quotation from Table-of-Contents page.

8. Ibid., 10.

9. Ibid., 95–96.

10. Ibid., 117.

11. Ibid., 34, 32.

12. Ibid., 34.

13. Ibid., 45.

14. Thomas Cooper, "Preface of the Translator," in F. J. V. Broussais, *On Irritation and Insanity* (Columbia, SC: S. J. M'Morris, 1831).

15. Thomas Cooper, "A View of the Metaphysical and Physiological Arguments in Favor of Materialism," in Broussais, *On Irritation and Insanity*, 342–43.

16. Susanna L. Blumenthal, "The Mind of a Moral Agent: Scottish Common Sense and the Problem of Responsibility in Nineteenth-Century American Law," *Law and History Review* 26 (2008): 99, 122.

17. Charles L. Barzun, "Common Sense and Legal Science," *Virginia Law Review* 90 (2004): 1051, 1077 fn 123.

18. David Hoffman, *Course of Legal Study*, 2nd ed., (Baltimore MD: Joseph Neal, 1836; repr., New York: Arno Press, 1972), 111.

19. Ibid., 109.

20. See William Paley, *The Principles of Moral and Political Philosophy* (1785; Indianapolis, IN: Liberty Fund, Inc., 2002).

21. After listing the course readings for each title, Hoffman followed up with explanatory notes for some, but not all, of the works listed. For example, the notes on Beattie and Reid take no more than one page total. However, the 1836 note on Paley takes up four pages, expanded from the one page it occupied in the 1817 edition. See Hoffman, *Course*, 101–5. The only notes to the first title longer than that on Paley were those on the Bible and Aristotle's Ethics.

22. Hoffman, *Course*, 101.

23. Ibid., 104.
24. See David Hoffman, *Legal Outlines* (Baltimore, MD: Edward J. Coale, 1829).
25. Hoffman, *Legal Outlines*, 464–69. Hazlitt seems like an odd choice to use for one who generally admired Bentham. Hazlitt had a personally rocky relationship with Bentham and the utilitarians. The most notorious incident included Hazlitt's eviction by Bentham from a property Hazlitt had rented for a number of years. Hazlitt's recent biographer makes a special point of mentioning how unfair Bentham treated him in his time of financial need. Bentham claimed that he had never heard of Hazlitt's name despite his seven-year residence just around the corner, and thus showed this "stranger" no mercy. Duncan Wu, *William Hazlitt: The First Modern Man* (New York: Oxford University Press, 2008), 277–78.
26. Hoffman, *Legal Outlines*, 604, app I.
27. Hoffman, *Course*, 105.
28. Ibid., 362.
29. Ibid., 434.
30. Hugh S. Legaré, "Hoffman's Legal Outlines," *Southern Review* 4 (1829): 47.
31. Ibid.
32. Ibid., 52.
33. Ibid., 53.
34. Ibid., 58.
35. On Bentham's critiques of the judicial and legal establishments, see Philip Schofield, *Utility and Democracy: The Political Thought of Jeremy Bentham* (Oxford: Oxford University Press, 2006), 114–17.
36. David Hoffman, *Miscellaneous Thoughts on Men, Manners, and Things* (Baltimore, MD: Coale & Co, 1837), 325.
37. David Hoffman, *Legal Outlines* (London: John Miller, 1836), vii–viii. Although substantively the same as the original 1829 American edition, the London version contained a preface addressed "To British Students of Law," from which this quotation is taken.
38. Hoffman, *Miscellaneous Thoughts*, 330.
39. Ibid., 328.
40. David Hoffman, *Viator; or, A Peep into My Note Book* (Baltimore MD: Plaskitt & Cugle, 1841), 75.
41. Ibid., 75. For Bentham, "authority" was the primary political fallacy used in public debates; it was the first of four—the others being delay, danger, and confusion—discussed in his famous work on fallacies. According to Bentham, appeals to authority worked "to repress all exercise of the reasoning faculty." Jeremy Bentham, *The Handbook of Political Fallacies*, ed. Harold A. Larrabee (1824; New York: Harper & Brothers, 1962), 17.
42. Hoffman, *Viator*, 76–77.
43. Hoffman, *Course*, 104.
44. Ibid., 437 fn *.
45. Ibid., 364.
46. Nathaniel Chipman, *Principles of Government: A Treatise on Free Institutions, Including the Constitution of the United States* (Burlington, VT: Edward Smith, 1833), 161.
47. Ibid., 162.
48. Ibid., 162–67.
49. See Paul D. Carrington, "Teaching Law and Virtue at Transylvania University: The George Wythe Tradition in the Antebellum Years," *Mercer Law Review* 41 (1990): 673–99; Charles Kerr, "Transylvania University's Law Department," *Americana* 31, no. 1 (1937): 7–44; John D. Wright, Jr., *Transylvania: Tutor to the West* (Lexington, KY: Transylvania University, 1975), 87–144, 175–76.
50. Kerr, "Transylvania University's Law Department," 11.
51. Ibid., 32.
52. Carrington, "Teaching Law and Virtue at Transylvania University," 691.

53. William T. Barry, *An Introductory Lecture on the Study of the Law, Delivered in the Chapel of Transylvania University, on Monday, October 1, 1821* (Lexington, KY: W. G. Hunt, 1821), 10–12.
54. Jesse Bledsoe, *An Introductory Lecture on the Study of the Law, Delivered in the Chapel of Transylvania University, on Monday, November 4, 1822* (Lexington, KY: Joseph Ficklin, 1822), 3–14.
55. Jesse Bledsoe, *An Introductory Lecture, Preparatory to a Course of Instruction on Common and Statute Law, Delivered in the Chapel of Transylvania University, on Monday, November 3d, 1823* (Lexington, KY: William Tanner, 1823), 8–9.
56. Daniel Mayes, *An Address Delivered before the Trustees and Faculty of Transylvania University at the Opening of the Session of the Law Department, On the 7th Nov. 1831* (Lexington, KY: N. L. Finnell & J. F. Herndon, 1831), 3.
57. Ibid., 9.
58. Daniel Mayes, *An Address to the Students of Law in Transylvania University, Delivered at the Beginning of the Session for 1835* (Lexington, KY: J. Clarke & Co., 1835), 8, 12.
59. George Robertson, "Introductory Lecture, Delivered in the Chapel of Morrison College, on the 7th of November, 1835," in *Scrap Book on Law and Politics, Men and Times* (Lexington, KY: A. W. Elder, 1855), 173.
60. Ibid., 174.
61. Ibid., 183.
62. Letter from Jeremy Bentham to Benjamin Franklin (1780), in University College London Library, Bentham Manuscripts, Box clxix, folio 18. One scholar cites this document as a letter Bentham sent to Franklin, and this is the suggestion on the manuscript folder. Chilton Williamson, "Bentham Looks at America," *Political Science Quarterly* 70, no. 4 (1955): 543. Williamson also suggests that it was *A Fragment on Government* that Bentham contemplated sending to Franklin. However, by that time the *Fragment* was widely available; it was *An Introduction to the Principles of Morals and Legislation* that was printed in 1780 and did not reach a wide audience until its publication in 1789.
63. See Jeremy Bentham, *Political Tactics*, Michael James et al. eds. (Oxford: Oxford University Press, 1999).
64. Jeremy Bentham to John Jay, 8 April 1795, in *The Correspondence of Jeremy Bentham*, ed. Alexander Taylor, vol. 5 (London: Athlone Press, 1981), 128.
65. Jeremy Bentham to James Madison, October 1811, in *'Legislator of the World': Writings on Codification, Law, and Education*, ed. Philip Schofield and Jonathan Harris (Oxford: Oxford University Press, 1998), 5.
66. See Philip Schofield, "Jeremy Bentham: Legislator of the World," *Current Legal Problems* 51 (1998): 115.
67. Jeremy Bentham, *A Fragment on Government*, ed. J. H. Burns and H. L. A. Hart (Cambridge: Cambridge University Press, 1988), 8.
68. Jeremy Bentham to James Madison, October 1811, in *'Legislator of the World'*, 18.
69. James Madison, "Federalist No. 10," in ed. Terence Ball, *The Federalist* (Cambridge: Cambridge University Press, 2003) 41.
70. Jeremy Bentham to James Madison, October 1811, in *'Legislator of the World'*, 22.
71. Ibid., 25.
72. Madison famously wrote, "If men were angels, no government would be necessary." James Madison, "Federalist No. 51," in ed. Ball, *The Federalist*, 252.
73. It cannot be said for certain that Bentham had read the *Federalist*, knew which papers Madison had written, and then made these sly references, but they are uncannily similar. We do know that Bentham eventually acquired a copy of the *Federalist* in 1812 because Aaron Burr sent him a two volume set and Bentham acknowledged receipt. See Letter from Aaron Burr to Jeremy Bentham, 27 August 1812, in *The Correspondence of Jeremy Bentham*, vol. 8, ed. Stephen Conway (1988), 259; Jeremy Bentham to Aaron Burr, 23 February 1816, in ibid., 508.
74. Jeremy Bentham to James Madison, October 1811, in *'Legislator of the World'*, 32.

75. Jeremy Bentham, "Letter to the Citizens of the Several American United States," in *'Legislator of the World'*, 164.

76. James Madison to Jeremy Bentham, 8 May 1816, in *'Legislator of the World'*, 36.

77. Jeremy Bentham to James Madison, September 1817, in *'Legislator of the World'*, 173.

78. Even though Jackson received more popular votes than Adams in the 1824 presidential election, no candidate achieved the required majority of electoral votes and thus the House of Representatives selected the president, in this case Adams. Jackson and his supporters accused Adams of a "corrupt bargain" to secure the presidency. Jackson then spent the next four years campaigning against Adams.

79. Jeremy Bentham to Andrew Jackson, 26 April 1830, in ed. John Bowring, *The Works of Jeremy Bentham* (1843; Bristol: Thoemmes Press, 1995), 11:39.

80. Ibid., 41.

81. David Hoffman, *A Course of Legal Study*, 2nd ed. (Baltimore: Joseph Neal, 1836), 686, 688.

82. Timothy Walker, *Introduction to American Law* (Philadelphia: Nicklin & Johnson, 1837), 58.

83. Perry Miller, *The Life of the Mind in America from the Revolution to the Civil War* (New York: Harcourt, Brace & World, Inc., 1965), 242.

84. Ibid., 249.

85. Ibid., 251–52.

86. Charles M. Cook, *The American Codification Movement: A Study in Antebellum Legal Reform* (Westport, CT: Greenwood Press, 1981), 158.

87. Miller, *Life of the Mind*, 254, 255.

88. Craig Evan Klafter, *Reason over Precedents: Origins of American Legal Thought* (Westport, CT: Greenwood Press, 1993), 118–19.

89. Miller, *Life of the Mind*, 256, 263.

90. Edward L. Widmer, *Young America: The Flowering of Democracy in New York City* (New York: Oxford University Press, 1999), 158.

91. [David Dudley Field], *A Letter to Gulian C. Verplanck, on the Reform of the Judicial System of this State. By a Member of the New-York Bar. December, 1839* (New York: University Press, 1840).

92. Widmer, *Young America*, 176.

93. Miller, *Life of the Mind*, 264.

94. Widmer, *Young America*, 183.

95. Thomas Cooper, "On the Constitution of the United States," in *Two Essays* (Columbia, SC: D. & J. M. Faust, 1826), 58–59.

96. See *Swift v. Tyson*, 41 U.S. 1 (1842).

97. Cooper, "On the Constitution of the United States," 58–59.

98. Ibid., 59.

99. Walker, *Introduction to American Law*, 58–60.

100. Ibid., 60–61.

101. On the importance of publicity to Bentham's philosophy of government, see Schofield, *Utility and Democracy*, ch. 10.

102. Hoffman, *A Course of Legal Study*, 674.

103. Ibid., 675.

104. See "Jeremy Bentham, an Englishman, to the Citizens of the Several American United States," July 1817, in *'Legislator of the World'*, 141–46.

105. Ibid., 141.

106. Hoffman, *A Course of Legal Study*, 679, 686.

107. [Anonymous], "Hoffman's Legal Outlines," *American Jurist and Law Magazine* 3 (1830): 95–96.

Part II

Legal Scientists

THREE

Knickerbocker as Legal Scientist

Gulian C. Verplanck

This chapter tells the story of one of antebellum New York's most profound legal minds. In fact, a good case can be made that Gulian C. Verplanck rivaled Chancellor James Kent in his legal acumen. Verplanck is less familiar than Kent, however, because his career was so diverse and varied, and his contributions to the law did not always occur in the courtroom. I argue for an appreciation of Verplanck's larger importance among a unique group of early-American legal intellectuals who viewed the law as so much more than the pleadings of lawyers and the opinions of judges. Verplanck saw the law as interconnected with all fields of inquiry, especially moral philosophy, literature, and natural science. He vehemently argued that the search for legal knowledge was no different than the search for moral knowledge or the search for scientific knowledge. Thus Verplanck thought all lawyers should be liberally educated and that law should not be treated as a vocation. His theories led him to reject the common law doctrine of caveat emptor, to support an extension of copyright terms, and to make the case that the New York judiciary was in serious need of reform, a conclusion the legal community as a whole came to share within a decade. His proposals, however, were based, not upon precedent or established legal doctrine, but upon the science of political economy, a psychological theory of human motivation, and good old public utility. Verplanck's legal contemporaries were surprisingly supportive of his later endeavors despite his overt contempt for precedent and tradition.

What follows is an attempt to explore a strand of this concept of law in which the tension between an older natural law and a more modern concern with utility play themselves out rather seamlessly, at least in the hands of Verplanck. First, I examine Verplanck's foundational ideas in order to better understand the preconditions necessary for such legal conceptions to develop. Specifically, I consider the effects of his education on his intellectual development and then describe how Verplanck understood law not as a field of knowledge unto itself but rather part of a larger science of human inquiry, and, relatedly, how he viewed America as uniquely situated to foster the growth of legal science. Then, I show how Verplanck put these abstract ideas to practice. In this vein, I discuss Verplanck's treatise on contract law and consider the legal community's reactions to it, followed by a look at how Verplanck used the law of copyright to further his view that support of the fine arts helped to create a moral citizenry. Finally, I consider Verplanck's role in reforming the state court system of New York. On the practical front, I examine how Verplanck's membership on his state's highest court allowed him to shift the jurisprudence of New York to fall into line with his views on morality. On the more abstract front, I consider his proposals for reform of the judicial system in order to make the machinery of justice more amenable to moral legal outcomes.

NEW YORKER, LAWYER, AND INTELLECTUAL

Gulian Crommelin Verplanck of New York was in many ways a renaissance man of his time. He was deeply learned, but eminently practical. He was a public intellectual as manifested by his discourses and writings, but he had no disdain for public office, actively seeking it himself. Verplanck crafted an American morality from common sense and utility and applied it to his decisions on public policy. Though his sense of morality guided every public action, because its foundations lay where they did, he never seemed to be moralizing to inferiors. Verplanck had no commitment to any political party because parties were inconsistent with good sense and public welfare. As a result, he had difficulty realizing his full potential as a politician. When New Yorkers and Verplanck mutually decided his public services were no longer needed, he did not bitterly withdraw from public life, but instead took to editing the works of Shakespeare for the continued enlightenment of the nation.[1]

It is too bad that Gulian Verplanck's only published biography is more than half-a-century old.[2] It is likely that the lack of interest in Verplanck stems from his general partisan neutrality, which was sincerely and deeply felt, and thus makes him a rather unexciting actor in the high-stakes antebellum political world. He was elected to the House of Representatives as a Democrat in 1824, serving for four terms, including the tense years of the Nullification Crisis.[3] But policy was always more important to Verplanck than the party line. He did not hesitate to express his views on the plenary powers of Congress, but neither did he shy away from condemning tariffs as bad public policy, inconsistent with political economy, nor did he refrain from calling attention to the legitimacy of public opinion existing in the South; Verplanck was certain that intellectual proofs of constitutional principles would not change southern opinion, nor should they.[4] For Verplanck, the existence of public sentiment was never illegitimate and always had to be handled respectfully. It was this characteristic of Verplanck—his genuine respect for the potentiality of all ideas and his utter lack of pretension—that earned him few personal enemies, as well as the respect of his peers in public life.

As a young man Verplanck trained as a lawyer, but he never practiced law professionally. In 1825 he published a treatise on contract law, which proved far from the typical legal treatise one found at the time—much more speculative than descriptive. The *Essay on the Doctrine of Contracts* was not particularly well received in the legal community. Since Verplanck was not an active lawyer, it was easily dismissed as the ruminations of a closet philosopher. His years of office holding then intervened and he was all but forgotten about within the legal profession. However, thanks to New York's constitutional imitation of the English legal structure, when Verplanck was elected to the state senate in 1837 as a Whig, he was simultaneously elevated to the highest court in New York. The New York Senate, along with the chancellor and the justices of the Supreme Court, made up the Court for the Correction of Errors. When this court sat, it was common for the chancellor or the justices to take the lead and the senators to follow, but Verplanck had other ideas. During his one term in the senate from 1838–1841, he took an active part on the court, delivering the most learned opinions seen since the time of Chancellor Kent,[5] and rarely was he in the minority, though he did not hesitate to leave the chancellor and the judges in the position of dissenters. Because his biographer did not consider Verplanck's legal career,[6] and the few intervening law review articles have lacked a certain comprehensiveness to them, most of what is presented here is an attempt to link Verplanck's legal thought to his broader outlook on American society and to treat that larger set of ideas as the product of a certain historical-intellectual context. Even though Verplanck's time as a legal commentator and jurist amounted to no more than a half-dozen years of an otherwise varied and illustrious career in politics and letters, it does represent a strand of legal thought widely scattered throughout the minds of the creators of law in the early republic.

Verplanck was excited about being a first-generation American. His Dutch ancestors had settled in New York as far back as 1633, so he certainly was not new to the land in that sense. Having been born in 1786, however, he was a first-generation American in the sense that Joyce Appleby uses that phrase—he was among the first generation of Americans to grow up never having known colonial rule.[7] Much like the representatives of Appleby's generation, Verplanck had a clear sense that the United States presented special opportunities heretofore unavailable in history. However, Verplanck's nationalism was so understated, that critics eventually questioned its very existence.[8] Verplanck's own ambition was certainly enough to prove his belief in a sort of liberal individualism, yet his criticisms of unrestrained business dealings and selfish accumulation complicate any overly simplistic description of Verplanck as a laissez-faire capitalist, though that is how he has often been portrayed.[9] The Verplanck who will make an appearance here, is one who, above all else, desperately wanted to be known for positively contributing to his society. Learned enough to be considered by most, "a scholar," he was adamant that he never fall into some cloistered life, cut off from the concerns of daily intercourse. Although Verplanck had plenty of ideas ready to apply to society's ailments, he was not ideological.

Verplanck's Legal Education

Little is known about Verplanck's legal education. He graduated from Columbia College in 1801 at age fourteen. After reading law in the offices of Josiah Ogden Hoffman and Edward Livingston, he was admitted to the bar in 1807 by Chief Justice James Kent. He set up a practice with Nathaniel F. Moore, but apparently never had a single client. Moore said of his partner:

> Indeed I am not aware that he had, or cared to have, any legal business whatever. He spent much of his time out of the office and was not very studious when within, but it was evident that he read or had read elsewhere to good purpose, for though I read more Greek than law and thought myself studious, I had occasion to discover more than once that he was a better Grecian than I, and could enlighten my ignorance.[10]

A friend recalled that "in his legal studies he delighted in the reports of law cases in Norman French, that he was fond of old French literature, and read Rabelais in the perplexing French of the original."[11] His biographer speculates that it was in Livingston's office that Verplanck was first exposed to republican and Jeffersonian ideas, having previously been raised by loyalist grandparents and then attending a Federalist college.[12] The more interesting inquiry, for present purposes, is what Verplanck learned about the law from both Livingston and Hoffman. Of course Livingston went on to become the great codifier of Louisiana and was closely associated with the Francophilia of the Jeffersonians.[13] Thus, one can only image that the young Verplanck was exposed to this republican view of the law—the democratic impulse against the elitist common law and the appreciation of the civil law system.[14]

Beyond Mere Lawyer

American intellectuals of the early republic have been considered in any number of ways, but most often they have been cast as the progeny of conservative Federalists weighted down with an inferiority complex, constantly comparing themselves to the revolutionary generation of their fathers and coming to the realization that they could never live up to those standards. Their cultural baselines were often British and the mass of vulgar Americans disgusted them and further sent them into a malaise. For some this was surely true, and it was for these sour citizens that Verplanck was especially worried. But Verplanck himself fits nicely with Marshall Foletta's description of New England intellectuals. Foletta's cast was rather uninterested in political office holding, but they were very concerned with creating a high culture of which Americans could rightly be proud.[15] In a similar vein Verplanck was concerned with creating a legal culture better than any other in the world, one that borrowed liberally from foreign practices but that paid particular attention to the concerns of American society. However, we cannot begin to understand Verplanck's legal thought until we have said something about his views on intellectuals and their role within American commercial society.

Verplanck was a popular commencement speaker—a public figure with a depth of learning comparable to any academic in the audience. His college lectures, at least the ones he published, had a common theme: how does the educated American use his superior knowledge for the public good? We do not even have to infer that Verplanck was speaking in the vein of classical republicanism because he leaves us with no doubt that he was doing exactly that.[16] The message he wanted all his listeners to take with them was not to turn their backs on their fellow citizens, however tempting it was given the mass of ignorance and self-seeking that surrounded them. American scholars had a duty to their country—a country that had given them the opportunities of which they made good use to that point in their lives—to spread their knowledge to the rest of society so that all of America could rise up as a nation within the world community. This is precisely how the virtuous Romans conducted themselves and had managed to preserve that great republic for so many centuries. Upon evaluating his life, the American scholar should, "like Cicero, look back, with proud satisfaction, to his labors in the forum, the senate, and the field, disastrous ofttimes, but full of glory."[17]

The Necessity of a Liberal Education

In an address to the students at Geneva College on August 7, 1833, Verplanck asked, "what ought to be the moral influence of a sound and liberal education"?[18] Any answer to that question had to consider "the legitimate and awful claims of society, of our country, of the human race, of the moral constitution of our nature, of the great Author of being and fountain of all wisdom."[19] In providing examples of men who had lived lives worthy of emulation he listed Newton, Pascal, Franklin, and Mansfield. Lord Mansfield,[20] more than any other common law judge of recent memory, knew what do with his knowledge. "Every where and every hour," in Britain and the United States, an insurance or commercial contract was "affected by the influence of his clear and sagacious mind."[21] Mansfield had taken the common law and applied to it that element usually lacking in Anglo-American jurisprudence—reason. In the same way that math, physics, and astronomy had begun with sublime theory and then turned into sciences of great practical use, the moral sciences were following closely behind. "Like the Alchemist . . . the chemist of the mind was taught by long experience to check his roving fancy, and at last to learn."[22] Natural scientists and moral scientists were both seeking the same thing—truth—but common lawyers were further behind the quest for truth because they had been habituated to a system of mindless artificial precedent. What lawyers needed to do was more closely follow the methods of natural scientists:

> The severe analysis of Reason leads us step by step to the laws of universal and necessary Truth. Physical observation and experiment enable the Philosopher to infer the general truth of nature from millions of individual instances. Virtue, and Right, and Duty, are the great objects of moral and metaphysical science and of legal ethics; yet these are but other names for moral Truth.[23]

Mansfield had engaged in "physical observation and experiment" in taking into consideration the actual practices of the commercial community[24] and thus he came closer than the common law had ever before come to attaining justice, the legal equivalent of Truth. "A still more brilliant example" of legal accomplishment was Grotius's invention of international law[25] because in that system competing sovereigns could settle differences "upon claims of public justice and humanity" rather than by "arms and battle."[26] But Grotius could only have conceived of such a branch of law by close observation of the actual practices of nations and the nature of man.

Advancing Truth through Legal Science

The search for Truth underlay every endeavor of Verplanck. Because Verplanck's Truth was a metaphysical and singular truth, its attainment required the efforts of the whole citizenry. Advancements in math and physics had not been the result of any one mind working independently, but the accumulation of many minds, the aggregation of insulated intellectual efforts combining into "one immense and harmonious system."[27] The same was true of advancements in the law, which was why insular common lawyers with their noses stuck in reporters would not achieve

Truth by themselves. The truth-seeking lawyer must have a liberal education: "The broader his range of knowledge, the more extensive and accurate his acquaintance with the order, beauty, and the harmony of nature."[28] Treating the law so that is has scientific truth for its object, trains the student's mind so that "it cannot easily content itself . . . with blindly following the guidance of early prejudice, of transient impulses, of habit, of caprice, of some fascinating example, of popular opinion, of the fashion of some little circle, or of the authority of some great name."[29] Applying such rationality to the various branches of law would harmonize the whole system without any conscious attempt to do so. We will later see how Verplanck thought that the law of contracts, insurance, and intellectual property all had the same moral foundations once their practitioners had begun to treat them as part of a legal science.

Interestingly enough, Verplanck's understanding of the nature of law comes through most clearly when we examine one of his earliest publications—a book on religion. In that work, Verplanck assembled a series of essays in which he claimed to explore the "internal evidence" of Christianity.[30] Verplanck's goal was to connect the "purely rational" with the "moral and sentimental parts of our nature."[31] Borrowing a concept from William Paley, Verplanck concluded that the "evidence of revelation" was "cumulative."[32] Immediately thereafter, in a footnote, Verplanck tells us that the word "cumulative" is "borrowed from the civil law, where it has an analogous technical signification."[33] What Verplanck was getting at, not only in his essays on religion, but in all his writings, was that the historical stock of human experience was a mixture of the rational and the moral, mirroring the nature of man, who was himself a creature, equal parts rational and moral. How did Verplanck know that the gospels of Jesus were not just the products of good fiction writers? The same way he knew Justinian had not invented Roman law out of whole cloth—the evidence as to their authenticity was overwhelming; everything fit together too well to be coincidence or myth.[34] In discussing the actual study of religion or law, Verplanck thought, "The most satisfactory, and, at the same time, the most gratifying employments of the understanding, are those which most depend upon, or involve, general principles of human nature." In the context of studying "some admired work of genius," it is only when one has to turn from "the moral internal evidence of its doctrines, to the critical internal evidence of its books," that the scholar "ceases to feel the ennobling and animating consciousness of his character as an intellectual and moral being, and remembers only that he is a linguist, a lawyer, or an antiquary."[35] In other words, one should be able to read a great work, like the New Testament, Justinian's *Institutes*, or Pothier, as both a moral and a rational being without getting caught up on technicalities that detract from the work as a representation of the cumulative, interconnected, knowledge of mankind. It was only cumulative, scientific study of various fields of inquiry that recognized man as both rational and sentimental, and thus, only such studies that accurately represented the true view of nature.

America: An Ideal Home for the Legal Scientist

America was an ideal country for the advancement of all forms of science because she had "no prejudices in favor of time-honored usages."[36] Scientific advancements may well shock and alarm people, but the student of science was sure to advance "to certain victory."[37] What the American scientist had always to be mindful of was achieving that delicate balance between theory and practice. Theory certainly had its place: "The abstrusest speculations of the metaphysician, have found their place in those controversies of theologians that rend the religious world, as well as in questions of political discussions, of legislation, and of jurisprudence."[38] But the American man of letters who was naturally drawn to speculation, was frequently called off from his study by the "variety of human occupation" that the young country provided. If some scholar was longing for "alternating only between the book and the pen," Verplanck reminded him: "The great men of antiquity, the models of eloquence, the fathers of poetry, the teachers of ethical wisdom, the founders of that ancient jurisprudence, that still rules the greater part of the civilized world, were none of them solitary scholars; none of them were contented with the 'half wisdom of books' alone."[39] The American scholar had to take advantage of the unique opportunity the new country offered at allowing scientific truths to settle the great questions of public policy. Only in America could the scholar be of so much practical use to his nation.

The Benefits

The "American literary man" had reason to be grateful for being born among the first generation of the nation. One reason for this optimism was something rather indescribable for Verplanck. "It is not the parchment record of our constitutions, the bills of right, the trial by jury, the elective franchise, nor all the securities provided by the jealous wisdom of our fathers for the unrestrained exercise of liberty, that can call back this living spirit when once it has fled."[40] In other words, it was not the popular character of her institutions that made America so promising—it was not her democratic government. What *it* was, was an "ardent, restless spirit ruling our whole people."[41] Verplanck thought, "It is thus that the adventurous ardor, so efficient in external and material matters, naturally extends its energies to the moral and intellectual."[42] There was something in the air, so to speak.

The second and more tangible reason for Verplanck's optimism was one that was central to the vast bulk of his concerns in the law—the market. In Europe, the "market for intellectual labor is overstocked," and as a result, most intellectuals had to attach themselves to a "patron."[43] But in America, scholars were free from the servility that went along with patronage.[44] American scholars owed this optimal condition

> to the diffusion of knowledge amongst the people, to the rapid increase of commercial and manufacturing riches, all combining to build up the sovereignty of public opinion, and to make the patronage of aristocratic wealth more and more insignificant in comparison with the unpretending munificence of an educated people.[45]

The ability in America to sustain a "comfortable subsistence" had reversed "the humiliating example of European learning."[46] Rather than directing their efforts toward pleasing their patrons, American intellectuals could steer their work toward instructing and delighting the people. A broadly educated public went hand-in-hand with a thriving economy, and both factors permitted the intellectual to sustain himself—the public, by appreciating his endeavors, and the market, by rewarding his efforts.

Commercial success in America cut both ways. On the one hand it had the potential to reward intellect. On the other hand, it had the potential to reward dumb luck. Verplanck worried that intellectuals, especially scholarly youth, would become disgusted with their own lack of success while seeing those they knew to be "unworthy" and "unlettered" succeed in politics, trade, and speculation. The economically struggling scholar could become "a soured and discontented man." This was what happened to "the late Joseph Dennie," who "would have accomplished very far more, had he not yielded to a strange, unwise and unhappy morbid dislike for the institutions and social order of his own country."[47] Such a fate would not befall a young man who took Verplanck's advice and applied himself to practical pursuits, in addition to his books.

The Drawbacks

The American scholar was not, however, perfectly safe in this well-educated, middle-class society. One "intellectual danger" that had to be guarded against constantly was "falling into a conceited, smattering superficiality."[48] This vice "nourishes and sustains itself upon compends, abridgments, extracts, and all the other convenient subsidia of improved education."[49] These intellectual contrivances guided you through the subject matter, but "without permitting you to know much of the country you pass through."[50] The best example of this façade of learning was "judicial opinions, where facts, and numbers, and grave statements of argument and collations of authorities are all that is wanted."[51] Verplanck was one of the few to recognize the advent of legal abridgments, reporters, periodicals, and treatises as potentially having a negative impact on the profession. Certainly others had complained about the rapidly growing amount of case law,[52] but none had before perceived the danger as one of intellectual stagnation, on the contrary, most saw these new publications as an advancement in legal systematization. No one before Verplanck had worried that legal self-nourishment might lead to the law becoming emaciated as a field of inquiry—as a field of truth-seeking. Remembering that Truth was transcendent and that the lawyer must draw upon his liberal education and avoid turning inward was the only way to overcome this "intellectual danger."[53]

APPLIED LEGAL SCIENCE

A First Attempt at Legal Scholarship

An Essay on the Doctrine of Contracts has received more scholarly attention than any other element of Verplanck's legal career. Peter Stein described the *Essay* as characteristic of early-nineteenth-century American lawyers' attempts to use the civil law for an "academic revival in legal education."[54] Morton Horwitz thought Verplanck was an archetypal will theorist whose views reinforced "existing social and economic inequalities," though perhaps he had a bit more sparkle because he refused to separate law from morality.[55] M. H. Hoeflich thought that the *Essay* was "a juristic tour-de-force," exemplifying a pragmatic balance of morality and practicality.[56] Finally, and most interestingly, Charles L. Barzun has described the work as the product of Scottish Common Sense philosophy.[57] Unfortunately, Verplanck's biographer, Robert July, only mentioned the work in passing as part of his unnoticed efforts as a moral philosopher.[58] Thus, the *Essay* has never really been considered as a product of Verplanck's larger intellectual outlook, especially his understanding that law was but one element of a liberal field of inquiry that studied Nature and Truth.

An Essay on the Doctrine of Contracts

Verplanck claimed that he was motivated to write the essay when he read the 1817 case of *Laidlaw v. Organ*,[59] and was troubled by the lack of "reasoning or authority" in Chief Justice Marshall's opinion.[60] The case arose out of a commercial contract for tobacco, transacted just as the War of 1812 was coming to a close. In preliminary negotiations, the vendor had agreed to sell to the vendee a certain quantity of tobacco at a certain price. On the morning the parties formalized the contract, the vendee got word that a peace treaty had been signed with Britain and thus the price of tobacco would thereafter increase 30–50 percent. The vendee remained silent about the information he had received and concluded the contract. The seller delivered the product but then confiscated it after delivery because of the news affecting the price. The vendee sued for the sequestration of the tobacco and enforcement of the contract. The vendor pleaded fraud in the inducement and asked the court to declare the contract void. The trial went against the vendor and the Supreme Court affirmed the principle that the vendee was not required to share his information with the vendor. All Marshall said in support of this conclusion was that the opposite principle would be difficult to limit in practice.[61]

Verplanck thought that most people's gut reaction would be to view the decision as "somewhat revolting to their notions of sound morality."[62] He claimed that he was concerned when the "untutored moral feeling" was at variance with the law.[63] There must be a way, thought Verplanck, to distinguish between "the fairest gains of industry and enterprise" and "the arts of deliberate knavery."[64] Rather than attempting such a distinction, Marshall had based his decision "not so much on the ground of justice as of policy and convenience."[65] For the same reasons of tradition and convenience the common law had embraced the doctrine of caveat emptor. What Verplanck set out to do in the *Essay* was to develop "a few fixed and broad rules, founded in nature, conscience, and reason."[66] These rules would be "in unison with the great laws of universal jurisprudence; and not inconsistent with . . . a commercial country."[67]

Various scholars have interpreted Verplanck's stated concern about the "untutored moral feeling" to be an indication that he was invoking Common Sense philosophy in criticizing the *Laidlaw* case.[68] Indeed, taken out of context, one could mistake Verplanck's phrasing as a critique of moral philosophy. However, considering the whole of the *Essay*, it is impossible to conclude that Verplanck rested moral obligation on untutored feelings. Instead, he followed Paley both in countering those "who argue from innate moral principles" and in deducing the moral obligation to keep promises and perform contracts from "the necessity of such conduct to the well-being, or the existence indeed, of human society."[69]

In the part of his *Moral Philosophy* that concerned "relative duties which are determinate," Paley explained the morality of promise-keeping as arising out of social expectations. The interpersonal confidence that a promise entailed was "essential to the intercourse of human life."[70] Paley further illustrated his point: "every hour of our lives, we trust to, and depend upon, others; and how impossible it is, to stir a step, or, what is worse, to sit still a moment, without such trust and dependence."[71] So commonplace in human society was the practice of promise-keeping that its ubiquity created the moral obligation—or bound the conscience—to the point that the average member of society did not have to engage in any moral philosophizing to expect certain practices from his fellow man. But for Paley—and Verplanck—the untutored moral feeling that an individual should and would act a certain way arose from social organization, not from instinct, or rather, social expectations created social instincts. These same morally-based expectations also extended to the analysis of contracts of sale.

Merely considering these opening sentiments and plans of Verplanck's *Essay* we can detect his more foundational understanding of Truth, Nature, and the role of reason. Likewise, we can see how even a universally acknowledged great judge like Marshall could fall into the intellectual danger zone by becoming too comfortable with doctrinal consistency, which had turned into the conceited, smattering superficiality Verplanck would later warn college graduates against. Marshall's opinion in *Laidlaw* had only been one paragraph long and the only reason he gave for his decision was that it was too difficult for him to imagine the outcome any other way. But only a lawyer or judge conceited enough to think that doctrinal purity mattered more than anything else could possibly be satisfied with such a performance. Marshall and the rest of the court had forgotten that law was connected to the rest of nature and the true rule for settling such a case could only come about through the use of reason, not by attempting to follow artificial precedent.

Verplanck began his second chapter by examining the substance of the common law that had dictated the outcome in *Laidlaw*. He took notice of the major distinction between the common law and the civil law, namely the former's preference for caveat emptor and the latter's rule of an implied warranty of merchantability. Nearly all the states in the union had borrowed the English rule of caveat emptor; only "the very able and learned Bench of South Carolina" had adopted a notion of implied warranty of sale.[72] What made the common law rule so starkly unjust was the recent development within Anglo-American jurisprudence of the law of insurance. This had mostly been developed by "the liberal learning, and powerful mind of Mansfield, in the course of his long and brilliant career."[73] As developed by Mansfield and adopted in most American states, insurance law "prescribes to each part, not simply strict integrity, but unreserved frankness and candour."[74] Insurance contracts were voided for fraud in accordance with "pure ethicks," as well as for negligence, accident, or inattention.[75] Hence, insurance taken out on an unseaworthy vessel would be void even if the owner were ignorant of its poor condition. But Verplanck could find "little analogy between the law of insurance and the more anciently settled parts of the English law of contracts."[76] Moreover, he thought, "It is impossible to assign any substantial reason for this remarkable contrast, either upon the grounds of natural equity or upon those of policy."[77] To illustrate this startling disconnect, he offered the following hypothetical: Suppose *A* takes out insurance from underwriter *B* on cargo in a ship owned by *A*. *A* is ignorant that his ship is not seaworthy, but he also sells the ship to *B* in his personal capacity, representing that he believes the ship to be in good order. The law will void the insurance contract on "natural justice" but the contract for sale is good under the doctrine of caveat emptor. In other words, *B* would not have to pay out a settlement as the underwriter of the insurance contract, but he would be stuck with the faulty ship he bought according to the sales contract. Verplanck concluded, "if the law be founded in reason, there ought to be some reason for the difference, and I have searched reporters and elementary writers in vain to find it."[78]

The distinction between artificial and natural reason is key to understanding Verplanck's whole argument in the *Essay*. Simply put, the common law had generally been celebrated as the pinnacle of artificial reason, whereas the civilians had been more concerned with the relationship between their law and the law of nature. Thus in no sense had the common law been discovered in nature, unlike the civil law. The best illustration of this feature of the common law is the famous exchange between Chief Justice Coke and King James I. Coke scolded James to mind his proper province as one unlearned in the law, while at the same time celebrating the common law's artificial reasoning.[79] The law's artificiality had always been justified as the product of the common man's practices, with those practices being developed into rules of law by the best legal minds—the judges.[80] But early on, the common law developed a reputation for inflexibility and other tribunals were developed in England for more "just" results, most notably the conciliar courts and the Court of Chancery.[81]

After considering the sorry state of the common law of contract, Verplanck turned his attention to the Roman-based civil law. He noted that "the incongruities of our law" were due to its lack of systematization, unlike the civil law, which was "regularly digested into written codes, settled by authoritative definitions, and commonly reasoned out from first principles," and thus had "the method and dignity of a science, and the unity of a system."[82] The civil law never permitted an outcome to rest upon "naked precedent and authority."[83] Instead, this preferable legal system "laid down as a universal and fundamental position, that the contract of sale depends wholly upon natural law."[84]

Verplanck's relationship to the civil law has been subject to varying interpretations. Stein thought that Verplanck was typical among early-republic legal intellectuals in his use of the civil law.[85] Hoeflich concluded, "Verplanck possessed a scholar's knowledge of the civil law; whereas, both Kent and Story possessed a superficial knowledge, useful to the practicing lawyer and judge, but far from masterful."[86] On the other hand, Barzun found that what was most striking was "that Verplanck ultimately rejected the civil law principles."[87] Considering Verplanck's whole body of work, Hoeflich comes closest to the mark, while Barzun missed it by quite some distance. Unlike Kent and Story, Verplanck was never a professional, but rather a man of leisure; even his twelve years in elective office were more the result of his leisure than of his desire to be a professional politician. Verplanck had no vested interest in the dignity of the bench or the common law, only a gentleman's interest in Truth. Although he was well read in the civil law, most of his reading was from Pothier[88] and other contemporary civilian commentators, rather than intimate familiarity with the Roman sources themselves. If we want a complementary comparison for that of Hoeflich's, we need only consider that two South Carolinians, Thomas Cooper and Hugh Legaré, far surpassed Verplanck in their knowledge of Roman law. Nevertheless, Verplanck had a deep enough sense of the civil law to fit it into his grand scheme of liberal education. What misled Barzun into detecting a hostility towards the civil law was Verplanck's treatment of Pothier's explanation of the contract of sale.

Pothier had taught Verplanck that the Roman law required each party to a contract to disclose all extrinsic circumstances of interest to the opposite party. Thus, if the purchaser of tobacco in *Laidlaw* had discovered a new method of producing cigarettes that he thought would be quite profitable, under this understanding of the Roman law, he would be required to tell the tobacco vendor this information. Pothier noted that this was not the law in France, but it might well be required *in foro conscientiae*. It was this latter assertion of Pothier's that bothered Verplanck greatly. In the first place, Verplanck rejected the notion that *all* extrinsic circumstances of interest to one party must be disclosed by the other party. This he thought was inconsistent with "the wholesome stimulus to commerce and the arts, given by the prospect of profit to be acquired by superior skill and industry, by minuter attention to business, or by a more extensive correspondence and more authentic intelligence."[89] Moreover, Verplanck thought that morality, or the *forum conscientiae,* did not require this rule either. Pothier had no difficulty separating law from morality; for Verplanck, to do so was to pervert the whole social function of law: "sound policy is never in collision with sound morality."[90] Verplanck thought that the error originated with the Stoic philosophers, who were lovers of paradox and verbal distinctions, and either they had overestimated human character or it had changed from what it once was. Either way, the rule, as explained by Pothier, was a bad one from the view of both policy and morality.[91]

The second area where civilian moralists had overreached was on the concept of inadequacy of price. These writers thought "that every honest sale proceeds upon the supposition of exchanging equivalents; singular as it may seem, they require what never occurs, or is ever likely to occur, in any commercial transaction."[92] What Verplanck realized was that all commercial contracts were "avowedly made with a view to *profit,*" and neither party viewed the exchange as equal. He concluded that neither legal system had precisely captured the subjective mindset associated with a contract, and thus neither system of laws was perfectly just. Hence, what Verplanck set as his task, without the help of the common law or civil law, was to "deduce for ourselves, from the nature and reason of things, and our own intuitive views of right morals, the safe and sound principles upon which the true equity of contracts must universally rest."[93] But it is clear to close readers—as it was crystal clear to contemporary reviewers—that Verplanck's agenda was to justify implied warranties and to undermine caveat emptor through natural-law type reasoning. Even though the Roman law may have mischaracterized human nature, at least it was working with the right raw material—man as nature made him, not man as the common lawyers caricatured him.

In order to achieve contractual justice, Verplanck needed a starting point for his analysis, and in creating his own path he said, "The clue to the accurate solution of this question is, I think, not to be found, where the old lawyers and moralists alone sought it, in metaphysical definitions or logical distinctions. We should rather seek it in some of the plainer truths of political economy."[94] What Verplanck wanted to do with political economy was to provide a scientific explanation for why the instinctual injustice that occurred in *Laidlaw* was inconsistent with Truth. The easiest way to go about this task was to claim that the price the tobacco purchaser had paid to the vendor was "inadequate" in terms of political economy, and thus "inadequate" at law. But Verplanck did not fully flesh out his theory of Truth in the *Essay*, and once he finished his explanations based on political economy and morality, he merely asserted that "civil justice," which was "nothing more than the methodized and scientific knowledge of the just and unjust," had to coincide with both economic and moral truths.[95] One needed to appreciate Verplanck's view of the liberal arts to understand that this was not merely wishful thinking on his part, nor simply the speculations of a naïve young lawyer who had never had a client. What Verplanck had not made clear was that whatever outcome yielded truth in political economy, also yielded truth in law, and thus yielded Truth in Nature because of the interconnectedness of all scientific knowledge.

History taught Verplanck that mankind progressed from "a very rude state of society" to a more "civilized life."[96] A mark of an increasing civilization was the division of labor and the development of commerce. The result was that certain commodities, because of their frequency of bargain and sale, combined with demand, cost, and quality, developed a "market price." Goods subject to a market price were those of domestic consumption and wholesale staples—goods that could not be described as "unique." Associated with mass-produced goods were "common facts" that underlay the market price. Verplanck described these as: "those facts which necessarily, directly and materially, influence the estimate on which the market value is founded, and therefore enter, of course, into the calculations of all dealers of ordinary prudence, and acquaintance with the business."[97] In other words, the common facts that determined the market price of a non-unique good were objective. The existence of an objective market price did not mean, however, that contracts for commodities were wholly objective; subjective views always entered into contracts. What an objective price did mean was that variance from the market price in a sales contract was "strong presumptive evidence" of error or fraud.[98]

It seems that Verplanck had turned to Paley's basic rule for the interpretation and enforcement of contracts—"*Whatever is expected by one side, and known to be so expected by the other, is to be deemed a part or condition of the contract.*"[99] Regarding sales contracts, Paley added, "Where there exists no monopoly or combination, the market-price is always a fair price; because it will always be proportionable to the use and scarcity of the article."[100] When combined, these two premises meant that a seller never had to apologize for selling a sound article at the market price and that a buyer had an implicit promise that goods sold at such a price were sound *and* that the price was in fact the market price.

The next step was to prove that because the market price for the tobacco in *Laidlaw* was 30–50 percent higher than the contract price, the withholding of the peace-treaty information was tantamount to fraud. Political economy had completed its work and this next consideration was "the purely ethical part of the question."[101] Verplanck approached the matter by asking, "how far, and when, may a man, consistently with honesty, keep his superior knowledge [of common facts] to his own breast, and profit by mere silence, from the ignorance of others?"[102] His answer was "never," so long as "there is a confidence expressly or impliedly reposed in him that he will take no such advantage of it."[103] As existing legal examples of this sort of relationship, he pointed to a trustee, an executor, and a guardian. None of those legal actors could take advantage of the beneficiary, testator, or ward for his own benefit. These cases were analogous to what had occurred in *Laidlaw,* Verplanck thought, because there "the knowledge of the actual fact of peace, and the concealment of it, amount[ed] to the seizing an advantage, where the contract itself was formed upon the understanding that no such advantage would be taken."[104] Therefore, *Laidlaw* was a clear-cut case of fraud.

Reactions to the Essay

The most positive feedback Verplanck received on his *Essay* was from his fellow New Yorker, Henry Wheaton, who at the time was in his final years as official Supreme Court Reporter.[105] In his 1826 contribution to the *North American Review,* Wheaton began with what he thought was an apropos quote from Lord Bacon in describing those best suited to improve the existing laws of a country: they were "*statesmen,* whose views are large and comprehensive, and at the same time rectified by an extensive and practical knowledge of human affairs."[106] Verplanck was such a statesman as exhibited by his *Essay* and his recent election to Congress. In contrast to both "mere technical lawyers" and "speculative philosophers," Wheaton thought Verplanck focused "his attention to promoting the happiness of his fellow men, by an enlightened and anxious investigation of the laws by which they are governed, and by an honest effort to amend their glaring defects."[107] This unique gift of Verplanck's put him in the company of Montesquieu, Smith, Filangieri, Beccaria, "and, notwithstanding his eccentricities, we will add, Bentham."[108] It was the unfortunate conduct of governments to have ignored these public-spirited philosophers until only recently. The concern of British ministers with law reform demonstrated that the tide was now turning in favor of heeding the advice of statesmen. However, more improvement had already come about in the United States than in Britain, especially notable in the law reform efforts of both New York and Louisiana.[109]

Wheaton recognized Verplanck's *Essay* for what it was, a work of censorial jurisprudence, concerned "less with the purpose of reconciling the anomalies of the existing law, and of showing what *it is*, than of comparing its precepts with those of reason and conscience, and thus endeavoring to ascertain what *it ought to be*."[110] Because this was not an expository treatise "of mere technical law," it was precisely what was needed to carry forward the process of law reform. "Independently of their utility in this respect," Wheaton thought, "investigations of this sort must always be attractive to those who regard law as a science founded on reason, and not merely resting on positive institutions and the authority of precedent."[111] Wheaton was able to offer this praise only because he shared Verplanck's view that the common law as practiced in the United States lacked a solid foundation in reason.

The case of *Laidlaw* was reported in Wheaton's second volume of *United States Reports*.[112] Like in most early case reports, the arguments of counsel are given prominent coverage.[113] But what is especially striking in the report of *Laidlaw*, is the editorial addition to the argument of the vendor's counsel. The plaintiff's lawyer did raise the issue of the Pothier's treatment of contracts, but it was not asserted with any particular verve.[114] However, Wheaton dropped a footnote to this part of counsel's argument that ran six pages.[115] What this footnote consisted of, was a quotation from Pothier on the required disclosures each party was bound to make to the other. It was this same section of Pothier that Verplanck had treated in the *Essay* and rejected for its overestimation of human nature. It is quite possible that Wheaton was signaling, through his position as official Supreme Court Reporter, that he disagreed with Marshall's opinion. As reported with Wheaton's editorial additions, it appeared that Marshall ignored a great part of the argument made by counsel, when in fact, it was a post-decision add-on. It should not, therefore, be surprising that Wheaton would respond warmly to a book-length argument dedicated to criticizing *Laidlaw* and supporting civil-law type reasoning.

The only other lengthy and positive review Verplanck's *Essay* received was from "the flamboyant Irish émigré lawyer" and "legal gadfly," William Sampson.[116] Sampson, a strong proponent of codification and opponent of subservience to the common law, sounded much like Verplanck in claiming that law should be based, not on precedent, but on "natural reason, universal justice, and present convenience."[117] Nearly half-a-century later, one Verplanck admirer thought Sampson's praise of the *Essay* "was probably as detrimental" as were critics of Verplanck because of Sampson's reputation as a loose cannon.[118] Sampson's review, however, was very measured and interspersed with long extracts from the *Essay* itself.[119] The thrust of Sampson's review was that Verplanck had made a contribution to putting law on a scientific foundation. Verplanck accomplished this feat with his systematic critique of the common law. Thus, Sampson "was strongly inclined to agree with Mr. Verplanck, in the preference which he gives to the civil law in this particular. It coincides with the natural sentiments of equity."[120] Praising the author in words he might have found in Verplanck's own essays, Sampson wrote, "Every part of this essay bears evidence that its author is a liberal minded man, who had thought for himself, without an excessive regard to what men of great authority have thought and said before him, and who gives his thoughts to the public, because he believes them valuable."[121] Sampson closed with the thought that Verplanck's *Essay* was sure to contribute to "the advancement of the law from a *trade* to a science."[122]

Other leading lawyers responded with less enthusiasm. Story and Kent each sent Verplanck admiring letters of acknowledgment of dubious sincerity.[123] In his treatise on equity, Story went out of his way to explain that *Laidlaw* was good law as to "mistakes of fact." In his section on "Mistake," he explained, "Equity, as a practical system, though it will not aid immorality, does not affect to enforce mere moral duties. But its policy is to administer relief to the vigilant, and to put all parties upon the exercise of a searching diligence."[124] In *Laidlaw,* the vendor had not been vigilant, and since the intelligence of the peace treaty was "equally accessible to both parties," no mutual confidence was reposed in the parties and the vendee took no action designed to mislead the vendor. Nevertheless, Story recognized the opposite argument and cited Pothier as contrary authority; he did not cite Verplanck.[125] Had Story cited Verplanck, he would have had to deal with the section of the *Essay* where he directly addressed the issue of mutual confidence and said that it "forms the fundamental consideration of the contract" of sale, and that only in cases where the seller advertises he is "answerable for no faults or defects" is the buyer put on notice not to repose confidence in him.[126]

Unlike Story, Kent did mention Verplanck in his *Commentaries,* but Story had to correct him for not being careful enough in describing the duty of mutual disclosure. Kent had written: "As a general rule, each party is bound to communicate to the other, his knowledge of material facts, provided he know the other to be ignorant of them, and they be not open and naked, or equally within the reach of his observation."[127] Of course, in *Laidlaw,* the vendee knew well that the vendor was ignorant of the treaty information, which was not widely available at the time of the contract, and thus by Kent's reasoning, would have been bound to disclose the news. Kent's phrasing prompted Story to clearly define the concept of "undue concealment" as "the non-disclosure of those facts and circumstances, which one party is under some legal or equitable obligation to communicate to the other; and which the latter has a right, not merely in *foro conscientiae,* but *juris et de jure,* to know."[128] Moreover, Story specifically warned that Kent's "broader doctrine" threatened to undermine *Laidlaw.*[129] Kent acknowledged Story's rebuke and capitulated by the third edition of his *Commentaries*: "The rule here laid down, though one undoubtedly of moral obligation, is rather too broadly stated, as Mr. Justice Story has shown . . . to be sustained by the practical doctrine of the courts."[130]

Kent attempted to respond to Verplanck's argument about the supposed incongruity between the law of sales and the law of insurance. Specifically, Kent wanted to argue that concealment of a common fact affecting the market price of a commodity did not necessarily give rise to a presumption of fraud. He explained: "The fundamental error of his [Verplanck's] theory, consists in the assumption of a breach of implied confidence in the ten thousand cases in which no such implied confidence exists, and in which men deal with each other at arm's length, and with an entire and exclusive reliance upon their own judgment, knowledge and examination."[131] Whereas in a marine insurance contract, the underwriter relies on the representations of the seaworthiness of the vessel since "[t]he insurer is essentially *passive.*"[132] Despite Kent's attempt to reconcile these two fields of law, and to show that "there is no jar between them, as the learned author of the essay I have alluded to supposes," he never addressed Verplanck's own example that demonstrated this precise gap, the example being that of two contracts being executed by the same parties—one an insurance contract, the other a sales contract—wherein the insurer of cargo is also the purchaser of the unseaworthy ship. Instead, Kent maintained his doctrines, but omitted explicit mention of Verplanck by the fourth edition of his work.[133]

Another critic, Joseph Hopkinson of Pennsylvania, former Federalist congressman and future federal judge, reviewed Verplanck's *Essay* for the *American Quarterly Review* in 1827.[134] He immediately noticed that it was not the typical professional work commonly published at the time. Hopkinson observed, "an original treatise on the science of jurisprudence is a rare occurrence with us."[135] But aside from the *Essay*'s originality, Hopkinson found little else to praise. He thought Verplanck's plan of action was typical of "dreaming politicians." As Hopkinson understood that plan, it consisted of replacing the common law with the civil law. Such an "ungoverned spirit of innovation in the law" was worthy of condemnation from practicing lawyers and judges.[136] Because Verplanck was a politician and not an active lawyer, he was unable to understand that English common law "may be said to be a part of ourselves" and that "the very foundations of society rest upon it."[137] Hopkinson thought, "As easily could the pyramids of Egypt be replaced by a few modern brick-layers, as the common law of England by such jurists" as Verplanck.[138]

If Verplanck was a will theorist as Morton Horwitz explained, then Hopkinson certainly was not.[139] This difference is starkly revealed in comparing their understanding of a just administration of a contract dispute. For Verplanck, "substituting another bargain for that which was actually made" was an injustice.[140] The easiest way for the law to avoid this hazard was to develop positive regulations "drawn from the actual usages of society, and in conformity with our modes of thoughts and habits of business."[141] Otherwise, "the artificial reasoning and technical subtleties of the common law" would interfere with natural justice.[142] By contrast, Hopkinson thought that "disputed contracts" usually and rightly received "an interpretation never understood by those who used them. Yet such is, and must be, what is called the administration justice among men."[143] He explained this cold, hard fact by taking notice that "no legislator ever expected to give a law which would exactly fit itself to every transaction that rises every hour in the diversified business of men. The laws of nature," he further explained, "do not possess this universal beneficence."[144] What Verplanck and Hopkinson were really disagreeing over were their understandings of truth and nature.

What Hopkinson lacked was a unified theory of the natural order in which every action of man had a place on the moral spectrum. Otherwise, he would not have been able to say, "It seems to us to be a radical mistake in Mr. V.'s argument, that there is a standard of 'moral judgment,' or 'conscience' except in very clear and broad cases."[145] In condemning the common law's adherence to unjust artificial precedent as "the arbitrary inventions of men," Verplanck had made the claim, "to such variations are all man's inventions inevitably doomed. Truth alone is immutable and eternal."[146] Hopkinson replied, "It is very easy and pretty to say, 'truth alone is immutable and eternal;' but it is not the less difficult to discover what is the truth."[147] This disagreement over truth, nature, and justice is best analyzed using the *Laidlaw* case.

Like Story, Hopkinson thought that the tobacco vendor had not been vigilant enough. He also thought the purchaser had not committed any fraud by keeping the news of the peace treaty to himself: "We cannot understand that a man may not use his superior intelligence to his advantage in a bargain, if he says nothing, and does nothing to deceive and mislead the other party, and has not obtained the intelligence under any confidence that he will not so use it."[148] That news of the peace treaty was what Verplanck had called a "common fact" determining the market price of tobacco, Hopkinson thought of no importance. Of Verplanck's notion that "common facts" were not to be taken advantage of by one party, Hopkinson said, "we utterly deny both in fact and theory. No such supposition is in the mind of either party."[149] Instead, because the fact was common, Hopkinson thought, "Let each be left to his own vigilance or good fortune."[150] He further thought that a "common fact" could not be distinguished from "ingenuity or good fortune."[151] From his response to Verplanck, it seems that Hopkinson failed to appreciate the Truth of political economy and morality, and instead favored the contrivances of the common law.

As an example of the confidence actually reposed in the vendor in each typical sales contract, Verplanck had offered the following example: suppose a man newly arrived in town purchases flour from the first shop he enters at eight dollars per barrel, unaware that the market price for flour in that town was actually four dollars.[152] Even if no discussion of the price of the flour occurred in the course of the transaction, Verplanck thought the vendor must be considered, by the standards of morality, to have committed a fraud. This was because the vendee must have considered the market price—an objective fact—to be eight dollars; otherwise he would not have paid twice the price for an ordinary commodity. Additionally, the vendor's action of selling the flour at eight dollars was an implicit representation that that was the market price of flour. Therefore, in such a transaction, the buyer's implicit confidence that the seller would not take advantage of a common fact known only to the seller was breached.[153] On the contrary, Hopkinson thought, "Let it be known that if a man will make a fool's bargain, and, as our author supposes, give eight dollars a barrel for flour, when he can buy it at the next house for four, he must abide by his folly."[154] But in his rebuttal, Hopkinson seems to have abandoned his previous description of the actual practices of the marketplace, wherein he said that no such confidence actually existed between buyers and sellers. Indeed, Hopkinson found it difficult to counter Verplanck's tight reasoning, and thus turned to name-calling, pointing out the fool who was not suspicious enough to comparison shop.

Because Hopkinson was a practicing lawyer of some repute, he felt at ease in criticizing Verplanck for his lack of real-world experience. Thus he closed on the following note:

> The refined ethics of the civilian may be delightful to the philosopher—who, in his closet, makes himself happy with reveries of the perfectibility of our nature and condition; but if he will go into the warehouse, or on the exchange, he will find that some more plain and practical doctrines are required for the actual business of mankind.[155]

At this point, some might note an inconsistency in Hopkinson's argument. Recall that at the beginning of his review, he criticized Verplanck for wanting to base contract law on the actual usages of merchants in contrast to the common law's artificial imposition of rules never contemplated by either party. Here, he was suggesting that Verplanck's theories were based on ungrounded speculation rather than the practices at the warehouse. Verplanck would get the last word, however, when he was able to apply his more refined theory of public utility to commercial cases that came before him on New York's highest court a decade later.

A year after Verplanck's *Essay* was published, the *United States Law Journal* (*USLJ*) printed a fifty-page, unsigned attack on the work.[156] The first observation the review made was that Verplanck did not practice law. Moreover, the review claimed it could not discover Verplanck's principles. "We can see, however, without much difficulty, that he has a great dislike of the common law, and a very decided preference of the civil law; and we must tell him plainly, that as far as this goes, he will always find in us most determined and irreconcilable enemies to his opinions."[157] This set the tone for the rest of the article.

The most notable aspect of the *USLJ*'s review was its resentment of Verplanck as a man of literary society. This was quite a contrast to a critic like Hopkinson, who was from a literary family himself.[158] "That a man, who had devoted so much time to literature and the fine arts as Mr. Verplanck had done," noted the reviewer, "should feel no great relish for the writings of Lord Coke, or the works of Mr. Fearne or Mr. Cruise, is not surprising."[159] The lack of surprise was due to the fact that these studies "do not make men better judges, either of what is or of what ought to be law."[160] The overwhelming sentiment was that men like Verplanck should stick to their studies, galleries, and like-minded aesthetes and leave the working lawyers alone.

> We say, therefore, let their votaries and admirers confine themselves to their own favourite pursuits, or if, by way of variety, or because they happen to have studied law in their youth, they think proper now and then to make an excursion into the severer regions of jurisprudence, let them be content with reading books, which they are not, and cannot be, sufficiently at home to write about it. . . . We assure them they will not escape without harsh reproof; no more than we should escape it from them if we should unluckily take it into out heads to write a book on architecture or the Italian Opera, or to criticize and condemn the works of Raphael or Michael Angelo, or Peter Paul Rubens. With our want of skill and experience we might perhaps contemplate the works of those great masters with the most complete indifference, and our untaught and unpractised ears might prefer the simple melody and the touching pathos of a Scottish ballad, or the inspiring liveliness of a cotillion or a reel, to the most elaborate and intricate compositions of Handel, or Mozart, Winter, or Buthoven [*sic*], or Rossini—to all the choruses and cantatas, and oratorios and overtures, and bravuras and battle pieces, of the whole German and Italian schools.[161]

Unlike Verplanck, the *USLJ* thought the law was not to be admired like a work of art, or, more precisely, "We would not give a fiddle-stick more or less for a body of law, because it recommends itself by its 'beauty.'"[162]

So as to leave no doubt as to their conclusion about Verplanck, the *USLJ* reviewer, closed with this thought: "As a lawyer, we think him decidedly visionary, and we cannot recommend his essay to the perusal of our readers. In a legal point of view it is absolutely useless. It is even worse; for it inculcates opinions which we think are positively mischievous."[163] In order to place into context this criticism of Verplanck, "that king of foppery,"[164] we must understand where Verplanck placed the fine arts within his vision of a liberal education.

Creating Moral Citizens through Art and Law

A Theory of Aesthetics

Verplanck had a theory of aesthetics, which he best articulated after returning from a visit in which he toured the medieval colleges of Oxford:

> I saw the walls covered with the portraits of those great scholars and eloquent divines, whose doctrines are taught, or whose works are daily consulted by the clergy of all sects throughout our republic—of the statesmen and judges, whose opinions and decisions are every day cited as authorities at our bar and in our legislative bodies—of the poets and orators, whose works form the study of our youth and the amusement of our leisure, I could not but confess that the young man who lived and studied in such a presence, must be dull and brutal indeed, if he was not sometimes roused into aspirations after excellence, if the countenances of the great men who looked down upon him, did not sometimes fill his soul with generous thoughts and high contemplations.[165]

Verplanck saw no reason why Americans should not enjoy the same sort of inspirations as the English through publicly supported museums, government buildings, and colleges. The social value of the arts are what led Verplanck to author a new copyright law while in Congress, and what had initially led him to attempt prose and poetry early in life, and then edit Shakespeare in retirement.

Fine art was one way of preserving a nation's history. What Verplanck imagined motivated most men, was a desire to be a part of history, to be remembered for their lasting contributions to their nation. Certainly, the strength of any nation depended upon the motivation of its citizens to work for the public good. Thus, if the natural desire to serve one's country was not strong enough—as it was in men like Verplanck—then art could act as a catalyst for directing the intellect toward a more civic-minded path. Who, after all, would not want immortality in the form of a marble bust or an oil portrait inscribed with a Latin phrase detailing his greatness in life? No one, thought Verplanck. Therefore, the "aspirations after excellence" that Verplanck thought were roused by the countenances of great men looking down on the students were quite distinct from "inspirations to veneration," which had historically been the purpose of great art. And in this sense, Verplanck's theory of art is highly democratic.

Unlike European art that had been created to display greatness and keep the lower orders in check, American art was supposed to encourage a desire for greatness, a desire to rival—in life and in death—the man in the painting looking down on you. Recall that Verplanck thought the liberally educated American scholar would not fall victim to intellectual fads or to worshiping authority. It is only an individual of this constitution for whom Verplanck's theory of art makes sense. Standing under a portrait of Lord Coke or Judge Blackstone should have an awe-inspiring effect on the viewer, but it should not be an inspiration to start citing either Coke or Blackstone as authority. Instead, the appropriate democratic effect is for the law-student viewer to be motivated to want his portrait eventually hung next to both Coke and Blackstone. And the only way he can accomplish this is by being as original as both, not by imitating them, and certainly not by bowing to their authority.

This understanding of the role of art is extremely individualistic in one sense, as well as new in American thought. Americans never had an aristocratic or a ruling class that employed artists as patrons once did, and thus never had a subjective relationship to art the way Europeans did. Verplanck was well aware of this and thankful for it. But art during the revolution had a more ambiguous social role as described by Joseph Ellis. On the one hand, art well served the then-dominant republican concerns with classical virtue by depicting revolutionary scenes in Romanesque motifs. On the other hand, the fine arts seemed rather frivolous to stoic notions of moral sobriety, and hence, after the revolution, the artist struggled to find his social niche. For example, Ellis described how Charles Wilson Peale managed to become an entrepreneur by selling images in a republican spirit—ones that unified the nation.[166] But even this republican-cum-democratic use of art is quite different from Verplanck's theory of the value of art to the country.

Verplanck thought that the aesthetic of the artistic undertaking should appeal to the viewer's self interest, not necessarily cause the viewer to imagine himself as part of something larger. But for this self-interest to be channeled into works of public service, the art had to make the concept of the nation indispensable to individual glory. Verplanck thought that the framers of the Constitution had come to the same conclusion when they inserted the Authors and Inventors Clause under Congress's enumerated powers.[167]

> They knew that the best security of national union and national power, was to be sought in the influence of national literature, science, arts, and education. They saw clearly that their own legislation, and that of

> those who were destined to administer the government they had reared, would be but feeble and temporary without the aid of that more potent and far more lasting, though secret and silent legislation, which acts on the mind and the affections.[168]

Verplanck's use of the phrase "secret and silent legislation, which acts on the mind" might sound ominous in a postmodern age, but he had no sinister motives aside from public utility.[169] History had taught that without some sort of cohesive force, free governments fall apart. "If our country is to escape the fate of other free governments," Verplanck thought it was the arts that would save it: "Their agency works its way without noise or pomp; but it is felt in the hearts of the people."[170]

What artists and inventors did, was to transform the abstract truths of science, morals, and law, into "eventful stories," "tales of courage, virtue, and patriotism," "eloquence or poetry," or some other form that transcended "our own moral and physical state," thus guarding "our liberties stronger than any laws can make, stronger than even our mutual interests (great as they are) can create, far, far stronger than can be imposed by arms or power."[171] Verplanck asked, "How much, then, can our country just claim from her authors, her artists, and all her sons ministering directly or indirectly to the mental wants of the people"?[172] The least the nation could do was not divest them of their moral right to their intellectual property.

The Law of Literary Property

In 1831, Verplanck delivered a speech in celebration of the recent passage in Congress of a new copyright law.[173] The new law extended the maximum copyright term to forty-two years and permitted the bequeathment of the copyright to widows and children.[174] Under the old law, authors and artists were only permitted a fourteen-year term, once renewable during the life of the copyright holder. The new law was also retroactively applied to holders of copyrights under the old law.[175] Three years earlier, in the Twentieth Congress, Verplanck had introduced a similar bill, but the tariff issue consumed all debate and he was unable to see it through at that time. The bill reported out of the House Judiciary Committee was basically Verplanck's old bill with some "useful modification."[176] But when brought to the floor for debate, it ran into some difficulties. The new bill "was decidedly objected to by a gentleman whose experience, ability, and faithful public service had acquired for him much influence in the House."[177] The member who raised the objection was Verplanck's fellow New Yorker, Congressman Michael Hoffman.[178] What Hoffman objected to, was the retroactive extension of old copyrights. He based his objection on the "vested rights of the individuals who compose the public."[179]

Hoffman argued against establishing "a monopoly of which authors alone would reap the advantage, to the public detriment." Referring to the copyright holders, Hoffman said, "There was an implied contract between them and the public. They, in virtue of their copyright, sold their books to the latter at an exorbitant rate; and the latter, therefore, had the right to avail themselves of the work, when the copyright expired."[180] Verplanck was moved to respond to such an argument out of "a sense of justice and the duty of asserting what I believe to be the rights of mind."[181] In order to make his argument, however, he first had to deny that intellectual property was the mere creation of positive law. Hence, the Constitution's recognition of Congress's power to legislate in this area merely provided a legal remedy for something the founders presumed to exist prior to the formation of the union.

> I therefore denied that the right of the author or inventor was the mere creation of the positive law of the land. I maintained that the right of property in the productions of intellectual labour was as much founded in natural justice as the right of property in the productions of corporeal labour—that he who toils with the mind is as honestly entitled to the fruits of that toil as he who works with the hands.[182]

Verplanck thought he was in line with Mansfield, "whose reasoning in the great English case of the law of Literary Property, was founded upon this principle."[183] Like most lawyers and lawmakers who had disagreements with Verplanck, Hoffman approached the issue with a logical detachment Verplanck found incompatible with his morality. In debate, Verplanck referred to a copyright as "a natural right," which the statute law was merely designed to recognize.[184] Hoffman thought this was "a contradiction in terms" because he could conceive of "no right but a remedial right."[185] Clearly Verplanck and Hoffman were working from different foundational premises, with Verplanck's view of the matter solidly anchored in a theory of human nature.

But if intellectual property was as much a natural right as private corporeal property, then how could the legal order be just with any expiration of a copyright term? Would this not be tantamount to suggesting that someone's estate be valid for only forty-two years? Verplanck thought the principled answer was "yes." But he recognized a public policy exception to natural justice just as he had articulated in the *Essay on the Doctrine of Contracts*. In the *Essay* Verplanck had justified statutes of limitation in a similar fashion.[186] After the statute had run, one's claim was barred in law even though it might remain a valid moral claim. Similarly, the copyright "may be longer or shorter according to the views of public policy, the natural and moral rights of property remaining unchanged."[187]

Unfortunately, Verplanck did not share his formulation for calculating the point at which considerations of public policy came to outweigh considerations of morality; all we know is that he considered the existing twenty-eight-year copyright term inadequately short. It was no secret that Verplanck ran in literary circles in his early years in public life and maintained literary friends throughout his career. He was sensitive to the appearance of self-interest and thus asserted that the benefit to his personal friends was of no consideration. Instead, he was motivated by his conversations with "those who had practically experienced the difficulties and imperfections" of the old law.[188] He likewise had the support of the legal press, most notably two articles by Willard Phillips in the *American Jurist*.[189] But if we recall Verplanck's theory of art, then we should have less need to be concerned that he was looking out for his own. Originality, not imitation, is what made one great and what inspired others to greatness, and, in the process, benefited the nation with advances in truth. Efforts at greatness and thus national preservation were "exerted not less in the humblest literary effort to instruct the infant mind, than in the labours of the teacher of high science, or in those of the philosophical historian, or statesman, or in the glorious inspirations of the orator, the painter, or the poet."[190] It is no wonder intellectual property deserved such significant legal recognition.

SCIENTIFIC RETOOLING: RE-CONCEIVING THE JUDICIARY

"By Senator Verplanck": His Time on the Bench

When members of the New York legal profession opened their volumes of *Wendell's Reports* spanning the years 1838–1841, they must have delighted upon seeing the words, "By *Senator* VERPLANCK."[191] It did not take long to realize that what followed such an ascription was usually a lengthy analytical essay, examining first and foremost the policy and moral implications of the legal questions presented in the case at bar. To be certain, Verplanck's opinions contained notice of relevant precedent from his own state, especially the opinions of Kent, as well as plentiful citations to English authorities, and when the case called for it, citation to parallel European judgments. But for Verplanck, authority was never controlling. It might be important in rendering justice if legal precedents had seeped into public practices and expectations, but it was never decisive for its own weight alone.

The Court for the Correction of Errors

It would be an untoward sight today to open a law reporter and see the name of an elected politician delivering the judgment of a court of law. Such was not the case in the New York of the early republic. Nor is it entirely correct to rest upon the analogy offered earlier in this chapter, wherein New York's legal system was compared to that of the English.

Certainly New York had borrowed from the English legal system the idea of having the upper legislative chamber act as the final court of appeals. However, the starkest difference is that the New York Senate was a fully elected body, whereas the British House of Lords was entirely unelected, being composed of hereditary and appointed members. Even though lay peers were not prohibited from participating in the adjudication of cases when New York was still a British colony, it was a fast fading practice by the early-nineteenth century.[192] In New York, the state senators, the chancellor, and the supreme court justices composed the Court for the Correction of Errors. Like the custom in the British House, the chancellor of New York and the justices of the Supreme Court usually took the lead in advising the court and delivering their opinions. Although all senators had the right to participate in the court, full senatorial participation was rare. When a case at law came before the court, the chancellor almost always delivered the first recorded opinion, followed by interested senators. When it was an appeal from chancery before the court, it was usually the chief justice who began with his opinion, again, followed by the participating senators.[193] Even in cases in which most of the eligible members of the court participated, it was highly unusual for more than two or three senators to give any reasoned opinion at all, instead just casting votes for affirmance or reversal. In cases of lesser moment, it was common only for the chancellor to speak, followed by a unanimous vote concurring in his opinion.[194]

It is difficult to measure the extent to which Verplanck's role on the court was made even more prominent by the fact of the contemporaneous occupation of the office of chancellor by Reuben H. Walworth. Little has been written about Walworth, and what has been said amounts to a mixed lot.[195] Walworth is perhaps best known as a failed US Supreme Court nominee of President John Tyler.[196] But it is unclear whether this failure was purely political or at least partly based upon a sense that Walworth was somewhat lacking in legal learning. In cases in which Walworth and Verplanck differed, it is quite clear who the more devoted jurist was; and even in cases when they agreed, Walworth's opinions were often superfluous next to Verplanck's broad-ranged reasoning. Considering some of these opinions will allow us to understand how Verplanck put his lifelong concern with a moral order into practice. We will then consider whether Verplanck's unique role as a judge-politician permitted him to contribute what he did to the law and how such a political order facilitated his use of the law to those ends.

Public Utility: The Rule of Decision

The most consistent theme in Verplanck's judicial opinions is his concern with what he called "public utility."[197] Regardless of the branch of law, public utility was always his primary concern. In commercial cases, public utility was usually determined by looking to the actual practices of the mercantile community in which the transaction took place. The vast majority of cases on which Verplanck expounded at length were of a commercial nature. In examining Verplanck's commercial jurisprudence, we must negotiate between the socioeconomic context and the intellectual climate as represented by the multi-faceted portrait I have been trying to paint of Verplanck using the whole of his social theory. Even if we wanted to read Verplanck as unabashedly pro-market, we would have to contend with his unique view of the value of the marketplace to the intellectual growth of America. In other words, we could understand his decisions as not promoting an upward redistribution of wealth, but instead as further aiding the country's search for Truth and furthering the advance of democracy. But a close examination of his actual judicial opinions reveals that Verplanck never forgot why the commercial community was important. His reasoning never resembled the formalistic jurisprudential mode that would come to characterize the late-nineteenth century. Rather, we know explicitly why Verplanck believed every decision he rendered, even if in dissent, was good for the public as a whole, not just for the benefit of one party or the other, and certainly not because it fit some prefabricated legal category.

The very first case Senator Verplanck heard and decided was a commercial shipping case, *Saltus v. Everett*,[198] in 1838. The case appeared rather uncontroversial by the fact that the judgment was unanimous in reversing the lower court, but Verplanck delivered a twelve-page, fully reasoned opinion, explaining the moral and policy implications of what had transpired. Everett, a New York resident, purchased a quantity of lead from merchants in New Orleans. The vessels on which the lead was being transported were twice involved in accidents and the cargo eventually landed in New York on a different ship than on which it began its journey. As a result, the captain of the incapacitated ship signed an intervening bill of lading, even though he was not the owner of the cargo. Upon arrival in New York, the firm that had accepted delivery sold the lead as ordered to do so by the captain of the first ship. Saltus was the bona fide purchaser of the lead from the New York firm and refused to sell the lead to Everett when approached to do so. The New York Supreme Court had ruled in favor of Saltus, believing the law preferred genuine bona fide purchasers who were without notice of competing claims on the property.[199]

Verplanck began by noticing that "the main question in the case is of great importance and must frequently arise in a commercial community. It ought, therefore, to be distinctly settled on principles of general application."[200] That main question was, "of these two innocent parties, which of the two is to bear the loss arising from the wrong-doing of the third?"[201] Posing the question in that fashion, it is easy to see that Verplanck was not going to shy away from evaluating the case on moral terms. But once he looked into the matter, he concluded that both claims were "equally meritorious";[202] Everett had a moral right to the property for which he contracted, and Saltus had a moral right to the property he purchased with pure motives. The only conclusion was that "public policy must draw an arbitrary line somewhere, and the greatest merit of such a rule must be its certainty and uniformity."[203]

In considering the public policy of the question, Verplanck thought that the arbitrary rule should favor the original owner over the bona fide purchaser for several reasons. First, a rule in favor of a purchaser was more easily susceptible to collusive fraud. One claiming to be a bona fide purchaser may in fact be in agreement with the intermediate agent who falsely claims the right to sell the cargo in his possession. Also, a rule in favor of purchasers would have a chilling effect on the use of agents in commerce. If every merchant had to worry that his agent might defraud him with impunity, then commercial transactions would suffer. Verplanck was aware that his preferred rule might sometimes put purchasers at great peril, but he thought public policy counterbalanced this possible inconvenience. With the law settled on this point, however, it would be easier for purchasers to be wary of purchasing cargo from unknown ships of foreign origin.[204]

In another commercial case, Verplanck again reiterated his belief that the use of agents should be promoted and not hampered. In *Kirkpatrick v. Stainer,*[205] an Italian mercantile house arranged, through their American agent, for the purchase of coffee from an American merchant. The American coffee merchant obtained an agreement from the agent that insurance would be taken out on the cargo, but the agent failed to do so. The ship was lost at sea and the coffee merchant sued the American agent for breach of contract. Over the Chancellor's dissent, and against the authority of *Story on Agency,* Verplanck held that the agent of a foreign principal was not liable in *assumpsit.*[206] Walworth, following Story, thought that a foreign agent should be liable because of the difficulty of reaching the principal through ordinary legal process. For his own part, Verplanck preferred to look at "usage and the particular course of trade."[207] But in so doing, he could not find a clear practice of departing from the ordinary law of agency, which held only the principal liable if his identity was known to the party opposite. However, it was public policy that really set Verplanck's mind at ease. He thought, "it would be of the greatest public inconvenience to assume a general rule applicable to and exonerating every principal residing in another state, . . . or even to principals not resident within the United States."[208] Moreover, agents were often transient and irresponsible, and thus not the real recipients of the credit extended to the principal. The opposite rule "would exonerate the foreign trader not only here, but by the application of the doctrine of *lex loci contractus,* it might also do so in the courts of his own domicile."[209]

One final case on agency is that of *Davis v. Shields*, heard in 1841.[210] The plaintiffs had contracted to purchase a quantity of iron from England through a broker. The broker agreed to the following terms: $70/ton, arrival in a "reasonable time" and six-months credit. The iron did not arrive until four months after what was commercially acknowledged as a "reasonable time" for delivery, but the buyer still demanded compliance with the other terms. Most importantly, the market price of iron had risen to $98/ton by the time of arrival. The vendor refused to comply with the contract and pleaded the statute of frauds because the broker had not obtained the seller's signature. Verplanck recognized that the "probable motive" for noncompliance was the "rise in the market price." But, he added, "whatever may be the merits of the controversy as between the individuals, the transaction is governed by general rules of public utility and positive legislation; and upon these it must be decided."[211]

The *Davis* case, like so many cases of interest to Verplanck, turned on nothing more than his calculation of public utility. Because New York's statute of frauds had recently been amended with the intent that "the party to be charged" give his explicit written assent to the contract, Verplanck thought that "manifest considerations of public utility" required the conclusion that the broker's negotiation had not satisfied the mandates of the statute. Aside from considerations of legislative intent, which Verplanck seems to have construed as coextensive with public utility, he also felt constrained "to add a single remark as to the policy of the law": "I do not see how we can sustain this entry as a binding note of sale, upon any presumed equity of this particular case, without giving a very dangerous extension to the implied authority of brokers or other agents for sale."[212]

For Verplanck, a healthy commercial economy required the use of intermediaries to carry out the intentions of the contracting parties, and as such, their use should not be deterred. However, these agents appeared to have no legally relevant wills of their own within any particular transaction—in *Saltus* the agent had no legal authority to sell to a bona fide purchaser, in *Kirkpatrick* the foreign agent was not liable for his inaction, and in *Davis* the agent was not permitted to negotiate contract terms without his principal's explicit authorization. This view certainly facilitated commercial intercourse, but no one class of people appears to have benefited to the detriment of another. The decision in the *Kirkpatrick* case clearly shows that Verplanck had no difficulty ruling against an American merchant. I highlight Verplanck's treatment of agents as unresponsible actors simply to emphasize his overt use of utility—what we might call his instrumental use of the law to reach a certain policy preference. There was absolute logic to Verplanck's opinions and no "legal fiction" was employed in the course of his reasoning. Public utility was the goal and support of commerce was generally useful, therefore the law was used to promote these preferences. Verplanck never asserted that agents actually lacked a will, or even that they should be treated in law as lacking a will. Rather, he thought their wills were of no moment in commercial cases because an agent's will was not usually in the contemplation of the parties to the contract. Any suggestion that legal consequentialism was only maintainable through a tortured formalism that sought to mask class preferences is quite wrong in the case of antebellum New York.

So far was Verplanck from being caught up with formalism or legal fictions that he often ridiculed legal precedent. When his court held that a promissory note written on a piece of paper separate from the underlying debt was not negotiable, he vigorously dissented, claiming, "Independent of legal authority, I think it must commend its own validity to the common understanding of men."[213] He thought "public policy" required the conclusion that "the contract is as fair and just in itself, as it is useful to the public."[214] When insurance companies tried to deny claims because of the negligence of the insured, Verplanck required that the burden be on the insurer to prove negligence. Thus when a claim for theft of insured cargo was denied because the thieves were not "assailing thieves" but merely covert thieves, the insurers offered English precedent on the legal interpretation of the word "thieves." But for Verplanck, "mere book authority" was "entitled to little weight."[215] All that mattered was that the theft could not be shown to have been the fault of the insured. But when the insurance company could show negligence, Verplanck did not hesitate to sustain the denial of the claim.[216]

Verplanck had no preference for creditors as most "conservatives" usually had. When a mortgagee underbid at a foreclosure sale on the very property on which he held the debt, Verplanck thought he had committed a fraud. "Where the buyer is the holder of the mortgage he must surely be content if his debt is paid."[217] Instead, the mortgagee had purchased the property for less than the debt and tried to continue his claim against the mortgagor. Verplanck called the auction, "a sale for a totally inadequate price,"[218] reversed the chancellor's decree approving the sale, and ordered a resale of the property. He wrote, "The respondent has no just claim to make a profit out of the transaction; nor can he complain if he gets his whole debt, with interests and costs."[219] In other words, profit by any means was inconsistent with justice, and therefore, inconsistent with the law.

Nor did Verplanck have a soft spot for corporations as opposed to individuals. Thus he approved of strict liability against common carriers for the loss of private property of passengers. When a steamboat gave a passenger's luggage to a Negro with a forged order for the luggage, Verplanck held the company liable for the loss even though no negligence had been proven.[220] "The policy of this severe rule, founded as it is on the necessity of the case, as the only possible means to prevent fraud and collusive thefts, and to enforce strict vigilance, by thus throwing the burden of loss, no matter how explained or excused, upon the carrier, applies practically to the traveler's trunks in the great majority of cases as much as to the merchant's bales."[221] The severity of the rule was somewhat tempered by the notorious knowledge that this was consistent with "usage," the "course of business," and the "common understanding of the parties," and hence, the rule was "founded in principle and in conformity with public utility."[222]

In 1840, a defendant convicted of murder and sentenced to death came before the Court for the Correction of Errors taking numerous exceptions to the conduct of his trial.[223] The case of *People v. White* took up more pages of the reporter than any other case in Verplanck's tenure because of the number of senators interested in giving opinions. It must also have been the case that lay senators felt more at home in expounding upon the rare criminal case than the run-of-the-mill, dry commercial cases. The court was unanimous in ordering a new trial. Some thought the trial court had been improperly composed, others thought the mid-trial retirement of one judge was improper, and still others thought the charge to the jury was in error. Verplanck agreed with this last point. The judge had instructed the jury to return a guilty verdict upon a finding of malice aforethought, and explicitly rejected the idea that premeditation was a necessary element of common law murder, or, as the judge charged, "The averment of premeditation is mere surplusage"; Verplanck's response: "I think otherwise."[224] He was troubled that the judge had relied on the common law when the defendant was charged under New York's revised statutes. Because the statutory scheme contained several different types of homicide, Verplanck thought the state could not simply elide those distinctions without placing in danger "the rights of every person accused of any of the graver crimes."[225]

What bothered Verplanck most in the *White* case, however, was the prosecutor's introduction of character evidence:

> The public prosecutor had no right to introduce evidence of bad general character against a prisoner. The offence must be proved substantially. The humanity and justice of the law give the prisoner the right of adducing evidence of virtuous character to show the improbability of the charge, but otherwise, the law must hold every man, whether virtuous or vicious in his course of life, to be innocent of any specific crime until he is proved guilty.[226]

Verplanck gave the standard argument that bad character evidence had the propensity to unduly prejudice the defendant, and thus could only be offered in rebuttal to the defendant's own effort to put his character into evidence in the first instance. But Verplanck followed this standard explanation of the rule with a concern based upon his understanding of human nature:

> Yet those who know or who feel how mysteriously virtue is mixed with vice in human nature—how much of evil there is in the good, and how much of better feeling is often left in the profligate, what does calm and sound reason infer from such testimony as to any malignity of heart capable of deliberate premeditated murder on slight provocation? I think it should have no such weight or tendency at all, even when such proof of character was presented in its most direct form.[227]

The senator recognized that there existed "an adjudged case or two to the contrary," but Verplanck concluded, "I do not hesitate to say . . . we ought, upon principle, to overrule them."[228]

The ease with which Verplanck cast aside precedent and traditional form was noticeable, yet it did not trouble his peers who publically and privately offered their own evaluations of his legal performance. One might think the obsessive focus on utility resulted from his simultaneous role as a legislator and judge. But only in the very first opinion he wrote did he explicitly acknowledge his constituents as a factor in his decision, but then again, public utility requires at least implicit considerations of constituent desires in every case.[229] Moreover, one suspects that had Verplanck ever served on a lower-court bench, he would have acted no differently. Perhaps Verplanck's judicial opinions should not be compared to contemporaneous opinions in terms of form. The senator seems to have received nothing but praise for his performance as a jurist. In 1842, Kent wrote to Verplanck:

> I have just now finished the Perusal of . . . Wendell's Reports . . . & I have been very much struck with the ability & learning displayed in the discussions & decisions, & especially with your excellent Opinions replete with profound & accurate learning & accurate views of the law. . . . [As] I may not have an opportunity to meet you very soon, I have taken the liberty to express in this way my sense of your distinguished merits, & my sincere regret that you are now withdrawn from that Senatorial House, where you so much & so usefully contributed to enlighten & adorn our jurisprudence.[230]

In later years, Chief Justice Daly, recalled, "These opinions, which were perspicuously and elegantly written, were not simply his conclusions, but elaborate judgments, founded on the closest investigations of the questions submitted, the most careful and exhaustive examination of authorities, and a practical, comprehensive, and familiar acquaintance with legal rules and principles, even those of the most technical kind."[231] Daly also recognized that Verplanck "was the controlling power" as judged by the frequency with which he carried the court over the dissent of the chancellor. Daly claimed that in only three instances was Verplanck in the minority. But here his enthusiasms for Verplanck led him astray, for Verplanck's dissents numbered slightly higher, especially during his first year in that body.[232]

What does it mean that the most committed Federalist judge and a sitting chief justice thought so highly of Verplanck's legal opinions? Despite Kent's and Daly's praise, any honest assessment of Verplanck's opinions must emphasize their dissimilarity from the judicial norm. While both judges were correct to note Verplanck's "accurate views of the law" and "familiar acquaintance with legal rules and principles," what both conveniently ignored was his constant rejection of those views, rules, and principles. The better explanation for this seeming inconsistency is that Verplanck said what the judges only wished they could say, but for political and professional reasons were unable to say. Kent had always been attracted to Verplanck's practical reason, and Story's short leash notwithstanding, he continued to admire his work into his senatorial career. But, as we will see in chapter 6, even Story's conservatism was more superficial than substantive, as his report on codification and law reform would eventually show. Verplanck's fulfillment of his judicial role tapped into a widespread reform-minded and progressive sensibility that he would also extend into the institutional realm of the court system.

A Proposal for Law Reform

New York went through several major constitutional changes in the early republic, and was considering the reformation of its legal system at the time Verplanck served in the Senate.[233] This bout of reform was not complete until 1848, six years after Verplanck left public office, but many of his ideas were incorporated into the final product. What is of most interest in the category of law reform is to see how Verplanck proposed to put his highly theoretical views into practice in the very concrete realm of the organization of legal institutions.

The best source for Verplanck's views on law reform come from a very lengthy speech he delivered in the Senate in 1839 on the judiciary system. The speech, later published and distributed, represents Verplanck's most mature thought on law in the abstract.[234] As a result, we get to see how he applied his distaste for imitation, his theory of individualistic motivation, his belief in combining practice and theory on the bench, as well as his explicit thoughts on the relation of the common law to the civil law.

According to Verplanck, a fellow senator, one Col. Young, proposed to adopt *en masse* Britain's recent law reform package. This senator was willing "to sweep away the whole of" the laws "and supply their place by a code like that of the civil law, or those which illustrate the name of Napoleon."[235] Instead, what Verplanck wished New York would do was imitate the British method of law reform, not the substance. There should be a full investigation of the judicial structure with evidence taken from those whom the law affects most, like the "business population" and the bar. That way, any proposed reform would respond to the real needs of society. Attention to real-world practices was always preferable to "the mere theories and projects of the Chancellor and all the Judges" anyhow.[236]

Verplanck displayed his desire to unite theory and practice, not only in the methods of law reform, but also in the form of substantive proposals. He was critical of the previous set of reforms in which the judges of the Supreme Court were taken off circuit duty and shut up "to hear and decide law arguments and nothing more; leaving the circuits for jury trials to inferior judges, confined to their own districts."[237] As we will learn momentarily, Verplanck used the term "inferior" in all senses of the word. But aside from leaving trials in less capable hands, the 1828 changes had cut the judges off from the real world of interacting with the parties to the litigation, on which they now only passed judgment from afar. Verplanck explained the problem as such:

> It is the nature of things—of the human mind, of the character of legal science itself. In all sciences, and above all in those which, like law, depend much upon authority, precedent, verbal logic and the interpretation of language, men shut up to the contemplation of the mere theory of the science, without applying it practically, are liable to even more than the ordinary share of human error. They are often misled by general rules and conclusions which prove false when applied to the workings of actual business. Hence I believe that in the hands of a court, confined to their books, and the hearing of legal arguments only, the law, if it does not deteriorate, will certainly never improve. Look at the history of our modern commercial law. Can any one believe that its great founder, Lord Mansfield, would have been able to form that admirable body of commercial jurisprudence which he left behind him, if he had been shut up in Westminster Hall, or his own library, whilst some inferior judge of some other court held sittings at Guild-Hall for the trial of commercial issues?[238]

There are clear echoes of the warnings he had earlier given to audiences of college graduates not to become men who alternated only between the pen and book. And Mansfield was again invoked as someone who never fell into that temptation. What made Mansfield's commercial law so great was the weight it gave to "the custom of merchants."[239] Practical experience allowed theory to be put to good use, all the while, more closely approaching truth and justice because of the interaction with man in his natural state—in this case, the marketplace. Under the old constitution, the judges sat in New York City, and took "the evidence of merchants" and gave "the charges to the commercial juries," and it was that experience that gave "Kent and Spencer that training which enabled them to turn the learning of the books to the best account."[240]

Verplanck also applied his theory of human motivation—which we saw explained earlier in his theory of the fine arts—to the recruitment of judges. The existing system of trial judges, vice-chancellors, and assistant vice-chancellors, all of whose decisions were subject to reversal for error, was yielding a low quality of justice. This was especially the case on the equity side where the main problem was that these inferior posts were attracting only inferior men because the jobs themselves were unattractive to the talented. Verplanck explained their failure to catch the interest of the learned and ambitious: "There is little opportunity given to a Vice-Chancellor for becoming known, through reports, to the profession, beyond the precincts of his own court, or to hand down an honored name to posterity. The inducement of fame, that which incites noble minds 'To scorn delights and lead laborious days,' is not held out to him."[241] The best way to acquire highly qualified judges to serve the public well was to appeal to man's natural desire for ever-lasting fame and glory. How else was a man going to have his portrait commissioned for the state house gallery, or his image sculpted in marble and placed in the halls of Columbia, unless he had a job worthy of such honors? Verplanck's solution was "a court of equity in place of the single Chancellor, consisting of three or more Judges."[242] The chancellors would sit individually in districts in the first instance and then sit en banc to hear appeals. Such a structure would offer "greater inducements to able men to accept the office; and would have greater respect in the eyes of the community, and procure greater confidence in the officers, and greater respect for their decisions."[243] Perhaps there is no clearer instance in which Verplanck so tightly linked individual interest and motivation to the public good as Bentham had done before him.[244] Undoubtedly Verplanck was aware of Bentham's theories because in this very instance he considered and rejected "the Benthamite theory of the superiority of 'single seated justice.'"[245] But his reasons for rejecting the idea were based on a very fact-intensive public utility calculation.

Chancery as an institution caused Verplanck all sorts of frustrations. The long-range goal of Verplanck's chancery reform was to phase it out entirely. New York's court was "but a bad imitation of the English System," especially the patronage powers associated with the office.[246] Another problem was the lack of jury trials, which meant a lack of clear separation between law and fact, which, in turn, was "the best security for the fair administration of justice yet invented by man."[247] Finally, in recent years, equity had been growing too fast as a field of practice and this resulted in the concomitant growth of a bar dedicated to theory over practice. Rather than a bar dedicated to jury trials, and thus the "wants and usages of a free people," equity had "led to the prevalence of opinions among lawyers, agreeing with those of the philosophical theories of speculative reasoners, and the admirers of civil and continental law."[248] It is important to note, however, that this criticism of admiration for the civil law was meant as criticism for the lack of jury trials and nothing else. Verplanck wanted to slowly move the areas of practice that fell under chancery's jurisdiction to the courts of law, in essence enlarging their province with equity powers.[249]

But these institutional issues are difficult to separate out from the problems caused by the chancellor himself, Ruben Hyde Walworth. Even the proposal just discussed, which called for three judges instead of one, was supported by the offhand remark that a single chancellorship ran the risk of being filled by someone grossly incompetent.[250] Verplanck was quick to add that New York was lucky to have had only distinguished men serve in that position, but other remarks were less veiled. "Equity, as a separate system, can hardly be said to have worked well any where," remarked Verplanck, who then backed up his claim with a historical example, in which he appeared to draw on his old talents as a political satirist.[251] Verplanck thought New York should follow "the sagacity and common sense of Oliver Cromwell," who "perceived and for a time checked similar evils in his day."[252] Sticking with seventeenth-century England, he gave this explanation for extinguishing chancery, which draws on history, poetry, and politics to make the point:

> If Edward Hyde, Lord Clarendon, at once the first law officer and Prime Minister of England,
> "By Kings protected, and to Kings allied"—
> Aye, or Lord Somers, with all the glory of the revolution, or Talbot or Cowper, had for a moment entertained jurisdiction on such causes as Reuben Hyde Walworth takes cognizance of as a matter of course, what an insurrection would it have occasioned at Westminster Hall. The King's Bench would have lifted up its voices unto the Common Pleas. The whole corpus of Judges and Sergeants and Barristers would have been mustered to repel the inroad on the territory of the common law. Articles of impeachment would have been moved in Parliament, and the presumptuous Xerxes of the courts would have shared the fate of his Persian prototype, and been driven back from the territory he had invaded, ungowned, un-wigged, and un-chancellored.[253]

It was too much for Verplanck to resist that Walworth shared his middle name with King Charles I's chancellor. Although he assured his listeners, "I ask for no violent revolution."[254]

Verplanck closed his thoughts on law reform with an unsurprising pragmatic tone. He thought any flaw in the system could be fixed by legislation and that the legislature should not be prevented from trying new things by constitutional prohibition. Although he had been critical of the common law case method throughout his life, he was not in favor of radical codification if that meant throwing out the existing case law in one broad sweep. The decided cases surely contained some history and wisdom from which one could learn even if they did not provide all the answers. On the multifaceted question of codification, he claimed to agree with Story's report on codification in Massachusetts, which was far from conservative.[255] Of all his proposals, he said, "I am far from stating any of them positively or dogmatically, as the certain and infallible, or as the only remedies for those evils of our jurisprudence of which the public complain."[256]

The Boston *Law Reporter* took note of Verplanck's speech in June of 1839. So impressed was the reviewer, that he excerpted about ten pages of the speech, but not before offering this praise:

> We are at a loss which most to admire, the general soundness of the views presented by Mr Verplanck, or the spirit and temper with which he urges a thorough reform in long existing abuses, and the eloquent manner in which he expresses himself, establishing every position with a depth of reasoning evincing a profound knowledge of the law, and illustrating his subject in the happiest manner by classical allusions.[257]

Verplanck must have been pleased to know that both his rationality and his liberal education continued to make their marks on his public endeavors.

VERPLANCK'S LEGACY

Gulian Verplanck's legacy lies not in his success as a lawyer or a lawmaker, but in his success as a thinker. Verplanck's sustained and systematic efforts to rein in the law according to a natural order would be unremarkable if it were not for the intricacy of the philosophy that underlay his view of legal science. Few, if any, lawyers who today practice commercial law, or intellectual property, or serve in state legislatures or in Congress, are motivated in their professional endeavors by anything resembling Verplanck's view of justice. With the increasing specialization, not only of law, but of life in general, perhaps it is expecting too much to think that lawyers can claim expertise in philosophy, literature, and economics, and then apply those fields to their daily practice. However, keeping in mind that such a feat occurred at one point in history, with the results described above—success in copyright extension and judicial reform, failure in vanquishing caveat emptor—we can better understand how the intellectual realm contributed to these outcomes should we desire to repeat or improve upon them in the future.

NOTES

1. *Shakespeare's Plays: With His Life*, ed. Gulian C. Verplanck (New York, 1847).
2. Robert W. July, *The Essential New Yorker: Gulian Crommelin Verplanck* (Durham, NC: Duke University Press, 1951).
3. For the legal arguments over nullification, see Richard E. Ellis, *The Union at Risk: Jacksonian Democracy, States' Rights, and the Nullification Crisis* (Oxford: Oxford University Press, 1987).
4. See Gulian C. Verplanck, *A Letter to Col. William Drayton, of South-Carolina, in Assertion of the Constitutional Power of Congress to Impose Protecting Duties* (New York: E.

Bliss, 1831). Although Verplanck did not question the constitutionality of the tariff legislation, he urged Congress to look to what is *practical* in the actual state of public opinion, and of the wishes, feelings, and personal interests of various large classes of the community—to what is *just*, alike in regard to the large interests vested under the existing laws, and to those which have languished or suffered under their operation—and more especially to what is *prudent* and *expedient* towards establishing a permanent plan of impost under which the capital and enterprise of the nation may be enabled to give a secure and uninterrupted direction to their hourly augmenting energies. Ibid., 30.

5. Irving Browne, *The Judiciary Through 1870*, (n.p., n.d.) 20, www.courts.state.ny.us/history/pdf/Library/History/Browne_The_Judiciary.pdf. ("Senator Verplanck's were among the most numerous, and are among the most learned and elegant judicial essays ever written in this State. Mr. Verplanck was a man of remarkable scholarship, and has left behind him an enviable reputation both in law and letters.")

6. July only considers the legal aspects of his Senate career very briefly. July, *Essential New Yorker*, 227–30.

7. See Joyce Appleby, *Inheriting the Revolution: The First Generation of Americans* (Cambridge, MA: Harvard University Press, 2000).

8. For example, one critic thought Verplanck's endorsement of the civil law led him to prefer European ways to American life. See "Doctrine of Contracts," *United States Law Journal* 2 (1826): 72, 91, where the anonymous author referred to "Mr. Verplanck, and the school he belongs to" and "their unpatriotic preference of the civil law."

9. July refers to Verplanck as a "conservative" on economic and banking issues. July, *Essential New Yorker*, 219. Another historian says, "Verplanck was more successful than his friends in incorporating the liberal ideology into the world of urban capitalism. . . . [He] came very close to building his vision around the business community, around successful managers of materially oriented enterprise." Edward K. Spann, *Ideals and Politics: New York Intellectuals and Liberal Democracy, 1820–1880* (Albany: State University of New York Press, 1972), 93.

10. William Cullen Bryant, *A Discourse on the Life, Character and Writings of Gulian Crommelin Verplanck* (New York, 1870), 15 (quoting Nathaniel F. Moore).

11. Ibid.

12. July, *Essential New Yorker*, 30.

13. See William B. Hatcher, *Edward Livingston: Jeffersonian Republican and Jacksonian Democrat* (Baton Rouge: Louisiana State University Press, 1940).

14. See ibid., 245–88, for Livingston's work in crafting a civil code for Louisiana.

15. Marshall Foletta, *Coming to Terms with Democracy: Federalist Intellectuals and the Shaping of an American Culture* (Charlottesville: University of Virginia Press 2001), 168. ("Perfecting the machinery of the American judiciary and clarifying the character of American law were tasks made necessary by the American Revolution.") Foletta acknowledges the criticism of the common law that occurred among New England intellectuals, but nevertheless concludes, "the defenders of the common law carried the day." Ibid., 171. I would qualify this conclusion by arguing that their defense of the common law, which Foletta nicely sets out, ibid., 167–72, was more rhetorical than substantive because they recognized the political dangers of appearing more innovative. Verplanck, though claiming to agree in substance with New Englander, Joseph Story, was less veiled in his rhetoric, and thus came in for harsh criticism as a radical from the populist elements of legal society.

16. For studies that show the influence of classical concepts on early American lawyers see Robert A. Ferguson, *Law and Letters in American Culture* (Cambridge: Harvard University Press, 1984), 73. Where he argues, "Already inclined toward classical study, lawyers used their training in Greek and Latin to solve specific professional problems." See also, M. H. Hoeflich, "Roman Law and Forensic Oratory in Antebellum America," *Zeitschrift der Savigny-Stiftung für Rechtsgeschichte. Romanistische Abthei-*

lung 120 (2003): 189, for a discussion on the influence of Cicero on John Quincy Adams's courtroom style.

17. Gulian C. Verplanck, *The Advantages and the Dangers of the American Scholar* (New York: Wiley & Long, 1836), 23 [hereinafter Verplanck, *American Scholar*].

18. Gulian C. Verplanck, *The Right Moral Influence and Use of Liberal Studies* (New York: J. & J. Harper, 1833), 18 [hereinafter Verplanck, *Right Moral Influence*].

19. Ibid., 18–19.

20. William Murray, Lord Mansfield, was the influential chief justice of the court of the King's Bench from 1756–1788. See James Oldham, *English Common Law in the Age of Mansfield* (Chapel Hill: University of North Carolina Press, 2004).

21. Verplanck, *Right Moral Influence*, 27. Mansfield was especially renowned for his innovations in commercial jurisprudence. See, e.g., David Lieberman, "Mansfield and the Commercial Code," in *The Province of Legislation Determined: Legal Theory in Eighteenth-Century Britain* (Cambridge: Cambridge University Press, 1989), 99.

22. Verplanck, *Right Moral Influence*, 11.

23. Ibid., 21.

24. As Lieberman notes, Mansfield had two key objectives for his commercial jurisprudence: "First was his firm insistence that commercial matters, as on the continent, had to be decided under the separate system of legal rules known as the 'law merchant.' . . . Secondly, he was equally clear that the common law courts needed to adjudicate cases in such a way as to establish a settled system of general legal rules, rather than a collection of individual precedents." Lieberman, *Province of Legislation Determined*, 104. One of the ways Mansfield approached these objectives was to use special juries composed of merchants for fact-intensive analyses of the "reasonableness" of the actions of the parties to a commercial dispute. See Oldham, *English Common Law*, 22–25, 74–75. It was this highly practical aspect of Mansfield's jurisprudence that Verplanck admired.

25. Hugo Grotius, *De Iure Belli ac Pacis* (1625).

26. Verplanck, *Right Moral Influence*, 28.

27. Ibid., 13.

28. Ibid., 34.

29. Ibid., 35–36.

30. Gulian C. Verplanck, *Essays on the Nature and Uses of the Various Evidences of Revealed Religion* (New York: Charles Wiley, 1824), iii [hereinafter Verplanck, *Essays on Religion*]. By "internal evidence" he meant to include only the rational coherence of biblical history and other religious writings, that is, he was not concerned with external evidence like miracles and other non-rational phenomena.

31. Ibid., vi.

32. Ibid., 2.

33. Verplanck, *Essays on Religion*, 2 n.*.

34. In exploring the evidence of the truth of Christianity, Verplanck noted "the single and striking exception of the history of the Roman law, and the authenticity of its code, digest, and institutes, which tried by these rules, is supported by any thing like the same strength of testimony as the history of the miracles and death of Jesus Christ." Ibid., 7–8.

35. Ibid., 169–70.

36. Verplanck, *American Scholar*, 18.

37. Ibid.

38. Ibid., 20.

39. Ibid., 22.

40. Ibid., 26–27.

41. Ibid., 28.

42. Ibid.

43. Ibid., 33–34.

44. Another problem with patronage, which I will discuss in the section on copyright, is that it frustrated the concept of intellectual property. See also Mark Rose, "The

Author as Proprietor: *Donaldson v. Becket* and the Genealogy of Modern Authorship," *Representations* 23 (1988): 51, 55. ("The concept of owning a work did not fit the circumstances of a traditional status society that functioned largely through patronage.")

45. Verplanck, *American Scholar*, 33–34.

46. Ibid., 35.

47. Ibid., 51–54. See also William C. Dowling, *Literary Federalism in the Age of Jefferson: Joseph Dennie and the Port Folio, 1801–1812* (Columbia: University of South Carolina Press, 1999).

48. Verplanck, *American Scholar*, 41.

49. Ibid., 41–42.

50. Ibid., 42.

51. Ibid.

52. See, e.g., Thomas Cooper, *Introductory Lecture to a Course of Law* (Columbia, SC: Telescope Office, 1834) (complaining that "the reports and other books necessary to a good library for a practising lawyer, will amount to 350 or 400 volumes of American Law."); Caleb Cushing, "Law Reports," *North American Review* 18 (1824): 371, 377. (Noting "the lapse of only one fifth of a century has added to the number *one hundred and ninety* volumes, exclusive of many valuable report of single cases" and worrying, "what mind will be adequate to the task of storing up the infinite multiplicity of decided cases?")

53. Verplanck, *American Scholar*, 41. My reading of Verplanck has been with an eye toward his views on the legal profession, but Spann has read the same material and concluded that much of the criticism directed at isolated scholars was a veiled attack on James Fenimore Cooper, whom Verplanck thought had too romantic a view of rural life. Spann, *Ideas and Politics*, 92–94. Cooper may well have been on Verplanck's mind, but the attack seems just as much leveled at the bench and bar, a group not considered among Spann's group of intellectuals. Moreover, there is good reason to reject Spann's argument, namely, because Verplanck was a romantic himself. This point is most clearly explicated in Perry Miller, "The Legal Mentality," in *The Life of the Mind in America from the Revolution to the Civil War* (New York: Harcourt, Brace & World, Inc., 1965), 97. Miller argues that the great issue in antebellum American law was "the never-ending case of Heart versus Head," in other words, romanticism versus legal logic. Ibid., 100. Verplanck's obsession with morality and nature mirrored Cooper's concerns. See ibid., 99–104. Miller specifically notes that Verplanck was in sympathy with "romanticizing pioneers like Natty Bumppo," one of Cooper's literary characters. Ibid., 246.

54. Peter Stein, "The Attraction of the Civil Law in Post-Revolutionary America," *Virginia Law Review* 52 (1966): 403, 425–26. (Discussing Verplanck's *Essay* as an example of one of the "detailed studies of a particular topic, in which the common law and civil law reached different solutions, and a comparison of the advantages and disadvantages of each.")

55. Morton Horwitz, *The Transformation of American Law, 1780–1860* (Cambridge, MA: Harvard University Press, 1977), 181–83. The famous Horwitz thesis of contract law is that early nineteenth-century lawyers and judges rejected "the longstanding belief that the justification of contractual obligation is derived from the inherent justice or fairness of an exchange," and instead, "they asserted for the first time that the source of the obligation of contract is the convergence of the wills of the contracting parties." Ibid., 160. For a famous challenge to this see A. W. B. Simpson, "The Horwitz Thesis and the History of Contracts," *University of Chicago Law Review* 46 (1979): 533. It is not my intention here to challenge the Horwitz thesis, but simply to correct his errors about Verplanck.

56. M. H. Hoeflich, "*Laidlaw v. Organ*, Gulian C. Verplanck, and the Shaping of Early Nineteenth Century Contract Law: A Tale of a Case and a Commentary," *University of Illinois Law Review* (1991): 55, 63 [hereinafter Hoeflich, *Laidlaw*].

57. Charles L. Barzun, "Common Sense and Legal Science," *Virginia Law Review* 90 (2004): 1051, 1079–91. Craig Evan Klafter makes a similar point about the influence of

"the moral sense philosophy of the Scottish Enlightenment" on Verplanck's *Essay*. Craig Evan Klafter, *Reason Over Precedents: Origins of American Legal Thought* (Westport, CT: Greenwood Press, 1993): 58–62. The influence of Scots law, or more generally, Scottish philosophy, on the development of American law has been surprisingly understudied. See C. Paul Rogers III, "Scots Law in Post-Revolutionary and Nineteenth-Century America: The Neglected Jurisprudence," *Law and History Review* 8 (1990): 205. One influential American legal intellectual who was much more influenced than Verplanck by Scottish philosophy, especially that of Dugald Stewart, was Hugh S. Legaré of South Carolina, who studied law at Edinburgh and eventually served as US Attorney General from 1841–1843. Unfortunately, legal historians have almost completely neglected Legaré. For an exception, see M. H. Hoeflich, *Roman and Civil Law and the Development of Anglo-American Jurisprudence in the Nineteenth Century* (Athens: University of Georgia Press, 1997), 50–73; Michael O'Brien, *A Sketch of Hugh Legaré* (Knoxville: University of Tennessee Press, 1985), 137–49; Stein, 427–32. The chapter on Legaré herein is an attempt to correct this omission.

58. July, *Essential New Yorker*, 209–11.

59. 15 U.S. (2 Wheat.) 178 (1817).

60. Gulian C. Verplanck, *An Essay on the Doctrine of Contracts: Being an Inquiry How Contracts Are Affected in Law and Morals, by Concealment, Error, or Inadequate Price* (1825; repr., New York: Arno Press, 1972), 5 [hereinafter Verplanck, *Essay*].

61. *Laidlaw*, 15 U.S. (2 Wheat.) at 195. ("It would be difficult to circumscribe the contrary doctrine within proper limits, where the means of intelligence are equally accessible to both parties.")

62. Verplanck, *Essay*, 5.

63. Ibid., 7.

64. Ibid., 10.

65. Ibid., 12.

66. Ibid., 14.

67. Ibid., 15.

68. See Barzun, "Common Sense and Legal Science," 1080–88, 1087, where he claims Verplanck derived contractual obligation from neither "grounds of expedience nor on theories of political economy, but rather on a 'common sense' moral intuition." Craig Evan Klafter, *Reason over Precedents: Origins of American Legal Thought* (Greenwood Press, Westport CT 1993) 60–61, also claims Verplanck relied on "moral sense philosophy" in the same vein as Thomas Reid and James Wilson. Interestingly enough, unlike Barzun, Verplanck never uses the word "intuition" to describe "unstudied impressions" or "untutored feelings." Moreover, while serving in Congress during the tariff and nullification crises, Verplanck urged settling the matter according to what was "just," which he equated with what was "practical" and "prudent and expedient." Gulian C. Verplanck, *A Letter to Col. William Drayton, of South-Carolina* (New York: E. Bliss, 1831), 30.

69. William Paley, *The Principles of Moral and Political Philosophy* (1785; repr., Indianapolis, IN: Liberty Fund, Inc., 2002), 73.

70. Ibid., 74–75.

71. Ibid., 74.

72. Verplanck, *Essay*, 34–35. Verplanck cited the case of Whitefield v. M'Leod, 2 S.C.L. (2 Bay) 380, 383 (1802) (holding "the doctrine of a sound price deserving a sound commodity" to be "a very wise and salutary one"), for this proposition. It is my suspicion that lawyer Thomas Cooper was responsible for the dissemination of much information about the justness of the South Carolina judiciary. Cooper was an English immigrant who originally settled in Pennsylvania in 1794. In 1820 he was appointed president of South Carolina College. But even before his arrival in the state, he was praising its rejection of caveat emptor in *Whitefield* in his edition of *Justinian's Institutes*. Thomas Cooper, ed., *The Institutes of Justinian with Notes* (Philadelphia: P. Byrne, 1812), 610–11. ("The rule of *caveat emptor*, ought to be changed into *caveat venditor*. It is a disgrace to the law that such a maxim should be adopted, and I rejoice to see that the

good sense of the South Carolina bench has revolted at it.") In 1826, Cooper sent a letter to Verplanck praising the *Essay*, see July, *Essential New Yorker*, 210 and 285 n.15. Moreover, in his law lecture, Cooper had boasted of the superiority of his state's judiciary: "Our South Carolina reports are cited by the lawyers of the middle States." Cooper, *Lecture*, 11. Verplanck's New York was one such middle state.

73. Verplanck, *Essay*, 37. Indeed Verplanck was correct about Mansfield's contribution to the field of insurance law. See Oldham, *English Common Law*, 124–51.

74. Verplanck, *Essay*, 37.

75. Ibid., 39–40.

76. Ibid., 37.

77. Ibid., 43.

78. Ibid., 48.

79. In 1607 Chief Justice Coke informed King James "that the king in his own person cannot adjudge any case," either criminal or civil. J. P. Kenyon ed., *The Stuart Constitution, 1603–1688: Documents and Commentary*, 2nd ed. (Cambridge: Cambridge University Press, 1986), 80. Coke then described the following exchange: Then the king said, that he thought the law was founded upon reason, and that he and others had reason, as well as the judges. To which it was answered by me, that true it was that God had endowed his Majesty with excellent science and great endowments of nature, but his Majesty was not learned in the laws of his realm of England, and *causes which concern the life, or inheritance, or goods, or fortunes of his subjects are not to be decided by natural reason but by the artificial reason and judgment of law*, which law is an act which requires long study and experience before that a man can attain to the cognisance of it, and that the law was the golden mete-wand and measure to try the causes of the subjects, and which protected his Majesty in safety and peace. With which the king was greatly offended. Ibid., 81 (emphasis added).

80. Blackstone best described this aspect of English law: "general immemorial custom, or common law" was that which was "from time to time declared in the decisions of the courts of justice." William Blackstone, *Commentaries* 1:73. In other words, as David Lieberman explains, the common law was not "a series of deductions from principles of reason or nature," rather, it was "an historical artifact." Lieberman, *Province of Legislation Determined*, 45. However, this whole notion of the law fitting the character of a particular nation was undergoing fundamental challenges in both England and America, and Verplanck was an active participant. For example, in England, Bentham famously argued, "That which *is* Law, is, in different countries, widely different: while that which *ought to be*, is in all countries to a great degree the same." Jeremy Bentham, *A Fragment on Government* (1776; reprint, J.H. Burns & H.L.A. Hart eds., Cambridge: Cambridge University Press, 1988), 8. Likewise, Mansfield argued "that the mercantile law is 'the same all over the world.'" Oldham, *English Common Law*, 124 (quoting Mansfield). While Henry Wheaton welcomed an American translation of a work by Pothier on maritime contracts "because the law of contracts is necessarily the same, or very nearly the same, in every civilized and commercial country; since it depends not so much upon positive institution, as upon general principles applicable to human conduct in an advanced stage of society." Henry Wheaton, "Pothier's Maritime Contracts," *North American Review* 13 (1821): 1. It was this sense of the cumulative and universal—the interconnectedness of mankind—to which Verplanck was appealing in his discussions of science and knowledge, and to which he applied to the theory and practice of law.

81. See J. H. Baker, *An Introduction to English Legal History*, 4th ed. (London: Butterworths, 2002), 109, 118 (describing "the essence of equity as a corrective to the rigour of the law," and the jurisdiction of the Star Chamber, the most famous of the conciliar courts, as "at first indistinguishable from that of the Chancery").

82. Verplanck, *Essay*, 59–60.

83. Ibid., 60–61.

84. Ibid., 63.

85. Stein, 425–26.

86. Hoeflich, "*Laidlaw*," 61. Hoeflich has been the leading authority on the influence of civil law on early American jurisprudence and is especially qualified to expound on Story. See M. H. Hoeflich, "John Austin and Joseph Story: Two Nineteenth Century Perspectives on the Utility of the Civil Law for the Common Lawyer," *American Journal of Legal History* 29 (1985): 36.
87. Barzun, 1083.
88. Robert Joseph Pothier, *Treatise on Obligations* (1761).
89. Verplanck, *Essay*, 75.
90. Ibid.
91. Ibid., 74
92. Ibid., 89.
93. Ibid., 105.
94. Ibid., 106.
95. Ibid., 156.
96. Ibid., 107, 110.
97. Ibid., 112.
98. Ibid., 116.
99. Paley, *Principles of Moral and Political Philosophy*, 85. Verplanck explicitly criticized the "too great latitude of this rule." Verplanck, *Essay*, 129. But his criticism was limited to its application to speculative contracts, and he thought that Paley "had the right view of the subject in mind, though imperfectly developed." Ibid., 131.
100. Paley, *Principles of Moral and Political Philosophy*, 86.
101. Verplanck, *Essay*, 117.
102. Verplanck, *Essay*, 118.
103. Ibid.
104. Ibid., 123–24. Paley, *Principles of Moral and Political Philosophy*, 90. ("But if I have access to secrets of state at home, or private advice of some decisive measure or event abroad, I cannot avail myself of these advantages with justice, because they are excluded by the contract, which proceeded upon the supposition that I had no such advantage.")
105. Wheaton was an important legal intellectual who has not received the recognition his body of work deserves. For the only biography of him, see Elizabeth Feaster Baker, *Henry Wheaton, 1785–1848* (Philadelphia: University of Pennsylvania Press, 1937).
106. Henry Wheaton, "An Essay on the Doctrine of Contracts," *North American Review* 22 (1826): 253.
107. Ibid., 254.
108. Ibid.
109. See ibid., 257.
110. Ibid., 258. Wheaton was clearly drawing on Bentham's distinction between the expositor and the censor. Bentham, *Fragment*, 7. ("To the province of the *Expositor* it belongs to explain to us what, as he supposes, the Law *is*: to that of the *Censor*, to observe to us what he thinks it *ought to be*.")
111. Wheaton, "An Essay," 258.
112. See Laidlaw v. Organ, 15 U.S. (2 Wheat.) 178 (1817).
113. See ibid., 184–94.
114. C. J. Ingersoll for the plaintiffs in error noted, "Pothier, in discussing this subject, adopts the distinction of the forum of conscience, and the forum of law; but admits that *fides est servanda*." Ibid., 185. But he said no more.
115. To the sentence quoted above, Wheaton added a six-page footnote, justifying it as follows: "As Pothier's discussion throws great light on this subject, a translation of this part of his admirable treatise may not be unacceptable to the reader." *Laidlaw*, 15 U.S. (2 Wheat.) at 185 n.c. That this was Wheaton's addition seems clear based upon his concern with "the reader." Moreover, Wheaton was widely known for his editorial additions. See, e.g., John Gallison, "Wheaton's Reports," *North American Review* 5 (1817): 110, 114. ("He has scattered through his volume notes upon some of the most

important points connected with the cases reported, in which he has given a compendious view of the law, as it is to be found in the most approved foreign writers."); Daniel Webster, "Wheaton's Reports, Vol. III," *North American Review* 8 (1818): 63, 71. ("Mr. Wheaton has not only recorded the decisions with accuracy, but has greatly added to the value of the volume by the extent and excellence of his notes. . . . His quotations from treatises of the continental lawyers are numerous and well selected.")

116. Maxwell Bloomfield, "William Sampson and the Codifiers: The Roots of American Legal Reform, 1820–1830," *American Journal of Legal History* 11 (1967): 234, 235, 236.

117. Ibid., 241 (quoting Sampson).

118. "Gulian C. Verplanck," *Albany Law Journal* 3 (1871): 26, 27.

119. William Sampson, "Verplanck's Essay," *New York Review and Atheneum Magazine* 2 (1826): 106.

120. Ibid., 114.

121. Ibid., 118.

122. Ibid., 125.

123. See July, *Essential New Yorker*, 209 and 285 n.14. ("Chancellor Kent dismissed it as an 'ingenious performance,' while Justice Joseph Story treated it with conventional politeness.")

124. Joseph Story, *Commentaries on Equity Jurisprudence, as Administered in England and America*, vol. 1, § 148, p. 161 (2d ed., Boston: Little & Brown, 1839).

125. Ibid., § 149, pp. 161–62.

126. Verplanck, *Essay*, 120, 125.

127. James Kent, *Commentaries on American Law*, 3rd ed. (New York: O. Halsted, 1836), 2:482.

128. Story, *Equity*, § 207, p. 216.

129. Ibid. §207, § 208. ("[T]he doctrine of Mr. Chancellor Kent would seem to require some qualification by limiting it to cases, where one party is under some obligation to communicate the facts, or where there is a peculiar known relation, trust, or confidence, between them, which authorizes the other party to act upon the presumption, that there is no concealment of any material fact.")

130. Kent, *Commentaries*, 2:482 n.b. Kent also acquiesced in Story's formulation that some legal obligation must exist on the part of the discloser: "The qualification of the rule is, that the party in possession of the facts must be under some special obligation, by confidence reposed, or otherwise, to communicate them truly and fairly." Ibid.

131. Kent, *Commentaries*, 2:487 n.b.

132. Ibid.

133. See James Kent, *Commentaries on American Law*, 4th ed. (1840), 2:487 n.d.

134. Joseph Hopkinson, "An Essay on the Doctrine of Contracts," *American Quarterly Review* 1 (1827): 106.

135. Ibid.

136. Ibid. (Arguing that alteration in the law should be based upon "long experience, not sudden emergencies or brilliant speculations.")

137. Ibid.

138. Ibid., 106–7.

139. It seems to me that "will theorist" is a fine term with which to describe Verplanck. For him, the morality of any obligation was ultimately judged by the expectations of the parties entering into the agreement. What Horwitz missed in his description of Verplanck was the existence of objective facts that entered into many contracts and formed a part of the expectations of the parties, and thus he was exactly wrong to suggest that for Verplanck, "there can be no objective measure of the fairness of a bargain." Horwitz, *Transformation*, 182. In the case of commodities, unless one party had an idiosyncratic reason for departing from the market price, there were objective measures of the fairness of every such sale. See also, Simpson, 541 n.44, where he points out how Horwitz specifically misrepresents Verplanck's criticism of just price doctrines. Perhaps Horwitz simply did not take Verplanck's *Essay* very seriously.

140. Verplanck, *Essay*, 142–44.
141. Ibid., 169.
142. Ibid., 169–70.
143. Hopkinson, *Essay*, 107.
144. Ibid.
145. Ibid., 111.
146. Verplanck, *Essay*, 177.
147. Hopkinson, *Essay*, 111. I do not think it is over-attention to detail to point out that Verplanck capitalized the "T" in truth in this instance and Hopkinson did not.
148. Hopkinson, *Essay*, 116.
149. Ibid., 118.
150. Ibid.
151. Ibid., 119.
152. See Verplanck, *Essay*, 116.
153. See Paley, 84–88. It is remarkable how much of this material Verplanck borrowed from Paley. It seems all he did was extend this example of Paley's: Whoever opens a shop, or in any manner exposes goods to public sale, virtually engages to deal with his customers at a market-price; because it is upon the faith and opinion of such an engagement, that any one comes within his shop-doors, or offers to treat with him. This is expected by the buyer; is known to be so expected by the seller; which is enough, according to the rule delivered above, to make it a part of the contract between them, though not a syllable be said about it. The breach of this implied contract constitutes the fraud inquired after. Ibid., 87.
154. Hopkinson, *Essay*, 120.
155. Ibid., 127.
156. "Doctrine of Contracts," *United States Law Journal* 2 (1826): 72 [hereinafter *USLJ* review] (book review). The *Albany Law Journal* noted of this review, "the whole article bears internal evidence of having been written by a personal or political enemy," *Gulian C. Verplanck*, 27, but I have been unable to identify who that enemy might have been.
157. *USLJ* review, 76.
158. See Burton Alva Konkle, *Joseph Hopkinson, 1770–1842: Jurist: Scholar: Inspirer of the Arts* (Philadelphia: University of Pennsylvania Press, 1931). Hopkinson was the first editor to bring out an American edition of Shakespeare beginning in 1795. Verplanck's edition was not published until 1847.
159. *USLJ* review, 82.
160. Ibid., 83.
161. Ibid.
162. Ibid., 86.
163. Ibid., 117.
164. Ibid., 91.
165. Gulian C. Verplanck, "Address on the Fine Arts," in *Discourses and Addresses on Subjects of American History, Arts, and Literature* (New York: J. & J. Harper, 1833) 123, 141 [hereinafter Verplanck, "Fine Arts"]. This address was initially delivered in 1825.
166. See Joseph J. Ellis, *After the Revolution: Profiles of Early American Culture* (New York: W. W. Norton & Co., 1979), 41, 71. ("His [Peale's] effort to forge alliances between the arts and the revolutionary tradition, the arts and the American public, the arts and the government, was a pioneering if premature attempt to place American culture, like American government, on a broad public foundation.")
167. See U.S. Const. art. I, § 8, cl. 8. ("The Congress shall have the power . . . To promote the Progress of Science and useful Arts, by securing for limited Times to Authors and Inventors the exclusive Right to their respective Writings and Discoveries.")
168. Gulian C. Verplanck, "The Law of Literary Property," in *Discourses and Addresses*, 224 [hereinafter Verplanck, "Literary Property"].

169. This is an excellent example of what Foucault later called the "art of government." Michel Foucault, "Governmentality," in James D. Faubion ed., Robert Hurley et al. trans., *Power: Essential Works of Foucault, 1954–1984*, vol. 3 (Harmondsworth, UK: Penguin, 2000), 201, 207. Foucault identified a shift in the eighteenth century, away from positive legislation as a method of governmental control toward "a range of multiform tactics." Ibid., 211. Verplanck was praising the framers for making good, economical use of political science and psychology, rather than positive law, to secure the idea of "United States citizen" as an end in itself.

170. Verplanck, "Literary Property," 225.

171. Ibid., 225–26.

172. Ibid., 227.

173. See ibid.

174. Act of Feb. 3, 1831, 4 Stat. 436. The act provided for an initial twenty-eight year privilege, followed by a once renewable fourteen year privilege.

175. §§ 15–16, 4 Stat. at 439.

176. See H.R. Rep. No. 21-3 (1830).

177. Verplanck, "Literary Property," 220.

178. Although Verplanck does not mention Hoffman by name in his address, an examination of the congressional debates reveals that Hoffman was the only member who spoke in opposition to the bill. See 7 Reg. Deb. 422–24 (1831).

179. Verplanck, "Literary Property," 220.

180. 7 Reg. Deb. 423 (statement of Rep. Hoffman).

181. Verplanck, "Literary Property," 220.

182. Ibid., 220–21.

183. Ibid., 221. In 1769, Mansfield had held that authors had a common law property right in their writings. See Millar v. Taylor (1769) 98 Eng. Rep. 201 (K.B.). That decision was overruled in 1774 by the House of Lords, where copyright was held to be entirely statutory. See Donaldson v. Beckett, (1774) 1 Eng. Rep. 837 (H.L.). For background to these cases see Oldham, *English Common Law*, 190–95; Rose. Verplanck, as well as the House Judiciary Committee that reported out the 1831 Copyright Act, thought that the Lords had set a mischievous precedent. The Committee's report read, "In England, the right of an author to the exclusive and perpetual profits of his book was enjoyed, and never questioned, until it was decided in Parliament, *by a small vote*, in the case of Miller v. Taylor." H.R. Rep. No. 21-3, at 1–2 (emphasis added). The report also noted how the United State was "far behind the States of Europe in securing the fruits of intellectual labor, and in encouraging men of letters." Ibid., 2.

184. 7 Reg. Deb. 424 (statement of Rep. Verplanck). ("It was a right of property existing before the law of copyrights had been made. That the statute did not give the right, it only secured it; it provided a legal remedy for the infringement of the right, and that was the sum of it.")

185. 7 Reg. Deb. 424 (statement of Rep. Hoffman).

186. See Verplanck, *Essay*, 158–62. Verplanck recognized statutes of limitations and rules of prescription as instances in which positive law varied from conscience, but which were necessitated by "the imperfections of human evidence." Ibid., 160.

187. Verplanck, "Literary Property," 220–22.

188. Ibid., 217.

189. See "Literary Property," *American Jurist and Law Magazine* 1 (1829): 157; "Literary Property," *American Jurist and Law Magazine* 2 (1829): 248. Neither of these articles is signed, but according to Verplanck, "Literary Property," 218 and n.*, at least one of these was written by Phillips. Moreover, the second article appears to have been written by the same person as the first.

190. Verplanck, "Literary Property," 225.

191. It is not an exaggeration to say that the appearance of a volume of reporters was cause for celebration at this time. See, e.g., "Wendell's Reports," *American Jurist and Law Magazine* 2 (1829): 290. ("The publication of a volume of reports of decisions in the

Supreme Court and Court of Errors in New York, is always an event of some interest in the legal community.")

192. Until 1844, voting on judicial matters was a power of all members of the House of Lords, whether they had legal training or not, yet it was bad form to vote according to personal or party preferences. However, "most peers abstained from participating in the judicial business of the House, although a small number was required to sit with the judicial members." A. H. Manchester, *A Modern Legal History of England and Wales, 1750–1950* (London: Butterworths, 1980), 175–77.

193. This unusual inversion, the chancellor handling the law appeals and the justices handling the equity appeals, is explained by the fact that these were appeals from those very same judges and thus, the judges were not expected to hear appeals from themselves. Hence, the chancellor sat out the equity appeals and the justices sat out appeals from their court.

194. See Browne, *The Judiciary through 1870*, 19–20.

195. See "The Last of Our Chancellors," *Albany Law Journal* 14 (1876): 224 (tempering praise with notice of his shortcomings).

196. See J. Myron Jacobstein and Roy M. Mersky, *The Rejected: Sketches of the 26 Men Nominated for the Supreme Court but Not Confirmed by the Senate* (Fremont, CA: Toucan Valley Publications, 1993), 38–39.

197. Trying to trace the intellectual origins of Verplanck's use of the concept of "public utility" is far beyond the scope of this article, although Paley appears to have been the one utilitarian he most frequently cited with approval. Certainly he meant to invoke the concept that the balance of social happiness was paramount over any individual desire, however, it is not clear when utility came into the picture in any given legal situation. There is good reason to think Verplanck invoked utility only when he was satisfied that no individualistic natural right was at stake in the dispute resolution. For a good overview of the various strands of utility, see generally Frederick Rosen, *Classical Utilitarianism from Hume to Mill* (London: Routledge, 2003).

198. 20 Wend. 267 (N.Y. 1838).

199. See Everett v. Saltus, 15 Wend. 474 (N.Y. Sup. Ct. 1836), rev'd, 20 Wend. 267 (N.Y. 1838).

200. *Saltus*, 20 Wend. at 274.

201. Ibid., 275.

202. Ibid., 283.

203. Ibid.

204. See ibid., 283–86.

205. 22 Wend. 244 (N.Y. 1839).

206. See Joseph Story, *Commentaries on the Law of Agency, as a Branch of Commercial and Maritime Jurisprudence, with Occasional Illustrations from the Civil and Foreign Law* (1839) § 268, at 265–66, § 290, at 290–91 (resting the liability of a foreign agent upon "the presumption, that the party dealing with the agent intends to trust one, who is known to him, and resides in the same country").

207. *Kirkpatrick*, 22 Wend. at 259.

208. Ibid., 262–63.

209. Ibid., 263.

210. 26 Wend. 341 (N.Y. 1841).

211. Ibid., 352.

212. Ibid., 361–65.

213. McLaren v. Watson's Ex'r, 26 Wend. 425, 441 (N.Y. 1841).

214. Ibid.

215. Am. Ins. Co. v. Bryan, 26 Wend. 563, 585 (N.Y. 1841).

216. Am. Ins. Co. v. Ogden, 20 Wend. 287 (N.Y. 1838).

217. Tripp v. Cook, 26 Wend. 143, 158 (N.Y. 1841).

218. Ibid., 159.

219. Ibid.

220. See Powell v. Myers, 26 Wend. 591 (N.Y. 1841).

221. Ibid., 596.
222. Ibid., 596, 597–98.
223. See People v. White, 24 Wend. 520 (N.Y. 1840).
224. Ibid., 569.
225. Ibid., 572.
226. Ibid., 573.
227. Ibid., 574.
228. Ibid., 575.
229. Saltus v. Everett, 20 Wend. 267, 286 (N.Y. 1838). ("The importance of the principles and rules not only of decision but of active business involved in this cause, especially in relation to that vast and busy community *which I immediately represent in this body*, has led me to examine this whole head of law with an interest and at a length wholly disproportionate to the amount of value in controversy.") (emphasis added).
230. July, *Essential New Yorker*, 229–30 (quoting letter from James Kent to Verplanck [Nov. 7, 1842]).
231. July, *Essential New Yorker*, 229 (quoting Charles P. Daly).
232. See ibid. My count puts the number of dissents at five: Allen v. Suydam, 20 Wend. 321 (N.Y. 1838); Cochran v. Van Surlay, 20 Wend. 365 (N.Y. 1838); De Groot v. Van Duzer, 20 Wend. 390 (N.Y. 1838); Stoddard v. Butler, 20 Wend. 507 (N.Y. 1838); McLaren v. Watson's Ex'r, 26 Wend. 425 (N.Y. 1841).
233. See Daniel J. Hulsebosch, *Constituting Empire: New York and the Transformation of Constitutionalism in the Atlantic World, 1664–1830* (Chapel Hill: University of North Carolina Press, 2005). Hulsebosch notes that New York had a constitutional convention every generation—five, to be exact—before the Civil War, and that each revision lengthened and complicated the document. Ibid., 260.
234. See Gulian C. Verplanck, *Speech When in Committee of the Whole, in the Senate of New-York, on the Several Bills and Resolutions for the Amendment of the Law and the Reform of the Judiciary System* (Albany, NY: Hoffman & White, 1839) [hereinafter Verplanck, *Judicial Reform*].
235. Ibid., 27.
236. Ibid., 3–4.
237. Ibid., 12.
238. Ibid., 13–14.
239. Verplanck, *Judicial Reform*, 14.
240. Ibid.
241. Ibid., 5–6.
242. Ibid., 6.
243. Ibid., 7.
244. Jeremy Bentham most famously developed a constitutional code that structurally linked the governors' self-interests with their duty to the people. See Philip Schofield, "Bentham on the Identification of Interests," *Utilitas* 8 (1996): 223.
245. Verplanck, *Judicial Reform*, 5.
246. Ibid., 8.
247. Ibid., 22.
248. Ibid.
249. See ibid., 21–25.
250. See ibid., 8.
251. Ibid., 24. See July, *Essential New Yorker*, 56–71 (describing Verplanck's participation in an anti-Clinton satirical publication).
252. Verplanck, *Judicial Reform*, 25.
253. Ibid., 26.
254. Ibid. The line of poetry is from Samuel Johnson, *The Vanity of Human Wishes*, the full stanza of which reads:

What gave great Villiers to the assassin's knife,
And fixed disease on Harley's closing life?
What murdered Wentworth, and what exiled Hyde,

By kings protected, and to kings allied?
What but their wish indulged in courts to shine,
And power too great to keep, or to resign?

—Samuel Johnson, *The Vanity of Human Wishes* (1749; Oxford: Clarendon Press, 1927) 12. With a name like "Ruben Hyde Walworth" there was just too much to play with here.

255. Joseph Story, "Codification of the Common Law," in ed. William W. Story, *The Miscellaneous Writings of Joseph Story* (1852; repr., Lawbook Exchange, Ltd., 2000), 698. This report was issued in January 1837. For a good overview of Story's report, see Charles M. Cook, *The American Codification Movement: A Study of Antebellum Legal Reform* (Westport, CT: Greenwood Press, 1981), 175–79.

256. Verplanck, *Judicial Reform*, 29.

257. "Administration of Justice in New York," *Law Reporter* 2 (1839): 33.

FOUR

English Radical as Legal Scientist

Thomas Cooper

Thomas Cooper was born on 22 October 1759, in Westminster, London. He completed his studies at University College, Oxford, in February 1779, and became a barrister at the Inner Temple in 1787.[1] That same year he penned a pamphlet condemning the international slave trade.[2] By 1792, Cooper was well into his radical phase, which would more or less spell the end to his residence in England. During that fateful year, the Manchester Constitutional Society asked him to prepare an abridgement of Thomas Paine's *The Rights of Man*. Then, in the spring, he travelled with a companion to Paris to witness the French Revolution firsthand. Back in London, Edmund Burke denounced Cooper for "carrying the British colors" in a revolutionary procession in Paris. In response, Cooper published his *Reply to Burke's Invective* in Manchester that May.[3] With Cooper and his associates, including the famed Joseph Priestly, fearful for their continued safety in Britain, Cooper set out on a prospecting trip to America and returned early in 1794, whereupon he published *Some Information Respecting America*, providing his home audience with demographic, economic, and political information on his soon-to-be homeland.[4]

Cooper's removal to America landed him in western Pennsylvania, where he quickly settled into a public life continuing on with his radical politics. It is perhaps not surprising that a follower of Paine and an enemy of Burke would find intellectual commonality with the party of Thomas Jefferson, and Jefferson himself. In fact, Jefferson was a frequent correspondent with both Cooper and Priestly.[5] So devoted to the political cause of democracy was Cooper, that in 1800 he suffered under the Sedition Law of the Adams Administration with jail time and a fine.[6] Once the Jeffersonians gained control of the state government, the Jeffersonian governor of Pennsylvania rewarded Cooper with a judgeship in 1804, although he was removed from office several years later for intemperate conduct.[7] Jefferson, however, maintained the utmost confidence in Cooper and, in 1819, appointed Cooper professor of chemistry and law at the University of Virginia. Although formally elected as professor, Cooper's appointment never panned out as the board of visitors received a number of objections to Cooper's philosophical materialism from prominent clergy. Instead, the board indemnified Cooper for his expenses and he moved on to another opportunity at South Carolina College.

It was during Cooper's time in Columbia that he made his most sustained contributions to legal science. Throughout the 1820s and 1830s Cooper published works on the US Constitution and free speech, he began giving formal law lectures, and he undertook the project of compiling the state statutes of South Carolina. However, it was also during this period that Cooper reevaluated his position on slavery. He concluded that slavery was a net benefit to the South and that his previous denunciations of slavery had been too abstract and lacked the empirical investigation upon which his approval now rested.[8] It was also during his time in South Carolina that he took sides in the growing sectional constitutional disputes. In the political debate over tariffs in 1827, Cooper delivered a speech condemning the "manufacturing monopoly" of the North in its aggregation of wealth at the expense of the South's agricultural interests. He ominously concluded his remarks by suggesting, "we shall 'ere long be compelled to calculate the value of our union."[9]

Despite his newly acquired sectional feelings, Cooper's other philosophical and political opinions remained steady. Over forty years after he had edited *The Rights of Man* in Manchester, Cooper continued to publicly praise Paine as "a truly kind, honest, and good man."[10] Just a few years prior to that, Cooper had praised the work itself as "a book much vilified, never refuted," and as containing "bold and fearless truths."[11] When he recalled his younger years to a friend, he said of his French Revolution activities, "those four months that I spent in Paris were the most happy and pleasant of my life. I laughed more than I ever did before or have since. I lived four years."[12] Neither did Cooper change his mind on his devotion to philosophical materialism. He continued to write in atheistic terms and once again, in 1833, the local clergy forced Cooper out of academia, this time the presidency of South Carolina College. The following year, he accepted the state legislature's appointment to collect the state statutes and organize them in volumes known as the statutes-at-large. This he pursued until his death in 1839.

More than any of the other legal scientists under consideration, Cooper wrote extensively on political philosophy, especially as it related to American constitutional law. It is important in appreciating Cooper's thoughts on legal science to fully understand how Cooper understood the relationship between legal science and democratic legitimacy. This chapter will begin by examining Cooper's writings on government and the Constitution before turning to his views on law reform, including educational reform and codification.

POLITICAL AND CONSTITUTIONAL THOUGHT

Dumas Malone, suggested that Cooper came to the idea of utility late in life. In fact, Malone discusses Cooper's thoughts on utility in his chapter, "Diversions of Old Age." There, he suggests that Cooper, who was by the 1830s an "avowed Benthamite," took up utilitarianism "in opposition to certain of his clerical foes" as a sort of reactionary step. Others have suggested that utilitarianism was a doctrine adopted by Cooper to justify slavery and the southern order. Thus, Daniel Kilbride also argues that Cooper came to utility late and for instrumental reasons, namely, for its polemical potential during the sectional crisis. Kilbride ultimately concludes that Cooper was "too much a partisan, and not enough of a philosopher, to appreciate the genuine critical potential of utilitarianism."[13] Finally, legal historian Alfred Brophy has recently suggested that a focus on utility in the decision-making processes of southern judges might help to shed new light on uniquely southern justifications for their way of life.

The existing literature merits two responses. First, Cooper did not come to the doctrine of utility late in life. We see it expressed as early as 1787 in his first published essays in Manchester. Moreover, appreciating Cooper's intimate friendship with Joseph Priestly adds to the context of Cooper as a serious philosopher and not a simple partisan who reached for the most convenient tools with which to craft a political argument. In fact, Bentham himself credited Priestly with inspiring his own formulation of utility.[14] Second, as we saw with Gulian Verplanck's legal career, appeal to the doctrine of utility had great attraction not only in New York, but also in the more general debates about the morality of caveat emptor and copyright law. Pleading utility as the basis for public morality was certainly a part of the emerging legal science's broader concern with rationality and universality.

In 1787, Cooper published *On the Foundation of Civil Government* while living in Manchester, and later republished the pamphlet in 1826, along with a new essay on the US Constitution.[15] *Foundation* is notable for its format—a series of thirty-four propositions dedicated to the support of civil liberty. Prior to launching into the enumerated principles, however, Cooper prefaced the essay with two motives for composing the work. First, he thought the subject one so important to general knowledge that he aimed to write an essay accessible to all—"so plainly as to be generally understood, and so briefly as to be easily remembered." He even risked being repetitious or redundant in the realm of political commentary because not enough could be said on the fundamentals of government. The second reason Cooper gave for his essay was his thorough rejection of the notion that all men are born equal, or with equal rights. As a materialist Cooper could not accept such a fanciful design. Thus "civil liberty must be placed on another basis; and other positions must be adduced to support it."[16]

Cooper's first seven propositions concerned the legitimacy of political power. His first, and paramount, proposition being: "*the right of exercising political power, whether about to commence or actually existing, is derived solely from the people.*" Before reaching this conclusion, Cooper rejected ten competing sources of governmental authority that had been popular among political philosophers. The second major feature of Cooper's work is what he considered to be "the great end and object of civil society," "the happiness of the community." As he phrased it, and continued to do so throughout his life, "the greatest good of the greatest number, is the polar star of all good government; and public utility the criterion by which every law is to be tested."[17] I will refer to these two features of Cooper's thought as his democratic and utilitarian impulses, and will explore below just how deeply these impulses run.

In defining "the people," Cooper was quite insistent that that term meant no more than "an aggregate of individuals." There was nothing metaphysical about a community once it was formed; it gained no new interest apart from the sum of the interests of its constituent members. Undoubtedly, a community would consist of individuals who were "*sui incompotes*, incapable of self-direction," such as infants, idiots, lunatics, and married women. For these individuals, their interests had to be determined for them. Cooper allowed for the possibility that the treatment of women might be "inequitable," but any reconsideration of their status still had to account for "the greatest sum of good to the whole community, male and female."[18]

When Cooper talked of the interests of individuals, he usually did so in terms of individual "rights." Although he never explicitly defined what he meant by a "right," his use of the term was fairly clear—Cooper took a Hobbesian approach to natural liberty, claiming that a "right" was anything an individual was capable of doing "previous to compact." When Cooper asked, why would any man submit himself to the authority of another, he answered, "for his own good" and because of the "prospect of living more happily." At the same time, however, no right was yielded gratuitously. Unless society was providing some benefit to the individual in return for his loss of liberty, one could not assume that any individual would surrender the right.[19] As we will see, this obsessive focus on the individual caused problems for Cooper in that he was led to the possibility of there being inalienable rights.

Cooper then grouped together six propositions "applicable to the subject of *religious liberty*." However, we are not told their commonality until after they have been thoroughly explained. Yet keeping this goal in mind does allow us to consider them in a fuller light. It is here that Cooper developed his notion of the equal protection, or equal application, of the laws. Cooper formulated the principle as follows: what cannot be demanded is the yielding of the right "of one individual which may not be equally required of every other individual of the community; otherwise society will be benefited at the expence of an act of injustice." The second major feature relating to religious liberty was Cooper's concept of a preexisting duty: it is not "to be presumed that on entering society we have surrendered the right of doing that, which, independent of society and antecedent thereto, it was our *duty* to perform." Examples of such preexisting duties included repaying personal debts and the worshiping of God in one's own way. The final element regarding religious liberty was the idea that the punishment of an individual was just only if it was done for an injury caused, not "because we think his conscience is misinformed." Here Cooper wanted to make some fine distinctions between internal and external actions, and place behavior solely on the side of external actions not affected by the conscience.[20]

Cooper's very next set of propositions concerned further refinements of what he meant by majority, and he seemed to get back on a utilitarian track. He recognized that "the interest of any one or any number of individuals constituting the minority only, must be presumed to be conceded where it interferes with the interest of the majority." Further, "for every practical purpose the majority is synonymous with the society." Thus, the collective opinions of the majority as to "any proposed means of compassing the ends of society" ought to be preferred to "the opinions of the few." However, to meet the ends of society, "a few must be deputed to act for the many." Hence, the penultimate set of propositions was devoted to controlling the few who govern. Given Cooper's early statements on governmental power deriving solely from the people, not much surprising is revealed here. The "few" "receive all their authority from their constituents," and the people may extend or limit, continue or annul, the delegated authority at will.[21] Cooper was silent in *Foundation* on the question of instructing representatives. In his 1826 essay he came out strongly against such a practice, especially in regard to members of Congress. Likewise, he contributed a short article to the Philadelphia-based *American Quarterly Review* in 1829, which was ostensibly a review of a speech by Burke that touched upon the topic. Cooper authored the review anonymously although he quoted himself liberally in the third person. Surely it was easier to agree with Burke if Cooper did not have to take direct responsibility for it.[22]

The issue of suffrage troubled Cooper a great deal. He took a less than fully democratic position and it was clear he was uncomfortable doing so, but he did take some relief in the thought that utility backed up his position. He said, "after much consideration, I incline to think that a line of exclusion *may* be drawn, and that no injustice is done by debarring those from voting in the choice of national representatives, who on account of their poverty, are exempted, for instance, from the payment of all taxes." Cooper gave six reasons for his position. He thought the poor contributed nothing to the enforcement of the laws and took no pledge to submission to the laws. Most laws related to and risked property, which was itself the physical basis of any political community. If these were not good enough reasons, "so small a portion of society" would be affected, that a majority of society would still be represented in the suffrage. Further, Cooper thought no exclusion would be necessary "if every individual in the community actually received a reasonable education." Should someone accuse Cooper of advocating government without the consent of the governed, he had a three-part reply. First, anyone was free to leave the United States. Second, all property benefits the poor, and therefore being called upon "to defend property which enables them to subsist, is no proper subject of complaint." Finally, and mostly importantly, "public utility" requires that notice be taken of "past experience" and "notorious facts." Just as we do not give liquor to a drunk, or a gun to a lunatic, we should not give the vote to "a certain class of the people" liable to abuse it.[23]

The final few propositions concerned the right of changing the form of government, which the people had the absolute right of doing. This follows from the observation that the people "*can* have no interest but that of the community at large (*i.e.*, of themselves) and of course can have no other object in determining, but the object itself for which society was formed." "Let it be remembered," Cooper noted, "that Government is not a compact between the governors and the governed." Thus on matters of constitutional significance, the governors' wishes were of no moment. If the governors proved inattentive to petitions for reform, the people "will be justified in rising to *compel* an obedience to their commands." Cooper realized that "it cannot be supposed that the majority of the people will rise at one and the same instant of time," and hence smaller numbers of men would be "justified in making a beginning." Though never making explicit reference to a utilitarian juncture of resistance, he said, "the good to be obtained by the alteration ought to be compared with the evils likely to ensue from the enforcement of it." Cooper concluded with his notion of the surest way of guaranteeing enduring liberty, and thus avoiding revolution: to insist upon "a greater freedom of the press, and a greater extension of knowledge, the necessary consequence of untrammeled discussion."[24]

LAW REFORM

Most of Cooper's writings on law reform come from the final decade of his life. That is not to suggest, however, that Cooper did write explicitly about legal science before then. To the contrary, Cooper published several works specifically aimed at reforming American law, that is, moving it away from the irrational precedent-based English system as well as integrating new findings in the natural science to the practice of law. He published a treatise on bankruptcy law in 1801, which he began while serving his jail sentence for sedition.[25] In 1812, he edited the first American edition of Justinian's *Institutes*, the primary source of Roman law.[26] To add value to the work for American lawyers, Cooper annotated the volume to reference US case law, indicating how Roman law principles could be imported into the domestic sphere.

Cooper's next major legal publication was his 1819 work on medical jurisprudence—the first compendium of its sort to be published in the United States.[27] In editing this work, Cooper thought himself ahead of the curve in preparing a work on a subject that would soon "force itself on the notice of the public." Up until this point, medical jurisprudence, as a field of study, had been more attended to "on the Continent of Europe, than in Great Britain or this country."[28] Cooper was successful in getting other legal scientist to at least acknowledge the value of the natural sciences to law. As one law professor explained to the graduating class at Transylvania University, "medical jurisprudence has been too generally neglected," and thus, further study would be necessary even after the student departed from school.[29] As with his edition of Justinian's *Institutes*, Cooper saw his work on medical jurisprudence, in part, as an opportunity to expose Americans to the more rational system of civil law. But he also saw the work as providing a similar opportunity to demonstrate to American lawyers the importance of chemical and medical knowledge to the legal topics of insanity, murder, rape, and other fields where scientific expertise could prove determinative of the legal outcome.

The law-reform spark seems to have been reignited when Cooper reviewed Jeremy Bentham's *Rationale of Judicial Evidence* in May 1830 for the *Southern Review*. His review was quite lengthy and contained an extended discussion of why Bentham was correct about everything he had reported in that work. Cooper's most original ideas came near the end of the piece, where he recommended codification for the American states.[30]

The only real criticism Cooper leveled against Bentham was that the "Benthamee dialect" in which the work was written required him to study every passage twice to appreciate the full implications of the work.[31] On the whole, Cooper agreed that the common law needed reform because it served the interests of the profession rather than the public. The review focused on a number of the evidentiary exclusions

Bentham had criticized as anti-utilitarian. It should be noted that Cooper disliked any general rule of evidentiary exclusion precisely because of its general nature—it allowed for no consideration of the utility of exclusion in a particular case. But what comes through most forcefully is Cooper's hostility to the religious nature of any part of the common law, specifically, those evidentiary exclusions based on religious grounds.

Sounding as though speaking from personal experience, Cooper lamented, "Even in this country of religious freedom under the constitutions of the several States, but we cannot honestly say in this country of religious toleration, a man is sure to encounter much obloquy, and great practical inconvenience who has the courage to run counter to the religious persuasions of his fellow citizens."[32] Among the features of evidence law that bothered Cooper, perjury was particularly troublesome because through the crime "we do not punish his offence against society, viz. the falsehood; but we let that alone and punish his offence against religion." Religion also worked to disqualify some, like atheists, from providing testimony at all. Yet if one confessed to such non-belief in the face of societal disapproval, Cooper thought, "can a stronger proof of devotion to the cause of truth, to veracity in public as well as in private, be exhibited? Can more decided evidence of undoubted honesty be imagined? . . . Language does not admit of expressing a case of more detestable absurdity." It astonished Cooper that judges in England and America continued to assert that Christianity was "part and parcel of the common law," especially after it was "so decidedly, so irrefutably exposed by Mr. Jefferson" to be a lie.[33] Realizing that his passions were getting the better of him, Cooper had to add this caveat: "Let us not be misunderstood: we are no advocates of Atheism, or any other kind of ism."[34]

Cooper chose an interesting example to further his point about religious disqualification. "Suppose a set of tipsy soldiers, were to enter a Quaker-meeting, bind the men and violate the women, how are the offenders to be convicted? not a witness present admissible in a court (of justice?—no, let us not be guilty of such misnomer) of law!"[35] The reason this example stands out is that Cooper had previously encountered trouble with the Quakers in Pennsylvania. In fact, one of the reasons he was removed from his judicial post was that he had allegedly yelled at a Quaker who had refused to remove his hat in the courtroom. Cooper always thought that he had been unfairly treated in that he had never been permitted to explain himself before he was removed by the legislature.[36] Perhaps this was his attempt to show he had no hostility to Quakers, only sympathy for their mistreatment by the law.

Cooper shared Bentham's objection to three particular privileges: self-incrimination, lawyer-client, and marriage. All three discounted public utility in favor of the pecuniary interest of the legal profession. Moreover, all three defied the sensible best evidence rule. The privilege against self-incrimination was designed "to screen guilt, to give impunity to crime, to cherish fraud, and counteract, in the most effectual way, the real ends of pubic justice." Cooper also made allusion to Bentham's fox-hunter analogy, in which he described the rule as one arising not out of sympathy with the accused, but in order to treat him like a "bag-fox; he will return, and we shall have our sport. Impunity of this kind created business." Cooper easily dismissed the lawyer-client privilege: "A contract between a rogue and his lawyer, to avoid the punishment of roguery, is no such a contract as need be treated with much respect." Nevertheless, it was "a fruitful source of causes and fees."[37]

It was his discussion of the marriage privilege that showed Cooper at his most eccentric.[38] Well aware that the rationale of such a privilege was to keep the family peace, Cooper completely rationalized his way around this rule. First he noted that the marriage contract was entirely voluntary, and sometimes evils are attendant on it. Second, there really was no rational reason for being angry with a spouse who was compelled by law to testify against the other. "Had it been voluntary, there might be some reason for anger; not where the disclosure is compulsive." Finally, bringing the argument back to public utility, "If the witness be the wife of a rogue, is that a reason why his roguery against me should be concealed and protected?" Such a privilege was also dangerous because it meant that "an evil-doer" would potentially "have a perpetual confidant and accomplice in the bosom of his family, from whom no law can wring the secret of his delinquency." If that were not frightening enough, the privilege would convert every family "into a nursery of unpunishable crime." This in turn "intermingles hostility to the public with the marriage tie, and inculcates concealment and protection of crime and dishonesty, as a marriage duty." Cooper got to the heart of the matter when he concluded that the fundamentals of marriage had not been fully thought out. Had they been subjected to close scrutiny one would have concluded, "Surely, the proper ethics of the marriage contract are, that love, respect, confidence and attachment are due only where those qualities exist, which reasonably call for them."[39]

While acknowledging that legislators and judges had too often deceived themselves "from the prejudice of legal education and long habit of thinking and acting in a legal routine," Cooper thought parts of America less worthy of condemnation than England. "In this country, and in our own State of South-Carolina, many glaring evils have been remedied or avoided; much has been well, because honestly done." Unfortunately, the same praise could not be laid on all states of the Union. "But look at the present state of the law and its practice in New-York, and who will say that reform is not required?" Cooper did not say what exactly it was about New York that was so egregious, but he did mention that they needed to be reminded, "the criterion of the propriety of every public law and every public measure is, the good of society—public utility." Clearly, the South was more utilitarian than the North. Always the democrat, however, Cooper thought that only "to the people must the people look for effectual reform."[40]

Whenever the people got around to actually reforming the common law, Cooper had a suggestion to them: look to the civil law. The civil law was a science, while the common law was merely a trade. No man could read the Code Napoleon or Pothier "without being wiser in the science of law." Whereas under the "artificial technical system," the common lawyer is trained "as a shoe-maker learns to make shoes: it has no tendency to enlarge the mind." The first step toward moving in the direction of a more scientific legal system was to simplify the existing law.[41]

American common law was wrought with examples of its ostensible failures. The fundamental shortcoming of the common law was its looseness of principle, which allowed self-interested lawyers and judges to create mischief with the public's business. For example, a legal novice in Pennsylvania in the company of his elders once remarked that it was the virtue of their state bench that "party spirit" never invaded judicial proceedings. According to Cooper, no one present could keep a straight face because of the manifest absurdity of the newcomer's statement. Cooper knew well how partisans used the Pennsylvania legal system as a weapon in their political arsenal. But the federal courts were even starker examples of judicial opportunism. According to a *New York Evening Post* article that Cooper had recently read, the US Supreme Court affirmed lower courts at a rate of only 56 percent. This proved that the common law was no better at providing predictability than a coin toss.[42]

The solution for the United States was to follow "the simple and natural code and practice of Louisiana; thanks to Edward Livingston." Cooper urged for each state that a committee be appointed to collect the laws and list them under "separate heads and branches." The legislature would then enact this code, with decennial revisions if necessary.[43] "But the great reform is that adopted in Louisiana. Substitute a [natural] system in lieu of a technical system."[44] Cooper was almost certainly drawing on what Bentham had termed a "natural" arrangement of law. A "natural" arrangement would produce a code of laws that classified and took into account "all men's needs," thus doing away with judicial legislation.[45] As further proof that Cooper intended the word "natural," Bentham himself explicitly contrasted his own "natural" arrangement with what he called Blackstone's "technical" arrangement—the same term Cooper uses for contrast.[46]

The court system should also be streamlined, believed Cooper. He suggested only two separate courts, one for civil and the other for criminal matters, although he allowed for the possibility of a family court if those sorts of issues occupied too much of the civil courts' time. Cooper also suggested reducing the number of jurors from the fetishistic twelve, which was fine for the number of months, zodiac signs, and apostles, but not particularly suited for achieving justice. Of course, this was not all just a "wild dream." Cooper asked rhetorically, "Have you been in a court in Louisiana lately?"[47]

Cooper carried forth his "wild dream" when he delivered his "Introductory Lecture to a Course of Law" at South Carolina College in 1834. The basic outline of his lecture was to begin with the origins of civil society, discuss the role of utility and lawmaking within a political community, and then move on to the actual state of the American legal system and suggest ways it could be improved. Cooper began with five principles that formed "the foundation of a whole system of Ethics," principles "plainly founded upon the necessary character and constitution of human beings, met together in a community." The first principle was the existence of a "Law of Nature" that sounded oddly Hobbesian. The second principle was the necessity of the institution of marriage, created to prevent "revenge and blood" that would otherwise occur without it. The third principle followed from the second, the parent-child relationship with its attendant obligations and duties. Fourth was the existence of obligations and contracts, without which there would be "a resort to the remedy of violence." Finally, there was the owner-slave, master-servant relationship, which originated from theories of a just war. These five principles presumed a natural default to a state of war, man against man, all against all. The first four also mirrored what in 1787 he had verged on calling, inalienable rights, which no government could legitimately claim to invade.[48]

Repeating his formulation from his 1787 *Foundation* essay, Cooper proclaimed that "in all communities of voluntary origin, the modern axiom is true: the polar star of morals and of law, is, *the greatest happiness of the greatest number*." It was only a wise legislature that could ably adopt laws in keeping with utility. And the only way to ensure a wise set of lawmakers was to ensure a wise set of electors, which could only be achieved through a high level of education that yielded moral citizens. Only with regard to appropriately educated citizens would the sanctions of laws adequately act on their motives. Any man properly educated would consciously consider the good of the community at the expense of "his own temporary gratification."[49] Despite Cooper's overt use of the axiom of utility, his plan was far afield from a Benthamic legislative scheme that relied on no one's selflessness, but instead depended on a deliberately designed constitutional code that kept the governors in check.

Cooper also seemed to be relying on some sort of anthropological evidence for his conclusion that a state of nature was "far from visionary." It is not at all clear what evidence he had in mind, but he seems to have had a notion of material societal progress, or a linear understanding of civilization. The point is, Cooper saw the civil law system—a code of written law—as the pinnacle of civil society.

According to Cooper a great civilization once existed, namely, "in the early days of Rome." It must be said, however, that this was not at all a new idea. Cooper's own 1812 edition of *Justinian* was the result of his belief that the study of Roman law would provide American lawyers with insight into a more ordered and rationale legal system. But he does not appear to have followed up on the idea until the 1830s. Cooper's goal in his law lectures was to show how far the English common law was from Roman law and how this gap could be bridged.

As Cooper had alluded to in his review of Bentham's *Evidence*, there was a great need for the simplification of American legal sources. Cooper figured that a lawyer in the United States needed "350 to 400 volumes of American law" in order to practice competently. As usual, the South was ahead of the rest of the nation such that "Our South Carolina reports are cited by the lawyers of the middle States." Nevertheless, Cooper feared that as society became more complex, the more difficult it would be to simplify the law if steps were not undertaken immediately.[50]

The goal of simplification was to eventually make the common law case method obsolete. In order for law to be a science, one had to be able to "deduce general principles," which could only occur if the voluminous source material was compacted "into a few pages of settled maxims." "Like all other sciences, the science of Law will be simplified by a patient accumulation and review of separate facts, to deduce from their comparison the leading rule involved in each of them."[51]

The United States hardly had any examples to follow when it came to creating a science of law, largely because "British sources" had been so blindly adopted. There was one major exception: "Louisiana had a peculiar system of its own; perhaps the best in the United States; certainly worth more investigation than it has yet received." In terms of legal literature, Cooper knew "of no book that [would] serve to direct him [the student]." Kent's *Commentaries* were good, "but that learned man is not, upon every point, to be relied on implicitly." Of course there was always Blackstone, but his "doctrines on politics and prerogative are so abhorrent from our republican principles, and so much of his book is filled with matter, worthless to the American student, that some other system had become desirable, for home use." Wilson's *Lectures* were out of the question: "Little is to be said in their praise, excepting that it is praise enough to have been the first in a laudable career."[52]

As outlined by Cooper, the plan for the series of lectures was to create a legal system better understood by the many, where it could not be said, as it was now, "Common Law is one thing, common sense another." "I shall endeavor, therefore, to treat Law as a branch of knowledge, in itself intrinsically of high value; and show that no plan of liberal education, for a legislator and a gentleman, can be complete without it." Cooper concluded his introductory lecture with the promise that the next topic would be political economy taught out of his own manual: "no lawyer in the country can permit himself to be ignorant of this absolutely indispensable portion of the elementary knowledge of a statesman."[53]

It is unclear what happened to Cooper's plan for his remaining law lectures, which were quite bold in scope. Malone opines that because only the introductory lecture survived, the lectures "did not proceed according to the original expectation."[54] However, a more likely explanation is simply that the subsequent lectures were never published. As Angela Fernandez has pointed out, law lecturers in the early republic had to be cognizant about student enrollment since their salary was usually tied to the number of paying students in class. Thus, it was in their interest not to have their lectures published as potential students might choose instead to read the lectures rather than pay the tuition to attend them in person. However, it was common to publish the "introductory lecture" as a way of enticing students as to what was to come.[55]

By 1836, Cooper was making headway in his efforts to reform South Carolina law when he was appointed by the state legislature to compile all the statute law of the state since 1682. There had been three attempts at compilation before, but none like the present, that is, "a plan sanctioned by public authority . . . formed and executed to collect, revise or digest our written Laws." The best collection of laws was a hundred years old, but still quite useful to Cooper. A more recent 1790 collection had been too heavily edited, with the compiler deciding for himself what laws were good and which had been repealed or were obsolete. The most recent 1814 set of laws was only ever intended as a student's manual, and therefore was quite unsatisfactory for the grand ambition of full-scale law reform. Cooper's review of these earlier works led him to conclude: "Hence, I have carefully considered the wants of the profession and of the public in the respect, and have determined to submit to the Legislature, through the governor of the State, a publication that shall fulfil [*sic*] the idea of *the Statutes at Large*; and which shall serve as an adequate basis or platform for future operations by the Legislature, and more satisfactory decisions by the Courts."[56]

In undertaking this project, Cooper was adamant about one thing in particular: it was "better to insert somewhat too much than somewhat too little." This might seems counterintuitive for someone who was trying to simplify the law, but Cooper had his reasons. Including dated material of questionable validity would enable the present generation to learn from past mistakes and make progress toward more enlightened laws. This would also allow the people and the lawmakers to understand how old ways of reasoning had failed. Another reason why even repealed legislation should be included was that "rights" may have "vested" under old enactments, and courts would have an easier time doing justice with the statutes in front of them. But by far the most important reason for including even the kitchen sink, or in this case the Magna Carta, was because "although ministerial authority may be delegated, legislative authority cannot." And deciding what to include and what to omit was tantamount to saying what the law was and what it was not. This did not mean Cooper's work was opinion free: "I may (as I shall do) suggest that a law is obsolete, but I cannot leave it out, if it bears on the face of it, a public character."[57]

One of Cooper's charges from the legislature was to include an index with the statute books. Cooper envisioned this endeavor as "making up a full general Index of all the Laws of a public nature that have been enacted; arranged under appropriate heads, and comprising a digested summary or code of the Statute Law of the State as it stands." It is clear that this index was the first major step to convincing people of the benefits of a code of laws. "Indeed, the main object in view with many persons at the present time, is a full and accurate digested INDEX of all our statutory enactments—an Index that may serve as a Code and Manual of out Statute law, for popular use."[58]

One aspect of the compilation that appears to have troubled Cooper was that the arrangement began chronologically. It is unclear why the main plan was so organized, but Cooper immediately asked permission to compose certain volumes by subject matter. As Cooper explained to the legislature, the proposed subjects were so frequently recurring that it would be inconvenient to have to consult different volumes while researching one topic. In response, the legislature basically gave Cooper carte blanche, praising his efforts and providing him with assistants and money. Unfortunately, Cooper only lived to publish four volumes through 1838 and never the subject-matter volumes, which were completed after his death according to his plan.

Volume 1 is somewhat of a subject-matter volume in that it contains "acts, records, and documents of a constitutional character," whereas volumes 2, 3, and 4 are purely statutory and chronological. The first volume allowed Cooper to mix governing documents with commentary, and thus is not surprising that half the volume is devoted to the Nullification Crisis and various assertions of states' rights by South Carolina herself. Cooper even inserted an essay of his own, "Concerning Federal Regulations generally."[59]

The statutory volumes include a series of editor's notes at the end of the works. Cooper's goal was to cross reference similar statutes and list relevant judicial decisions for each statute, which he more or less managed to do, but not without letting the reader know of his toils: "This will add considerably to the labour of the Editor, but it is labour that in his opinion is demanded by the present state of our Law, and will become more difficult the longer it is deferred."[60] This was thought so useful, that readers complained to him that these notes should follow each statute, rather than being collected at the end of the volume. But the nature of printing the works prevented this useful suggestion from being implemented. What Cooper had originally wanted to do, was to give a brief summary of each judicial decision relating to a particular statute, but after attempting this method with the subject of wills, he gave it up as impracticable.

Of all the legal scientists discussed herein, Cooper was by far the most devoted to abstract philosophizing, yet as we have seen, he kept active in highly practical matters. The implications of Cooper's philosophical thought for his legal reform endeavors has only been glossed in this chapter. A whole work could be devoted to examining Cooper's judicial work in Pennsylvania, comparing and contrasting it with his later reform efforts in South Carolina. We know that his philosophy of government had not changed over the years, and his political radicalism was able to find some outlets early on in his stay in western Pennsylvania. His legal treatises, law lectures, and statutory consolidation efforts should all be seen as natural extensions of his utility-based legal science, which itself was rooted in philosophical materialism, likely initiated by Priestly, but certainly sustained by Bentham.

NOTES

1. Most of the factual details of Cooper's life come from Dumas Malone, *The Public Life of Thomas Cooper, 1783–1839* (New Haven, CT: Yale Univ. Press, 1926; repr., Columbia: University of South Carolina Press, 1961).
2. Thomas Cooper, *Letters on the Slave Trade* (1787; Warrington: W. Eyres, 1788).
3. Thomas Cooper, *Reply to Mr. Burke's Invective against Mr. Cooper and Mr. Watt in the House of Commons, on the 30th of April 1792* (Manchester: M. Falkner & Co., 1792).
4. Thomas Cooper, *Some Information Respecting America* (Dublin: William Porter, 1794).
5. See Seymour S. Cohen, "The Correspondence of Thomas Jefferson and Thomas Cooper: A Previously Unpublished Manuscript of Dumas Malone," *Proceedings of the American Philosophical Society* 147, no. 1 (2003): 39–64; Jenny Graham, "Joseph Priestly in America," in ed. Isabel Rivers and David L. Wykes, *Joseph Priestly, Scientist, Philosopher, and Theologian* (Oxford: Oxford University Press, 2008), 221–28.
6. Thomas Cooper, *An Account of the Trial of Thomas Cooper, of Northumberland; on a Charge of Libel against the President of the United States* (Philadelphia: John Bioren, 1800).
7. Thomas Cooper, ed., *Narrative of Proceedings against Thomas Cooper, Esquire, President Judge of the 8th Judiciary District of Pennsylvania on a Charge of Official Misconduct* (Lancaster, PA: William Hamilton, 1811).
8. Cooper claimed that "the inferiority of natural intellect among the blacks cannot be denied" when comparing free northern blacks and southern slaves. He thought, based upon his interactions with both groups, that there was no distinction in intellect. Thomas Cooper, "Coloured Marriages," *Carolina Law Journal* 1 (1830): 100.
9. Thomas Cooper, "Speech of Thomas Cooper, July 2, 1827," *Niles Weekly Register*, September 8, 1827.
10. Thomas Cooper, "Thomas Paine," *Free Enquirer* (NY), December 7, 1834.
11. Thomas Cooper, Preface, *Two Essays* (Columbia, SC: D. & J. Faust, 1826), iv.
12. Thomas Cooper, "Memoranda of Table-talk of Judge Cooper," D. J. M'Cord, ed., in Duyckinck, *Cyclopaedia*, 2:332.
13. Daniel Kilbride, "Slavery and Utilitarianism: Thomas Cooper and the Mind of the Old South," *Journal of Southern History* 59, no. 3 (1993): 469, 485.
14. Schofield, *Utility and Democracy*.
15. Thomas Cooper, *Two Essays* (Columbia, SC: D. & J. Faust, 1826).

16. Thomas Cooper, "On the Foundation of Civil Government," in *Two Essays*, 5.
17. Ibid., 9.
18. Ibid.
19. Ibid., 10.
20. Ibid., 10–11.
21. Ibid., 12–13
22. [Thomas Cooper], "Instructions to Representatives," *American Quarterly Review* 5, no. 9 (1829): 41–50. Based upon a review of the publishers' account books, Cooper is identified as the author in Ralph M. Aderman, "Contributors to the *American Quarterly Review*, 1827–1833," *Studies in Bibliography* 14 (1961): 163–76.
23. Ibid., 12–16.
24. Ibid., 16–18.
25. Thomas Cooper, *The Bankrupt Law of America, Compared with the Bankrupt Law of England* (Philadelphia: John Thompson, 1801; repr., Littleton, CO: Fred B. Rothman & Co., 1992).
26. Thomas Cooper, ed., *The Institutes of Justinian. With Notes by Thomas Cooper, Esq.* (Philadelphia: P. Byrne, 1812).
27. Thomas Cooper, ed., *Tracts on Medical Jurisprudence* (Philadelphia: James Webster, 1819; repr., Clark, NJ: Lawbook Exchange, 2007).
28. Ibid., iii.
29. George Robertson, "Valedictory Address to Law Class of Transylvania," in *Scrap Book*, 237. The address was delivered and published in 1847, yet Robertson noted that he had written the substance of it ten years earlier. Ibid., 234.
30. Thomas Cooper, "Bentham's Rationale of Judicial Evidence," *Southern Review* 10 (1830): 381.
31. Cooper was referring to Bentham's notoriously complex prose, which Bentham actually thought served to make his writing unambiguous. See Philip Schofield, *Utility and Democracy: The Political Thought of Jeremy Bentham* (New York: Oxford University Press, 2006), 11–14.
32. Cooper, "Bentham's Rationale of Judicial Evidence," 394.
33. Ibid., 396. Cooper was referring to Jefferson's famous essay disproving, through an examination of English treatises and case law, that Christianity was part of the common law. See Thomas Jefferson, "Whether Christianity Is a Part of the Common Law?" in *Reports of Cases Determined in the General Court of Virginia* (Charlottesville: F. Carr, 1829), 137.
34. Cooper, "Bentham's Rationale of Judicial Evidence," 393–96.
35. Ibid., 396.
36. Malone, *Public Life of Thomas Cooper*, 205.
37. Cooper, "Bentham's Rationale of Judicial Evidence," 399–401.
38. On Bentham's own radical views on marriage, based in part on the equality of the sexes, see Mary Sokol, "Jeremy Bentham on Love and Marriage: A Utilitarian Proposal for Short-Term Marriage," *Journal of Legal History* 30, no. 1 (2009): 1–21.
39. Cooper, "Bentham's Rationale of Judicial Evidence," 402–4.
40. Ibid., 406–7.
41. Ibid., 413.
42. Ibid., 414–19.
43. Ibid., 422–24. Virginia was the first state to take statutory revision seriously as early as 1792—a project in which legal scientist and future William and Mary law professor, St. George Tucker, participated. See Charles T. Cullen, *St. George Tucker and Law in Virginia, 1772–1804* (New York: Garland Publishing, Inc., 1987), 95–115.
44. Cooper, "Bentham's Rationale of Judicial Evidence," 424. In the text, "natural" reads as "national," but it is certainly a misprint. I have found this error in Cooper's commentary in the *South Carolina Statutes* as well. Perhaps his writing was difficult for printers to read; the error would be comical if the implications were not so extreme. Cooper was almost certainly drawing on what Bentham had termed a "natural" arrangement of law. A "natural" arrangement would produce a code of laws that clas-

sified and took into account "all men's needs," thus doing away with judicial legislation. Michael Lobban, *The Common Law and English Jurisprudence 1760–1850* (Oxford Univ. Press, 1991) 124–25. Moreover, Bentham explicitly contrasted his own "natural" arrangement with Blackstone's "technical" arrangement. David Lieberman, *The Province of Jurisprudence Determined: Legal Theory in Eighteenth-Century Britain* (Cambridge University Press 1989) 258–59.

45. Michael Lobban, *The Common Law and English Jurisprudence, 1760–1850* (Oxford: Oxford University Press, 1991), 124–25.

46. David Lieberman, *The Province of Jurisprudence Determined: Legal Theory in Eighteenth-Century Britain* (Cambridge: Cambridge University Press, 1989), 258–59.

47. Cooper, "Bentham's Rationale of Judicial Evidence," 425–26.

48. Thomas Cooper, *Introductory Lecture to a Course of Law* (Columbia, SC: Telescope Office, 1834) 4–5.

49. Ibid., 7.

50. Ibid., 11.

51. Ibid., 12.

52. Ibid., 18–21.

53. Ibid., 25–26.

54. Malone, *Public Life of Thomas Cooper*, 369.

55. Angela Fernandez, "Copying and Copyright Issues at the Litchfield Law School," *Connecticut History* 47, no. 2 (2008): 219–36.

56. Thomas Cooper, Preface to *The Statutes at Large of South Carolina. Volume First, Containing Acts, Records, and Documents of a Constitutional Character* (Columbia, SC: A. S. Johnston, 1836), iii–iv.

57. Ibid., iv–vi.

58. Ibid., x–xi.

59. Thomas Cooper, "Concerning Federal Regulation Generally," in *Statutes at Large of South Carolina. Volume First*, 201–25.

60. Thomas Cooper, ed., *The Statutes at Large of South Carolina. Volume Second, containing acts from 1682 to 1716, inclusive* (Columbia, SC: A. S. Johnston, 1837), 703.

FIVE

Southern Scholar as Legal Scientist

Hugh S. Legaré

In South Carolina, it is pronounced *luh-gree*. Harriet Beecher Stowe immortalized the name while mocking the South's provinciality with her character Simon Legree, the ugly, coarse, and profane slave master from *Uncle Tom's Cabin*. The fact that Simon Legree is a more recognized figure than Hugh Swinton Legaré is perhaps the cruelest irony for Legaré. Legaré himself could not have been more dissimilar to Stowe's character or to whichever distant French-Huguenot relative of Legaré's she is supposed to have based the character upon.[1] Hugh Legaré was born in 1797 and raised by a single mother; his father died in 1799 and his mother never remarried. After Legaré had been inoculated against smallpox at age four something went terribly wrong and he was incapacitated for a period of months. He eventually reacquired his mobility but his lower extremities were permanently stunted. As he matured, his torso became quite masculine and developed, and thus he was quite a respectable figure while seated. But once he arose, his deformity was obvious. Throughout his life Legaré was self-conscious about his appearance. From an early age he was attracted to the solitary world of intellectualism. It was only after he gained wide respect for his metal abilities that he became confident enough to take on a public life. In public he succeeded well, finally succumbing to illness while serving as both US Attorney General and acting secretary of state.[2]

Legaré died at age forty-six, never having had a family of his own. There have been numerous speculations for why this was so, the most obvious being the social limitations caused by his physical condition. What is important here, however, is the family into which he was born. During his childhood illness he became especially close with his mother, as she was his only means of survival. Legaré had an older and a younger sister, and thus he became the man of a family of three women who depended upon him for support. His older sister married early, but his mother and younger sister were always on his mind, if not for sentimental reasons, then for obligatory financial ones. He had to cut short his legal education abroad to return to John's Island to tend to the failing family plantation. Even at the zenith of his public career, he had to move his mother and sister with him to Washington and put them up in an apartment where they managed to make the most of his money. It is important to appreciate the role these women played in his private life in order to understand certain ways in which he interpreted and created high culture, mostly through the mediums of law and letters. Michael O'Brien has interpreted Legaré's intellectual life as a dialectical study between the contrasting impulses of romanticism and modernity.[3] In this vein, law, for Legaré, was the space in which he struggled with the competing impulses of sublimity and utility. Much of Legaré's contribution to American law and letters is characterized by a tension between classicism and romanticism, between order and chaos, between man and nature, in other words, the very tension that exists in all forms of cultural expression. Throughout his short career, Legaré made valiant efforts to merge the two opposing forces, and perhaps his creation of the *Southern Review* was his most successful effort. In that journal, he not only managed to expound upon legal matters in an orderly fashion, but he was also able to write literary criticism that further brought the natural order under his command. In the later years of his life, Legaré was undertaking his most sublime feat, an English translation of Heineccius, a Latin civil law text.[4] Unfortunately for Legaré, Mother Nature had the last word, and his lifelong quest to be free of irrational influence ended unaccomplished.

Unlike Verplanck, Legaré was not a man of leisure—he needed to work for his money. Yet, in the South, especially South Carolina, lineage mattered more than wealth to one's social standing. Being a fifth-generation native southerner, Legaré was assured of public notice provided he had something to offer. What he did have to offer was a keen intellect, nurtured by years of classical studies, supplemented by a year traveling and studying in Europe. Upon his return to his home state, he attempted to practice law, his chosen profession, but he was so frequently called upon to hold public office that he never really had a lengthy, uninterrupted law practice. Legaré served in the state legislature, as state attorney general, as a diplomat in the Jackson administration, one term in congress, then finally in President John Tyler's cabinet. The parallels with Verplanck's political career are interesting. Both men began as Jacksonian Democrats and held their final posts as Whigs. But more importantly, neither man cared deeply for partisan politics. South Carolina politics was just as personal as, if not more so than, New York politics. While Verplanck's hostility to the Clinton machine was at least surmountable in

New York, Legaré's falling out with Calhoun spelled his doom in South Carolina.[5] The national scene looked more promising for Legaré who seemed to be doing the impossible when he suddenly died—he was making the Tyler administration look competent and respectable.[6] Legaré's long-term goal appeared to be to secure an appointment to the US Supreme Court. With this in mind, we can explore the thought of someone who was well on his way to achieving that goal. We can see how Legaré was able to use law as an expressive medium for viewing social relations and what his agenda was for using the law to exact social change.

ADRIFT IN A SEA OF THOUGHT

Vernon Parrington thought enough of Legaré to give him a ten-page subsection all his own in his famous multi-volume work, *Main Currents in American Thought*.[7] Parrington divided up American writers into two camps: Puritans and liberals. The former, while important shapers of American thought, were decidedly the enemies of all that was good and progressive—they were the whole problem with America. Not surprisingly for a progressive living and writing in the 1920s, Parrington viewed lawyers with great suspicion.[8] Not only were lawyers responsible for the self-seeking constitution Charles Beard had recently uncovered, but they were presently the best friends corporate America could afford. Moreover, the craftiest of all lawyers—the members of the Supreme Court—were basing decisions "upon an economic theory which a large part of the country [did] not entertain," namely, laissez-faire individualism, and borrowing doctrines from "Mr. Herbert Spencer's Social Statics"—and that was according to one member of the court himself.[9] The main problem with lawyers throughout American history was that they knew nothing but law—no political philosophy, no social theory, no history, and worst of all, no economics. Their naive faith in law was so contemptible because those with sinister interests could manipulate it to their own ends.

Legaré clearly troubled Parrington because he could not easily dismiss him as another politician only interested in power, or another lawyer who read nothing but law. "As a lawyer he was rather a philosophical historian than a special pleader," wrote Parrington, who was clearly impressed with the depth of Legaré's historical knowledge, and probably not a little less than intimidated by his writings. In commenting upon Legaré's work Parrington surmised, "Probably not three men in America comprehended the signification of half the references that he offered for the consideration of his fellow lawyers, or were competent to question his deductions."[10] But this erudition in philosophy and history was not enough to escape Parrington's scorn because Legaré's study of those subjects had taught him that abstract political theory—especially liberal theory, but one could imagine Marxism as well—was not only useless, but possibly dangerous. "Intellectual revolutionaries," as Parrington called them, would have no place in Legaré's political order. In place of a Puritan theocracy, Legaré would have a secular "lexocracy," and Parrington was shrewd enough to recognize the replacement of one capitalist superstructure with another when he saw it.

In Legaré's distaste for political theory, Parrington discovered the "inherent conservatism of the legal mind."[11] "Back of this ingrained conservatism was a tender Puritan conscience that must twist his legal studies to ideal ends. After all it was no other than a juridical romanticism that Hugh Legaré discovered in the bottom of his scholar's cup." There is no doubt that Legaré reveled in the romance of classical history, but, as I will argue below, Legaré was mostly conscious of his bouts of romanticism and constantly struggled against them with the sobriety of classicism itself. Parrington thought that in his obsession with classical legal history, Legaré had equated law with justice. He thought that Legaré was just as overawed by "black-robed advocates" as a medieval lady was by knights in shining armor, when, in fact, one's capacity for justice or chivalry had nothing to do with the costume one donned. Hence, Parrington said of Legaré's supposed romance with law:

> It is a pleasant fiction still believed in by lawyers of the old school, and to Legaré in his study it bore the very semblance of truth. He had read too many law books; he had speculated too little on politics; immersed in his codes, he had forgotten to inquire into the hidden springs of sovereignty. In his contempt for practical politics he had neglected to study even the primer of economic determinism. To the economic historian, Legaré's boundless faith in the sufficiency of legal process is incomprehensible.[12]

As Richard Hofstadter recognized, this was "a strong reproach to a man who died five years before the *Communist Manifesto* was written."[13]

We can appreciate, today, the concerns of Parrington, but there is certainly no need to maintain this portrait of Legaré. Modern historians are more likely to see a nonpolitical judiciary as the agent of progressive reforms and populist politicians as the conservative force more in need of reckoning. However, Legaré wanted to be no one's champion; he served no party, interest, or region. He did not use the law to promote cotton interests, slavery, or Charleston in any localized sense. He performed his duties as lawyer, office holder, and journal editor, for one primary reason—self-amusement. Legaré was especially introspective and enjoyed theorizing about what made the world go 'round, so to speak. He took all his work very seriously, and appeared rather Puritan-like to others, but he believed in no metaphysical truths, or at least he saw none that had any serious bearing on day-to-day societal functioning. Although Legaré believed in Nature, law and politics were largely unaffected by that entity. Legaré saved the contemplation of Nature for his literary, philosophical, and historical endeavors. And here was the conflict. Legaré could express his rational nature in public, through his complete mastery of law and politics. Law required scientific study, but its foundation was completely man-made and thus entirely subject to historicization. Law was the realm in which man could perfect his dominion over man-in-society. Politics was the emotional, non-scientific counterpart to law. If any individual was to exert social control, he needed skill in both areas. Literature and poetry, however, were concerned with Nature. This was the realm of knowledge that contemplated man-in-nature. Nature was decidedly not man-made. Nature is what had deformed Legaré as a child, what had given him his mother and sister, and what he knew he could not control. His way of dealing with Nature was usually to ignore it, hence his disgust of natural-law philosophers so popular in Enlightenment Europe. Legaré was completely unsure whether Nature could be comprehended by man, and thus he had no patience for political and legal philosophies based upon dubious assumptions. Luckily for Legaré, human society was independent enough from Nature that it could be studied and managed in an entirely historicist fashion.

Legaré has usually been considered a man of letters as well as a man of law. However, given the legal scientists we have already seen in this work, more qualification is necessary. Legaré was an amateur literary critic, rather than a littérateur. Gulian Verplanck made his early career as a political satirist and edited Shakespeare late in life, Joseph Story published a book of poetry, and David Hoffman tried his hand at a multivolume literary history of Christianity. And although Verplanck, Story, and Hoffman were not on par with other literary lawyers like Hugh Henry Brackenridge, Washington Irving, William Cullen Bryant, or any of the other figures who earned Robert Ferguson's attention in *Law and Letters,*[14] they nevertheless had the drive to express themselves in such a distinct artistic fashion; Legaré was not so inclined. His first biographer, who came out of an English department, criticized his writing as self-centered, even his personal correspondence, and his standards of excellence as unreasonably high. She also noted his tendency "to judge every contemporary piece, regardless of its purpose, by the measure of the classics."[15] But this should not be surprising if we keep in mind that literary criticism was, for Legaré, his sanctum of self-exploration, the realm in which he could war with Nature. Literature was not law—it had no scientific or man-made basis to it. If Byron fascinated Legaré—as he indeed did—it was not because his poetry was excellent in comparison with the work of other poets, it was because Legaré saw Byron's work as the product of someone to whom he could relate, someone who had similar difficulties with a mother and a sister.[16] In short, Legaré's literary criticism was his attempt to grapple with the irrational Nature he would otherwise gladly ignore in his daily interactions with the social world through law and politics.

The other standard interpretive trope we must confront is the charge of political conservatism. This is a label applied to any public figure from the South, especially South Carolina, who was unable to extract himself from his cultural milieu to the satisfaction of modern historians. To Parrington's great credit, he engaged with Legaré's thought before passing judgment on his supposed intellectual conservatism. But too frequently, Legaré is written off in one sentence as just another states' rights demagogue. This interpretation must give way if we are to understand what animated someone like Legaré in jurisprudential affairs. Legaré took American society as he found it, complete with sectional politics and distinctive cultural characteristics. His years of study and contemplation of law and politics gave him a decided preference for purely material considerations over idealistic abstractions in matters of public policy. Legaré was a strong unionist in national politics but issues of morality played no role in this public realm. In law and politics there was no single way-things-were-supposed-to-be—no natural order. Slavery existed in America, especially in South Carolina, but Legaré had no inner-voice (no God-substitute) telling him this was wrong. However, his study of legal and political history convinced him it was far from a desirable condition for the American South. And if Legaré preferred to worry about the applicability of Roman law and Byron to American law and society instead of slavery, this did not mean that he was compromising on the issue. To pin the label "states rights southerner" on Legaré is to falsely ascribe to him moral views he never held. In order to morally compromise on an issue, one must think it a matter worthy of principled speculation in the first place, and no matter of public concern was such an issue for Legaré. Legaré's heart bled for no one, except perhaps himself, and even then the only solution was to brood over a poem, not to pass a law. Slavery did not morally trouble Legaré, Verplanck the New York Copperhead, or the English immigrant Thomas Cooper, and even the New England judge, Joseph Story, was able to treat slavery as a matter of political compromise. The ease with which Verplanck was reabsorbed into New York high society after the War tells us much more about the supposed morality of the great cause than anything else. Legaré comfortably interacted with black people both at home and in Europe, but he preferred to write about the more interesting legal institution of Roman slavery, which had a noble, masculine aspect to it, rather than fall into the trap of philosophical speculation about the morality of American slavery. American slavery, unlike Roman slavery, served no logical, scientific purpose, and should have been handled accordingly.

A NON-TRADITIONAL LEGAL EDUCATION

Legaré attended the South Carolina College and graduated a few years before Thomas Cooper was installed as its new president. After college he studied law for three years, but not in the usual fashion. Rather than enter the law office of an established attorney to serve a standard apprenticeship, Legaré's former teacher, Mitchell King, a leading practitioner in Charleston, acted as his patron, funding Legaré's own independent study at home.[17] After his years of domestic legal study, at the age of twenty-one, he decided a trip to Europe to study the civil law would be a good way to round out his legal education.[18] His mother caused some drama at the prospect of him leaving home, but he managed to get away. His intention was to study law at the University of Göttingen. While visiting Paris he learned of political disturbances in the area and the University of Edinburgh was recommended to him as a good alternative. He took the advice and spent the winter of 1818–1819 studying in Scotland, home of his maternal Swinton ancestors.

While at Edinburgh, Legaré studied four courses, natural philosophy, mathematics, chemistry, and civil law, as well as independently learning Italian. He decided to limit the study of his three non-legal courses to the one-hour daily lecture time in favor of spending eight to ten hours each day reading civil law. The professor of civil law at Edinburgh that term was Alexander Irving, whom Legaré's traveling companion, William Preston, described as "a man of small talent and moderate learning," although "earnest and attentive."[19] The class was conducted entirely in Latin with daily examinations on the course readings. Legaré threw himself into his studies fully: "On one occasion he found himself at breakfast Sunday morning, on the same seat where he had breakfasted the day before, having remained in it four and twenty hours."[20] Preston recalled another extraordinary occasion:

> It happened once, while Mr. Legaré was under examination, that some difference of opinion arose between him and the professor, on the construction of a passage in the *Institutes*. Mr. Legaré maintained his opinion with warmth, and at length astonished the class and the professor by the elegance and facility of his diction and the extent of his reading. Dr. Irving thought the character of the discussion such as to require from him a written exposition of the point in controversy, which he sent to a member of the class, a friend of Mr. Legaré.[21]

While we should expect a eulogist to exaggerate a bit, it seems certain that Legaré came to Edinburgh well prepared to study the civil law and took full advantage of his opportunities while abroad.

According to Preston, Legaré did not originally regard the civil law "as an object of systematic study," but rather as an addendum to his previous classical studies. However, "the judicious, or perhaps the lucky selection of Heineccius as a text book for the class, gave an interest to the study which it might not have derived from the professor." This surely explains Legaré's continued fascination with the work and his unfinished undertaking of translating the work for American publication. Indeed, twenty years after his study in Edinburgh, Legaré continued to judge new works on the civil law by that standard.[22]

More than a decade removed from his time in Edinburgh, but no less another study-abroad session, was his four-year stint as an American diplomat in Brussels. Legaré came to the attention of Louisiana codifier Edward Livingston, then serving as Jackson's secretary of state. Legaré gained Livingston's notice with his first oral argument before the US Supreme Court in 1829. Livingston was impressed "by the unusual display of civil law erudition" in Legaré's argument.[23] According to Preston, during the time that Legaré served as South Carolina Attorney General from 1830–1832, he was growing increasingly unhappy with the common law and thought that more intensive study of the civil law would allow him to eventually make useful contributions to the American legal system. Livingston, aware of Legaré's desires, wished to aid this undertaking, which would presumably help all those wanting to make civilian contributions to common-law America. The secretary of state offered Legaré the position of *chargé d'affaires*. "The mission to Brussels was accepted by him, and tendered by Mr. Livingston, mainly with a view to this object."[24] Legaré's appreciation and advocacy of the civil law, as we will see, came to be appreciated by many like-minded reformers.

THE ADVOCATE IN PRACTICE

One of the first cases Legaré argued before the US Supreme Court is quite telling on a number of levels. We see Legaré's desire to separate law and morality especially clearly. We also get to see the range and breadth of Legaré's learning and how he attempted to get the judges to follow along. However, we also get an insight into the author of the opinion, Justice Joseph Story, who ruled against Legaré, and had a more difficult time cleaving moral consideration away from legal ones.

Shanks v. Dupont was a property dispute arising out of occurrences dating to the American Revolution. Thomas Scott was a native South Carolinian and an American patriot who died intestate in 1782. Scott's sole heirs were his two daughters, Ann and Sarah, who each took one-half of the estate. Sarah married a South Carolina native and had children, but Ann married a British soldier, Joseph Shanks, during the occupation of Charleston and subsequently removed with her husband to Britain where she had five children and lived the rest of her life. Both Sarah and Ann died intestate in 1802 and 1801, respectively. Thomas Scott's property was involved in some litigation and the court ordered the land be sold. Thus, the case of *Shanks* was a dispute between Thomas Scott's grandchildren over whether the British-born children of Ann Shanks were entitled to half the amount received for their grandfather's land. Because English law forbade foreign-born children of foreign fathers from inheriting land, it was held in the court of appeals that the Shank children were not legal heirs to the proceeds of their grandfather's estate; this holding was not challenged in the Supreme Court. What was challenged, was the citizenship of Ann Shanks, because if it were held that Ann somehow became a British subject by the fact of her removal to Britain, then certain peace-treaty provisions would apply to allow for the inheritance of the estate by her children. Legaré was retained by Scott's American grandchildren to argue that their cousins were not entitled to the estate and that, as the sole heirs, they were entitled to the full sum of the sale of the land. The legal question of citizenship, however, verged close to—and in less able hands intersected with—the political aspects of the issue. Unfortunately for Legaré, his civil-law learning, which had impressed the South Carolina court, held no sway with Joseph Story, who carried the Supreme Court in reversing Legaré's initial victory. Even though Legaré lost the case, South Carolina native, Justice William Johnson, delivered a dissenting opinion that made Story's judgment look anemic by comparison. Although Story's opinion was more substantial than Marshall's *Laidlaw* opinion that had provoked Verplanck, it still lacked a solid rationale beyond summary citations to precedent and vague intuitions. On the other hand, it was obvious that Johnson had put Legaré's argument to good use in crafting his dissent because its breadth is astonishing by any standard.

As Chancellor Desaussure noted in his original decree, this was a "tedious case."[25] Not only did it raise questions of old English statutes on wills and inheritance, but also state reception statutes of English law, treaty interpretation, and most troubling, the common law of allegiance, which may or may not have been bound up with natural law and the law of nations. If anyone was capable of mastering this case, however, it was Legaré. Unfortunately, there was one non-legal factor Legaré could not control—the factor he never could control—nature, which worked against him through the irrational emotion of sympathy. Sympathy was on the side of his opponents, and even Desaussure recognized this while ruling in his favor:

> For it seems peculiarly hard that these unfortunate persons should lose their inheritance, because their father was an alien, and they being born abroad cannot inherit their American mother, on account of his alienage, and because their mother was a citizen, and therefore her children are not protected by the operation of the treaty of 1794, as they might have been if she had been a British subject. Judges however do not make, but administer the law.[26]

This language must have been triumphant for Legaré on several counts. Most importantly, he won over a majority of the South Carolina chancellors. His victory in the state court, however, was clearly a triumph for the logic of the law over the chaos of emotion. That this was explicit could only have sweetened the win because in Desaussure's words we have a clear recognition that law was capable of subduing nature as long as all the jurists played along. Story, however, was less than a team player in that he allowed his romantic instincts too much headway into the masculine realm of law, and thus spoiled Legaré's second appearance at the bar of the US Supreme Court.

Story's conclusion for the Court was that the peace treaty of 1783, in which Britain recognized the independence of America, fixed Ann Shanks's allegiance to the British crown, and therefore allowed her British-born children to inherit her half of her father's estate under the terms of the treaty of 1794. The common law of allegiance held that an individual could not renounce his citizenship or subjection to a particular state; only the state could dissolve those bonds. Thus everyone agreed that Ann's marriage to a foreigner and her removal to another country did not alter her American citizenship. What Story claimed altered her status, and thus made her a British subject, was the peace treaty of 1783, which "took the actual state of things as its basis." Since Ann had been in Britain since December 1782, and "adhered to her [Britain]," "the treaty deemed" her a British subject.[27] The problem for Story was that there were far too many gaps in his logic, especially the consequences. In 1783, before the federal Constitution was in existence, citizenship was entirely a state matter, and as Justice Johnson asked, "when did South Carolina renounce the allegiance of Mrs. Shanks?" Moreover, had Ann Shanks become a British subject in 1783, then, under South Carolina law, she would not have been eligible to inherit her father's estate at all. From the policy side of the issue, Ann never needed the protection of the treaty of 1794, which prevented the confiscation of British and loyalist land precisely because she was a South Carolina citizen. While alive, she could have sold, encumbered, or devised her half of the estate, but unfortunately for her children, she never claimed the property. Finally, there were innumerable American citizens who were in Britain in 1783 who later returned to America after hostilities cooled and were recognized as American citizens without any renunciation by the British crown.[28] But Justice Story was not troubled by any of these arguments, instead he expressed his true motivation for ruling as he did: "If the treaty admits of two interpretations, and one is limited, and the other liberal; one which will further, and the other exclude private rights; why should not the most liberal exposition be adopted?"[29] It should be clear why this sort of reasoning was troubling to Legaré, who sought more certainty from the law than, "let's be fair and generous," which is what Story's rationale amounted to. Elsewhere, we will take a closer look at how Story was never comfortable putting to rest the romantic poet he had once tried to become. For the present, we need to consider how Legaré approached the case of *Shanks* to see how romance, sympathy, and emotion, and hence, nature, played no role in law.

What Story had done was to allow Ann Shanks free agency to "adhere to" whichever government she wished; in other words, to elect which political society she wanted to join. Story's notion of political society, however, was far too liberal for Legaré. It sounded too much like Locke and Rousseau, those political theorists who had no business invading the realm of law and who only tended to cause trouble for one trying to make sense of things. Justice Johnson admitted that a number of years earlier, on circuit, he had once fallen prey to social compact theory. "But more mature reflection has satisfied me, that I then gave too much weight to natural law and the suggestions of reason and justice; in a case which ought to be disposed of upon the principles of political and positive law, and the law of nations."[30] There can be no doubt that it was Legaré who set straight Johnson's immature impulses and guided his entire dissenting opinion.

One of the incontrovertible aspects of this case was that the common law of allegiance and of descents favored Legaré's clients. Everyone also agreed that positive law could alter the common law, but there was disagreement over whether it actually had. Story claimed, through a liberal canon of construction, that the treaty allowed those American citizens residing in Britain in 1783 to elect allegiance to Britain. Johnson and Legaré claimed the common law required an explicit renunciation of allegiance owed by South Carolina citizens to the state, which had never occurred. Moreover, Johnson denied that "the right to elect [allegiance] is inherent and unalienable in its nature, and remains above the legislative control of society, notwithstanding the social compact."[31] Johnson wrote, "there is not a writer who treats upon the subject, who does not qualify the exercise of the right to emigrate." A state may limit the right because of "a state of war, want of inhabitants, indispensable talents, transfer of wealth to a rival, and various other grounds." Johnson viewed emigration from a state, not as a personal choice, but as the resolution of an obligation between the individual and the community he was abandoning. He asked, "what other mode [of resolution] is there but a reference to the positive legislation or received principles of the society itself?" Sounding as though he was channeling Hobbes, Johnson rejected the contract theory of government, and asked rhetorically, "why then should not those to whom we must be indebted for advantages so indispensable to the development of our powers, be permitted, to a certain extent, to bind us apprentice to the community from which they have been and are to be procured? [By] what rule is the limit to be prescribed, unless by positive municipal regulation?" Story's unfortunate opinion "[brought] man back to a state of nature; at liberty to herd with whom he pleases, and connected with society only by the caprice of the moment."[32] Johnson's most ringing legal-positivist sentence put the exclamation point to all this natural-law-theory nonsense: "It is of importance here, that it should be held in view that we are considering political, not moral obligations."[33]

Legaré's theory of law had no room for states of nature, inherent rights, or the humoring of any individual's caprice. It is through an argument like Johnson's *Shanks* dissent that we can most clearly see Parrington's error in claiming that Legaré thought excessive study of law revealed truth and justice. It is also an apt forum for exposing exactly what the "springs of sovereignty" were, and for Legaré, unlike for Parrington, they were not "hidden." Law, government, and society were entirely artificial; truth and justice were not. Perhaps all Thomas Scott's grandchildren should have gotten along and shared and shared alike. Perhaps Ann Shanks should have been able to ally herself to whichever government she wished that was willing to take her in. But the fact was, that in 1830, all these question were clearly settled by law, by those artificial rules of conduct that allowed man predictable control over those things outside himself. The suggestion, inherent in Story's "liberal exposition," that man's laws had to answer to some natural, non-artificial, principles, was to introduce disorder into a previously reasoned system. The only sovereign with which the law was concerned was artificial, not natural. The motivation for any particular law—the springs of action for legislation—as we will later see, was their logical fit with each other and their worth for organizing society as proven by historical example. As a result, Legaré was not overly concerned with democracy as a means of legitimating sovereign action, but neither was he concerned with—in fact, a good argument could be made that he was blind to—the class-based consequences of any law.

STATE LEGISLATOR AND CODIFICATION

Upon his return from Edinburgh, Legaré was elected to the state legislature and served for several terms in the early 1820s. It was during this time that South Carolina began to consider the codification of its law. The House named Legaré chairman of the legislative committee charged with exploring codification in 1826. The result was a committee report that deemed it "inexpedient to attempt to codify the whole body of Common Law."[34] This led the author of the only book on early American codification, Charles Cook, to call Legaré "a champion of common law orthodoxy."[35] Cook's conclusion could not be farther from reality. Legaré was opposed to a certain caricature of codification, but he was even more opposed to "common law orthodoxy." The fact that Cook could not understand Legaré's highly intricate views is not surprising given the generalist nature of his work. Cook, however, is the only scholar to have mentioned this aspect of Legaré's political career; even his biographers omit it. However, what we learn from studying Legaré's writings on codification is that he shared the fundamental concerns of the other legal scientists who more enthusiastically embraced codification, but at the same time he worried about the mechanics of its accomplishment more than they did.

The legislative report that Legaré authored in 1826 is interesting because it serves as a prelude to what Thomas Cooper began to accomplish the following decade—a compilation of South Carolina law. Legaré began by clarifying that he did not object to codification of "the whole body of the Common Law" based upon concerns of expediency or practicability. His concern was more substantive, namely, that such a change would be "great and momentous" and "ought not to be ventured on but upon very urgent motives." Nevertheless, Legaré spent the bulk of the report explaining that such reservations over codification did not lead the committee to object to the safer route to law reform, i.e., statute consolidation.[36]

Because "the whole body of the Public Law of this Commonwealth" was largely statutory in origin, Legaré concluded that the public would benefit from "a lucid arrangement, a simpler and more concise phrasing," along with "expositions of the Courts of Justice in relation" to the statutes. It is especially noteworthy that Legaré singled out the statute-based public law, as opposed to the common-law-based private law, as worthy of reformers' attention. It was the public law—such as the election law and the militia law—that concerned "the political rights and duties of the citizens." Thus, it was of far more public utility that the laws that affected the citizenry on a daily basis were of the greatest notoriety. However, there was more to Legaré's conclusion than just a concern for a greater publicity of rights and duties. The committee chairman was clearly troubled by positive law more generally.

According to Legaré's plan, the commissioners charged with consolidating South Carolina's statute law were to discuss the adjudications of the statutes in addition to simply laying out the statutory text. As explained in the committee report, this annotation of the statutes was designed to increase the public's understanding of its rights and duties. Since the law "is not the statute alone, but the statute as expounded by the judges who are its constitutional interpreters," a record of the judges' interpretations of particular statutes would be of immense use in understanding the applicable law. The problem with written law was that language was ultimately imprecise and "it is often impossible to foretell what construction will be put on it when it comes to be the subject of judicial discussion." As a result, the unadorned legislative enactment might mislead the public "for whose instruction and benefit the law is published."[37] Why then was Legaré less concerned about the lack of clarity of the unwritten common law? The answer lies in Legaré's evaluation that common law was actually more "scientific" than American statute law, although neither compared to the intellectual elegance of the Roman law.

Legaré's concern over existing South Carolina statute law was evident in his committee report. The commissioners' proposed charge extended beyond "merely collect[ing] and class[ing] [the statutes] under suitable heads." Legaré thought they should go further in effecting "an entire change . . . by expanding, abridging and consolidating them."[38] He reiterated as much in an article for the *Southern Review* several years later as his legislative committee's proposal had gone nowhere in 1826. There, he wrote, "All our statutes ought to be revised, condensed, amended, explained, digested. They are in a sad state, it must be confessed."[39] The problem with statutes was their "definite form." Written law "arbitrarily prescribed" what was "mere authority." "The question arising upon such a law is not what is reasonable, but what is commanded." Under a statutory regime, the judge is merely the interpreter, whereas the legislator is a "self-willed dictator." Hence, a written code of law would often sacrifice justice to form. In the hands of lawyers, written law would sacrifice "general reasoning" to "verbal criticism."[40]

Even though Legaré shared the utilitarian's suspicion of the legal profession's ability to thwart just outcomes in favor of its own self-interest, he clearly did not share their confidence in the ability of the written word to constrain an ingenious verbal argument. As we will see in the next section, Legaré was well versed in Bentham's general moral theory. However, it is not clear that he ever fully engaged with Bentham's codification proposals.

A number of years later, Legaré composed an article on the history of Roman law in which he further elaborated his view of the relationship between legal science and written law. One of his main points in this article was that the popular notion of the Roman law as existing in code form from the beginning was misplaced. "There are those who seem to imagine that the civil law has existed as a science only since Justinian published it in the form of a code. The very reverse is the fact." The *Institutes* merely tried to record what was already a well-ordered system.[41]

The deficiencies of common law treatises furthered Legaré's suspicion that mere text could serve to further the scientific enterprise. According to Legaré, most existing treatises merely collected the existing cases in a particular field of law and set about distinguishing them. Thus, their real value was limited to situations in which a case arose that had factual similarities to cases already decided. Of what value were these works to a practitioner who had a case of first impression? In such cases, the "English text book hardly ever affords the least assistance to an inquirer. They never think of the *elegantia juris* of Gaius, of a scientific distribution of their subject, of genus or species, class or category; a new case calls for its application, the most trifling difference in accidental circumstances, gives rise to embarrassing doubt. In short, there is a total absence of all philosophical analysis, and systematic exposition."[42]

The "folly of Codification" lay in its attempt to be comprehensive, yet setting out rules for specific situations only. For Legaré, legal principles were far more important than legal rules. Unlike the more committed American Benthamites, he could not accept the notion that the principle of utility was sufficiently fundamental so as to guide an entire legal system. But he did agree that practice mattered more than abstractions. Legaré wrote that the "history of law" was "the most important part of the annals of every country." But it was Legaré's definition of law that placed him squarely within the camp of the legal science reformers:

> We mean not the law as it is written, but the law as it is applied and executed—not the letter, but the spirit—not the statute, but the interpretation—not the pompous and hollow Bill of Rights, but the daily practice of the courts in regard to such things as *habeas corpus*, trial by jury, and the liberty of speech and of the press. The law, in this only practical sense of the word, reveals the inward life and true character of a people. It *is* that very life and character, and a deputy sheriff may know more about them than a De Lolme or a Montesquieu.[43]

Assuring that the daily manifestations of law, so defined, proved themselves just required more than a simple code of statutes. It required scientifically trained interpreters. A code not only provided a false sense of security, it potentially hampered the scientific judge from meting out justice.

However, not all written volumes were necessarily overly speculative or of little use because too specifically tied to case law. When Legaré set out to review the first two volumes of Kent's *Commentaries*, he immediately praised the chancellor for demonstrating that "use may be made in our courts of the enlightened equity of the Roman jurisconsults."[44] However, Kent's recognition of the value of Roman law had not necessarily translated into an accurate grasp of the subject, at least from Legaré's viewpoint. This fault was most notable in the first chapter on the law of nations: "We are by no means so well satisfied with the execution of the first part of Chancellor Kent's work, as with the rest of it." The problem was that Kent had not fully appreciated the tripartite nature of Roman private law, and especially the *ius gentium*—what Kent was referring to as the law of nations. This misconception was most likely due to the fact that Kent was not a fulltime scholar—"it is not such a book as Chancellor Kent would have produced, had he been all his life, like Cujas or Pothier, a professor of law, instead of a judge." Even though the work was not as philosophically grounded as it might have been, the content of Kent's substantive law still made it an "excellent work."[45]

To philosophize about the nature of American law more thoroughly, it was necessary to take a step back from the rigors of legal practice. One could then muse about "the influence of America upon the mind," and as one did just that, it was not long before he realized that it "should become first and chiefly, if not exclusively perceptible, in the department of politics and law." America had to set out on new paths in politics and law because those two subjects tended to exhibit "strictly national peculiarities." More importantly, it was necessary to consider what law and politics were not concerned with, and that was "nature." Nature was the subject of poets, philosophers, and scientists, and "is everywhere the same." "But the case is very different with the civil and juridical institutions of a country." In these fields, "only the general principles of government and jurisprudence" can be imported.

Yet even within the realms of law and politics there was a great degree of difference between them. Politics was not a science because "no constitution in the world is worth a straw but public opinion and national character," and thus, it was a subject that had no analytical method with any predictive success. Legaré was somewhat anomalous in his evaluation that a written constitution was bad because it promoted formalism to the detriment of philosophical thinking in political matters. His central worry was that, in America, politics had been rigidified like a science, with the Supreme Court pretending to superior knowledge on matters that were rightly settled by public opinion. Legaré reminded his reader, "Liberty is a practical matter—it has nothing to do with metaphysics—with entity and quiddity."[46] Because politics was not a science, Legaré had little interest in it. He was much more fascinated with law.

Law "is at once the most exact and the most complicated of all the *moral* sciences" and, Legaré believed, it was the Roman law that best exemplified this fact. Of the civilians he said, it is "impossible not to be struck with the superiority of their truly elegant and philosophical style of analysis and exposition"; "every thing savors more of a regular and exact science" with them. Legaré would not stand by while the English were given credit for others' accomplishments. Dare one speak of the "boasted improvements of Lord Mansfield," Legaré was there to remind him that "that great judge invented nothing." What about Blackstone, "with all his prepossessions in favour of whatever is English"? "The truth is, that 'the learned commentator' was any thing but an original or philosophical thinker." Most other commentators on the common law were "mere *pragmatici*," that is, they were too concerned with applying technical rules to factual cases. "They seem to dread nothing more than generalization, or the stating a proposition in the form of a theorem," Legaré lamented.[47]

Ideally, American lawyers would learn to treat law as a "higher *art*." That meant that law was more than mere "technical skill" and that the "discipline of the forum" would not help in its refinement. Instead, the art of law "discovered itself in a lucid order, in precise definition, in sound interpretation, in a systematic development of the whole doctrine in question, and a logical deduction of all its legitimate consequences, at the same time that everything false or irrelevant was rigorously excluded by the analysis."[48]

THE PROBLEM WITH BENTHAM: THE OMISSION OF NATURE FROM LIFE

In August 1831, Legaré reviewed the first American edition of Jeremy Bentham's *Principles of Legislation,* which had been published the previous year in Boston. The work was the editorial product of John Neal, who can only be described as a man of moderate talents in both law and literature, prone to exaggeration and full of a sense of self-importance.[49] Neal, a native of Maine, had lived with Bentham for a period of time at Queens Square Place, his London residence. That experience was enough for Neal to consider himself the most intimate friend of Bentham's then living, and to surmise, "probably no person alive knows more of the true character of Jeremy Bentham than I do."[50] That conceit and arrogance oozed from every page of Neal's introduction to Bentham's work, which comprised just over half the number of pages in the volume. Neal deserves much credit for the work he actually did, which was to translate Etienne Dumont's French version of the work into English. Both halves of the publication came under Legaré's scrutiny in the *Southern Review.* What we learn is that Legaré did not suffer fools gladly, nor had he gained any more tolerance for political theory. We also get a glimpse at how his experience with the Edinburgh crowd influenced his understanding of Bentham.

It is difficult to appreciate Legaré's criticism of the work without understanding Neal's overly familiar tone. Throughout his biographical sketch, Neal constantly referred to Bentham as "Jeremy," with the clear intent that the readers not forget his intimate acquaintance with the philosopher. As a result, Legaré began doing the same in clear mockery of Neal. We learn from Neal's "uncouth jargon" that Bentham was afraid of ghosts, that he never left his house nor changed his bed sheets, and many other personal eccentricities that seemed highly out of place. As Legaré accurately noted of Neal's portrayal of Bentham, "it is difficult to conceive a more ridiculous figure than he makes him cut in his pages."[51] For example, Neal related Bentham's first, and last, foray into the practice of law at the English bar. Bentham had argued a cause citing precedent based on his extensive researches, all of which proved for naught because the cases had been overruled without being reported, or as Neal quotes Bentham, "the law had been altered without my knowledge or consent." After this humiliating defeat, Bentham refused to practice law again.

Legaré interpreted the incident as such: "for the man who was destined to reform the whole body of the law, does not seem to have been fitted to excel in the most important part of it, viz. the application of its principles to practice."[52]

Legaré's most recent biographer called him a "snob,"[53] and his review of Neal and Bentham might well provide support for that evaluation. The majority of the overwhelming sarcasm, however, is really reserved for Neal, whose pretensions earned no respect from Legaré. Characteristic of Legaré's review is this observation: "It would be exacting too much of a biographer to require him to write the life of another, without occasionally alluding to his own, and Mr. Neal had, therefore, taken the liberty of detailing, with the greatest precision, all the circumstances which led to his acquaintance with Jeremy." When Neal defended the circuitous route of the American edition of *Principles* from Benthamee to French to English, Legaré was amused by the admission that "the only means of understanding many of the great Reformer's speculations, is to read them in a foreign language." The resulting precision from Bentham's language, which Neal likewise defended, was also lost on Legaré: "The progress which the Philosopher had been gradually making in this corruption of style, is rather a singular phenomenon in itself, but it is not more strange than his biographer's notion that it is to be explained by the tenderness of Mr. Bentham's conscience."[54] At this stage, we can already detect Legaré's disgust for Neal's hero-worship of Jeremy, the Reformer, and the Philosopher. That sort of subservience was a clear sign of intellectual weakness, especially since Neal was more interested in the irrational parts of the man, rather than the logical ideas that made any study worthwhile.

When Legaré considered the substance of the *Principles of Legislation*, he acknowledged, "That Jeremy Bentham is a most vigorous and original thinker cannot be denied." What Legaré could and did deny, however, was that Bentham's utilitarianism was an attractive philosophy for life. In short, Legaré thought Bentham wasted too much time on his theory of language, that he was mistaken in turning moral philosophy into a science, and that his whole theory was impoverished by its lack of appreciation of nature as an unknowable force. In other words, Bentham did exactly what Legaré counseled against—he attempted to bring nature into the realm of legal theory. Although the results of Bentham's utilitarianism were not disastrous like the state-of-nature philosophers, Benthamism was aesthetically unappealing.

Legaré's interpretation of Bentham seems to have been influenced by his interaction with the folks at the *Edinburgh Review*. Dugald Stewart was away from Edinburgh the year Legaré was in residence, but it is clear from his writings that Stewart had a large impact on Legaré's own theories. As John Dinwiddy has written, the Scottish philosophy of Stewart was dominant in the *Review* at that time, and his followers "had objections to utilitarianism as a general system of morality."[55] As we will see, Legaré's criticisms of Bentham also closely resemble those Thomas Carlyle published in the *Review*, in which he discussed utilitarianism's preference for "prudence rather than virtue."[56]

The first substantive criticism of Benthamism is Legaré's objection "to ethical *science*, strictly so called—to inquiries into the *principles* of morals."[57] Legaré assured his readers that he had no objection to ethical literature or art, just ethical science. Science, being entirely a human creation of much utility itself, had absolutely nothing to do with ethics or morals. The term "moral principles" had no meaning for Legaré because the realm of the moral was the realm of the natural, and therefore, unknowable to man, who was the sole inventor of principles. How did man come upon principles for legal and governmental conduct? Legaré's answer was through the study of history, from which one could detect what had worked and what had not. It is true that this assumed some sort of human nature that was unchanging, but that was not man's concern because it was not in man's control. Bentham, on the other hand, began with nature: "Nature has subjected man to the dominion of *pleasure* and *pain*. To them we are indebted for all our ideas. To them we refer all our opinions, and every judgment we give."[58] But Bentham did more than explain a phenomenon of nature, he laid down a rule of conduct, according to Legaré. Explaining nature was not problematic, it was what poets and artists did—it was a pleasurable experience. However, Legaré was unimpressed with Bentham's explanation: "We have searched in vain for any substantial addition which it has made to the previous stock of knowledge upon the subject—whether for theoretical or practical purposes." The theoretical aspect of utility, Legaré thought, was merely a repackaging of the obvious. With regard to knowledge of human nature, Legaré's rhetorical questions best establish his feelings on the matter: "What can you tell a man of himself, which he has not over and over again experienced? . . . But what discovery is to be made in human nature, at this time of day? What nook had been left unexplored in the heart?—what *terra incognita* in the mind of man?"[59] In other words, if moral philosophy was a species of self-exploration, like literature and art, then Bentham was not particularly original or creative because he offered nothing new for one to contemplate about man-in-nature. What Bentham said about man-in-society, however, was slightly original, although rather derivative of the Epicureans, and definitely problematic.

The practical aspect of utility, Legaré thought utterly impractical; he characterized it as "the absurd affectation of mathematical exactness, in a matter which does not admit of it."[60] It was not Bentham's utilitarian foundation Legaré found problematic, it was "the *spirit* in which [the] doctrine [was] preached and the purposes and the character" of the preacher. Legaré understood pain and pleasure as human motivators but absolutely disagreed that they alone should guide conduct. Legaré committed the Edinburgh error of supposing that Bentham was advocating utility as a code of personal ethics rather than as a purely political theory. However, he had plenty of reservations about the political, social engineering, aspects of Benthamism as well.

The spirit in which Bentham reduced all human motivation to pain and pleasure was cynical, thought Legaré. Moreover, it was arrogant to think that one could explain the whole of nature in one sentence. This is how Legaré saw Bentham treating nature:

> The presumptuous and reckless confidence which such views must needs inspire, is not the least pernicious of their effects. A thorough bred Utilitarian, or rather Benthamite, is never wrong. . . . Talk to him of the voice of nature or the instincts of the heart, he laughs outright at such childish and ridiculous superstition. To say that his sensibilities have been extirpated by the stern discipline of his school, is only to say that he is an Utilitarian—but a worse effect, if possible, of this discipline, is the inevitable extinction of that chastity of moral feeling, which has never sinned even in thought.[61]

Legaré was acknowledging that Benthamism, as a school of thought, could work, but at great cost. Most people did not realize that what they viewed as their own motivations for action—sympathy, desire to please God, parental duty—could be reformulated as nothing more than pursuit of one's own pleasure. Legaré thought it was not a good idea to start getting people to think this way, because then one would lose the unconscious—perhaps natural and inexplicable—virtue that most non-utilitarians possessed. The result, Legaré thought, would be quite startling:

> It is the boast of Jeremy, that by his version of the maxim just cited, he has exploded altogether, what he calls the system of sympathy and antipathy—that his disciples can very coolly argue propositions, of which the bare idea is revolting to people whose consciences are more nice than wise—and that, if his sect spread, civilized nations may not long have to envy savages the right of destroying their sickly children and superannuated parents, or Mr. Mill, jr. or Mr. Francis Place, or any other good Malthusian, boggle about teaching and practising infanticide as "the sovereignest remedy on earth" for a glut in population.[62]

For Legaré, there was something positively good about not analyzing and decomposing social and moral practices that had historically been shown to be longstanding or the result of progress.

In Legaré's desire to preserve nature, rather than make it the mere handmaiden of man like Bentham would have, we see his romantic tendency in full force. Who else but a romantic would celebrate "the instinctive love which springs up in a mother's bosom, as soon as she has an infant to press it for nourishment," and at the same time shudder at the alternative notion that a mother would have "to work an algebraic equation of utility" before her love settled upon the child.[63] Such a scenario touched too close to home for Legaré to give the practice of utility a second thought. Legaré feared that had it not been for his mother's natural "instinctive love," a fatherless, crippled four-year-old might have produced a negative sum, especially when two healthy sisters and a failing plantation were added into the equation. But Legaré's romanticism was not simply reactionary, it was well thought out.

Legaré's romantic rationale was indebted to Hume's theory on sentiment, in which he distinguished it from reason. "The origin of the *sentiment* is within, and its operation is what is commonly called instinctive or mechanical—and therefore not liable to the objection of explaining that by *reason*—which must be resolved into an original law of nature."[64] Yet, for one who objected to Bentham's dismissal of sentimental religion, Legaré analyzed the workings of the religious sentiment in a similar manner. The reason religion had been far more effective "than any scheme of philosophical teaching" in retaining adherents was because it "inspire[d] a certain degree of enthusiasm, a divine fervour of feeling, a holy intenseness of purpose." Legaré was not religious himself, but he understood and shared the empty void religion filled. More importantly, he thoroughly enjoyed his religion-substitute, which was, first and foremost, classical studies, as well as literature and poetry. Cold, calculating machines were not completely human: "he who can look out upon the material world, as it lies before him in its grandeur and beauty, or read of the heroic doings of the mighty dead, without feeling his bosom warmed with that enthusiasm which is the soul of poetry, falls, so far, short of what man ought to be." Legaré could not bring himself to cut man off from nature the way the utilitarians had. For Legaré, man would never be fully triumphant over nature. Nevertheless, man could, and should, compartmentalize the natural and social.

"What a difference is there between a cold compliance with the letter of the law . . . and the religious veneration, the fervid and holy love, the entire devotedness of soul which Sophocles has consecrated in the person of Antigone!"[65] Astonishing as it was to behold, it was a difference that had to be maintained. The reason was because sentiment was personal, whereas reason was public. Not everyone experienced nature the same way. In fact, the beauty of nature was the diverse reactions it inspired in man. Society, on the other hand, had to accommodate all persons. Law, therefore—the rules of society—had to be non-foundational, or, more precisely, law's foundation had to be created from scratch with absolutely no illusion that law had to answer to anything more than human needs, which consisted of more than maximizing pleasure and minimizing pain, however natural that utilitarian formula might be.

In public life, Legaré was even more pragmatic than the other legal scientists. Although a romantic in personal matters, he never let sentiment, even a sentiment based in utility, stop him from advocating for orderly rationality. As Legaré made clear from his writings, he opposed the *spirit* of Bentham's utilitarianism, but it is not clear that that philosophical opposition led him in any other direction. Even Legaré's position on codification was tinged with a public-spirited concern whose skepticism for the undertaking lie primarily with professional distrust. His unwillingness to defer to authority—whether in the form of the legal profession, the political bosses, or philosophical foundations—made him an unlikely public officeholder. In his recorded table-talk, Thomas Cooper said, "when you become a member of the legislature take my advice, conciliate the fools; for they are always the majority. . . . It prescribes the course Legaré should have taken, but he chose the opposite. Sense, eloquence, speeches won't do. You must work into their favor."[66] This shared, public-spirited, elitism was what united the legal scientists at the most base level.

NOTES

1. Harriet Beecher Stowe, *A Key to Uncle Tom's Cabin; Presenting the Original Facts and Documents Upon Which the Story Is Founded* (Port Washington, NY: Kennikat Press, Inc., 1853), 39–46.
2. Biographical details come primarily from Michael O'Brien, *A Character of Hugh Legaré* (Knoxville: University of Tennessee Press, 1985).
3. Michael O'Brien, "Politics, Romanticism, and Hugh Legaré: 'The Fondness of Disappointed Love,'" in *Intellectual Life in Antebellum Charleston*, ed. Michael O'Brien and David Moltke-Hansen (Knoxville: University of Tennessee Press, 1986).
4. See Johann Gottlieb Heineccius, *A Methodical System of Universal Law: Or, the Laws of Nature and Nations*, George Turnbull, trans. (London, 1741; Indianapolis, IN: Liberty Fund, Inc., 2008).
5. Legaré's dislike for Calhoun and his policies is most clearly on display in his review of one of his Senate speeches. [Hugh S. Legaré], "Bankruptcy, and the Bankrupt Bill," *New York Review* 7, no. 14 (1840): 440–75.
6. See Marvin R. Cain, "Return of Republicanism: A Reappraisal of Hugh Swinton Legaré and the Tyler Presidency," *South Carolina Historical Magazine* 79, no. 1 (1978): 264–80. On President Tyler's own praise of Legaré, see John Tyler, "The Dead of the Cabinet," in *The Letters and Times of the Tylers*, Lyon G. Tyler, ed. (Richmond, VA: Whittet & Shepperson, 1885), 2:384–87.
7. Vernon L. Parrington, *Main Currents in American Thought*, 3 vols. (New York: Harcourt, Brace & Co., 1927), 2:114–24.
8. Richard Hofstadter, *The Progressive Historians: Turner, Beard, Parrington* (New York: Alfred A. Knopf, 1969), 408.
9. Lochner v. New York, 198 U.S. 45, 75 (1905) (Holmes, J., dissenting).
10. Parrington, *Main Currents in American Thought*, 2:116–17.
11. Ibid., 119.
12. Ibid., 120.
13. Hofstadter, *The Progressive Historians*, 410.
14. See Robert A. Ferguson, *Law and Letters in American Culture* (Cambridge, MA: Harvard University Press, 1984).
15. Linda Rhea, *Hugh Swinton Legaré: A Charleston Intellectual* (Chapel Hill: University of North Carolina Press, 1934), 129.
16. See Hugh S. Legaré, "Lord Byron's Character and Writings," *Southern Review* 5, no. 10 (1830): 463–522.
17. Duyckinck, "Hugh Swinton Legaré," in *Cyclopaedia of American Literature*, 2:247.

18. W. C. Preston, *Eulogy on Hugh Swinton Legaré* (Charleston, SC: Mayor and Aldermen of Charleston, 1843), 9.
19. Ibid., 12.
20. Ibid., 11.
21. Ibid., 12.
22. See Hugh S. Legaré, "Origin, History, and Influence of Roman Legislation," *New York Review* 5, no. 10 (1839): 269–334, 278.
23. Preston, *Eulogy*, 17.
24. Ibid., 19.
25. *Ex Parte Dupont*, 5 S.C. Eq. (Harp. Eq.) 5, 16 (1824).
26. Ibid.
27. Shanks v. Dupont, 28 U.S. 242, 247 (1830).
28. For example, Peter Van Shaack, who was run out of New York during the War because of his loyalist leanings returned in 1786 and began an early law school and proved to be one of the most eminent members of the New York bar. See Maxwell Bloomfield, *American Lawyers in a Changing Society, 1776–1876* (Cambridge, MA: Harvard University Press, 1976), 1–31.
29. Shanks, 249.
30. Ibid., 258.
31. Ibid., 261.
32. Ibid., 265.
33. Ibid., 262–63.
34. H. S. Legaré, Special Committee Report on Codification of the Law, South Carolina House of Representatives, December 1826.
35. Charles M. Cook, *The American Codification Movement: A Study of Antebellum Legal Reform* (Westport, CT: Greenwood Press, 1981), 128.
36. Legaré, Special Committee Report on Codification of the Law.
37. Ibid.
38. Ibid.
39. Hugh S. Legaré, "Codification," *Southern Review* 7, no. 14 (1831): 395.
40. Ibid., 403–11.
41. Hugh S. Legaré, "Origins, History, and Influence of Roman Legislation," *New York Review* 5, no. 10 (1839): 284.
42. Ibid., 286.
43. Ibid., 299.
44. Hugh Swinton Legaré, "Kent's Commentaries," *Southern Review* 2, no. 3 (1828), 77.
45. Ibid., 89.
46. Ibid., 74, 95–97.
47. Ibid., 74, 80–82.
48. Ibid., 83.
49. See John Neal, *Wandering Recollections of a Somewhat Busy Life: An Autobiography* (Boston: Roberts Brothers, 1869).
50. Hugh Swinton Legaré, "Jeremy Bentham and the Utilitarians," review of *Principles of Legislation*, trans. John Neal, *Southern Review* 7, no. 14 (1831): 268.
51. Ibid., 261.
52. Ibid., 263-64.
53. O'Brien, "Politics, Romanticism, and Hugh Legaré," 125.
54. Legaré, "Jeremy Bentham and the Utilitarians," 266.
55. J. R. Dinwiddy, "Early-Nineteenth-Century Reactions to Benthamism," in *Radicalism and Reform in Britain, 1780–1850* (London: The Hambledon Press, 1992), 354.
56. Ibid., 357.
57. Legaré, "Jeremy Bentham and the Utilitarians," 280.
58. Jeremy Bentham, *Principles of Legislation*, trans. John Neal (Boston: Wells & Lilly, 1830), 196.
59. Legaré, "Jeremy Bentham and the Utilitarians," 280.

60. Ibid., 283.
61. Ibid., 286.
62. Ibid., 294.
63. Ibid., 290.
64. Ibid., 291.
65. Ibid., 296.
66. Thomas Cooper, "Memoranda of Table-Talk of Judge Cooper," in ed. Duyckinck, *Cyclopaedia of American Literature*, 2:333.

SIX

New England Justice as Legal Scientist

Joseph Story

Joseph Story occupies a unique place in the debate over legal culture, and the extensive Story historiography is set out in the introduction. He was at once an intellectual who never closed his mind to new innovations in the law, while at the same time a judge on the highest court in the land with a vested interest in conserving the dignity of the established legal order. But Story was remarkably adept at keeping in balance these oftentimes competing impulses, and this is especially exemplified when he was confronted with ideas that pulled him in both directions. Although Story never embraced any radical reform agendas, notably those of the radical codifiers, he was hardly a proponent of the status quo that was the common law. It would even be difficult to argue that Story occupied some sort of middle ground on the ideological spectrum because his fascination with the defects of the common law ran so deep.

In the areas where Story appeared to be conservative, it was often a professional conservatism he was exhibiting. For example, his opposition to codification, though seemingly principled, exhibits a good deal of professional self-interest. Story thought that a complete code was impossible because "the imperfection of human language and foresight" would never account for the "infinite varieties of distinctions as to civil justice," especially in a nation growing further complex in its business and commerce.[1] But the lack of human foresight at rendering complete justice was all the more reason "we must be content" with a learned bench and bar. Likewise, Story was highly skeptical about the effectiveness of standalone courts of equity. He thought such courts had the tendency "to give a popular cast to our jurisprudence; to make it a sort of arbitration law, or to decide cases upon their own peculiar circumstances, without reference to any general principles."[2] Clearly, Story was not opposed to equity—in fact, he was highly critical of the common law's lack of an equitable sensibility. What he was opposed to was popularizing legal proceedings and removing from them the professional attainments of the bar.

Story did occasionally have a few praiseworthy words for the common law. Frequently, however, these commendations were for the common law's form, rather than its substance. What appealed most to Story about the common law structure, was the centrality of the judge to its unfolding. Thus, liberty, privacy, and property rights were secured by "the principle of common law, as it has been moulded and fashioned from age to age by wise and learned judges."[3] One such wise and learned judge whom Story admired was James Kent, chancellor of New York. Kent was a judge for whom "the easy course of general reasoning, popular analogies, and fanciful theories, has no charms."[4] Personal acquaintances and self-interest aside, however, Story long exhibited a respect for the bench. His proudest accomplishment while in the Massachusetts legislature was the passage of an act to raise the pay of the judges to secure their independence from political opinion. Reflecting back on that 1806 struggle Story said: "The measure has . . . contributed more to give permanence to her institutions, dignity to her jurisprudence, and steadiness to her prosperity, than any one single measure of the State during the last forty years."[5] As a Republican legislator, Story thought judicial independence so important, even for an all-Federalist bench, that this achievement cost him political friendships.

Story's defense of Blackstone similarly advanced the profession's standing. Blackstone's *Commentaries* represented "a new epoch in the annals of the common law." Despite this achievement, according to Story, "There have not however been wanting of late years attempts to undervalue the importance of these Commentaries." But what Story was eager to defend, again, was not so much the substance as it was the form of Blackstone's work. Prior to Blackstone, legal treatises "were little more than a collection of decisions under general heads, without any attempt to systematize the matter, or subject it to a critical analysis." Once the *Commentaries* made their way to America, however, the common law took on new life. These four volumes made the common law, not only attractive, but also necessary, to up-and-coming statesmen in the United States. For Story, "the most incontestable proof of the excellence of the work is to be found in the striking effects which its publication produced in every department of the common law."[6] After Blackstone, all American leaders not only felt an increased ability to learn the various departments of the common law, but they also felt it their duty to do so. With American statesmen well versed in the common law, thanks to Blackstone, the bar and the bench were assured of the respect they were due and continued to experience during Story's tenure.

With the profession's position well secured and the bench leading the way, Story was able to focus critically on the substance of the common law, and he did not always like what he saw. If one thing is abundantly clear from Story's public writings, it is that common law desperately needed to acknowledge its past and future debt to the civil law when it came to substance.[7] This was especially the case with the branches most closely associated with commercial intercourse: maritime and admiralty law, insurance law, and even the foundational law of contracts. "The common law was an *utter stranger* to the principles of commercial jurisprudence, and slowly and reluctantly admitted them into its bosom; so that the age was always greatly in advance of the doctrines of the judicial tribunals."[8] Not "until the days of Lord Mansfield, was a victory gained by the spirit of the age and the influence of commerce over professional prejudices."[9] According to Story, the "character of Englishmen" was so jealous and insular that the common law of England rarely partook of foreign influence. "If the English common law were perfect in itself, and were susceptible of no improvement, it might justly refuse any foreign admixture. But no one would be so rash as to advance a pretension of any sort."[10] The problem with pure common law was its rigidity—best exhibited in the application of old forms of action to new situations arising within the commercial world. The solution for a nation "crowded with commerce and manufactures" was to search for "equitable principles to be applied to the new combinations of circumstances, which are daily springing up to perplex its courts."[11]

Equity, for Story, meant the application of "the general principles of jurisprudence" to "experience." What Story had in mind was clearly a sense of the Roman *ius gentium*. In fact he used the adjectives, "Roman," "Pretorian," and "masculine" to describe the application of equity to any given case.[12] But his sense of equity as universal justice is most explicit in his praise of the opinions of Lord Stowell: "One seems in them to be reading, not the law of England merely, but the law of the world—the results of human reason and human learning, acting on human concerns, with reference to principles absolutely universal in their justice and convenience of application."[13] Recall, however, that Story was also a critic of the establishment of courts of equity in the United States because of the tendency for them to assume a popular cast. But the deeper reason underlying his objection to chancery courts was that too much was left to judicial discretion, and thus it was "of infinite moment that it be administered upon determinate principles."[14] But where was a judge to look for the principles of equity and the "law of the world"? A good judge "draws from all sources, ancient and modern, the best and purest principles to aid, to illustrate, and to confirm his own judgment."[15] Valin, Emerigon, and Pothier, were but a few of the illustrious names dropped by Story. Regarding English judges' neglect of Pothier, it brought "a disgrace to the learning and literature of the nation."[16] It was thus a pleasure and a relief for Story to see a number of distinguished American legal scholars avoiding the disgrace of England.

CODIFICATION

Story's biographer, Kent Newmyer, determined to paint the justice as a "conservative activist," was forced to confront a "paradox" created by Story's persona as a "leading legal reformer" when it came to the subject of codification. Newmyer concludes that Story's hand was forced to embrace codification by the legal reformers around him. Story's reluctant arguments in favor of moderate codification "were addressed less to Benthamite radicals, of whom there were few in America, than to stubborn common lawyers who resisted any reform at all." Story himself assured a friend, "We have not yet become votaries of the notions of Jeremy Bentham."[17]

More recently, Blaine Baker has lamented the fact that "students of Story have tended to focus on his judicial and education activities, rather than on his actions as a legislative delegate on statutory consolidation and private law codification commissions." The unique and underexplored features that Baker sees in Story's codification efforts are the organizational aspects, which had "common roots in the contemporary natural sciences" and employed "the late-eighteenth century's spate of European doctrinal texts" as a model.[18]

My own reading of Story's law reform efforts echoes both Newmyer and Baker to a certain extent. It is within the codification debate that Story's desire for reform is most prominent. Yet his desire not be associated with "radicals" seems more political than philosophical. His more thoughtful essays in the *North American Review* and the *Encyclopedia Americana* display stronger strains of the reformist agenda, but in more intellectual tones. Certainly, the natural sciences and the civil law tradition both influenced Story's understanding of legal science, but that influence was not limited to codification, although, once again, it might be most visible within that realm.

In January 1837, the Massachusetts commission on the codification of the common law reported their findings. The commission consisted of five members and was chaired by Joseph Story, who also served as the sole author of the report.[19] He described the commission's legislative charge as exploring the "practicability and expediency" of reducing the common law of Massachusetts to a "written systematic Code." Before he could come around to the substance of the charge, he first thought it necessary to define what the "common law of Massachusetts" was. It turned out to be a mixture of two things: first, it consisted of the common law of England with numerous qualifications, and second, it consisted of "local usages and principles." Moreover, its "true nature and character" "consist[ed] of positive rules and remedies, of general usages and customs, and of elementary principles," all of greatly varying vintage. Thus, the common law was much more flexible than simple positive law, rather, it was "a system of elementary principles and of general juridical truths," which aided societal progress, especially in trade and commerce.[20] Its main mode of accomplishing this was through the methods of common law adjudication.

Story's description of common law adjudication is interesting in that it reveals a multi-layered process that eventually reveals the foundation of the common law as based in "natural justice." First, the common law judge looked for an applicable statute. One suspects, however, that if he failed to find one exactly on point, he did not care to extrapolate from anything contained in the statute books. Second, the judge searched for a "clear and unequivocal principle of the common law." If that also failed, then he attempted to uncover an analogous principle of common law. But again, reasoning by analogy appeared only to be legitimate for case law, and not statute law. If the judge was not inventive enough to find an analogous common law rule for the case before him, he then turned to "natural justice." If "natural justice" did not dictate the outcome of the case at bar, then the dispute was remediless at common law, and the legislature would have to pass a new statute to resolve the matter.[21]

We can take the field of obligations to show how this five-part process of common law adjudication worked in practice. Regarding an obligation in the abstract: "It is simply a dictate of natural justice, and from that source was adopted into the common law." It is not entirely clear what sort of obligation Story was referring to, but based on his next example, it is fair to assume it was some sort of explicit, voluntary undertaking. The second example was an implied obligation: "here, again, the courts acted upon principles of natural justice," and found that they could draw an analogy with the already existing law based upon the first example. Even though Story refers to the sense of natural justice in the case of an implied obligation, a court only had to go as far as step three, using existing common law that had been already reasoned upon natural justice. Story's final example was that of the negotiability of promissory notes. This example presented the case where the explicit common law offended a sense of natural justice by forbidding their negotiability. Hence, it was only a statute that could correct the error, not the common law court itself, which was strictly bound by its precedent. Had this error never been introduced into the common law, however, a court deciding the matter on a *tabula rasa* would have certainly been within its authority to recognize the analogy with other obligations and create a new common law rule in line with natural justice.[22]

With the definition of "common law" and its method of adjudication now settled, Story was ready to answer the question, whether it was practicable to reduce the common law to a code. His answer: yes and no.

"No," if it would mean that the common law would be arrested in its future development, but "yes" if the code was understood to be limited to the past and present state of the law only. If judges were limited by the code to a "direct application of the text," rather than being allowed to continue to create new common law, then "every case of wrong and injustice and oppression, not thus foreseen and provided for, would be wholly remediless."[23] Thus, Story's main hesitation in endorsing a complete code was that the bench might be limited in its development, and especially in its application, of principles of natural justice to the cases that came before it.

To allay his fears of a restricted judicial function, he created for his proposed code, three "fundamental rules for its interpretation and application." First, it was to be interpreted "as a code of common law . . . and not as a code of mere positive or statute law." This essentially meant that it was a restatement of the then-existing law, and as such, it was not "subject to a strict construction." The second rule was that the code was to be extended by analogy in appropriate cases. Finally, if the code was inapplicable, even by analogy, the common law was to govern the case under consideration "unless repugnant to the common law affirmed in the code, or to the statute law of the state."[24] By this Story must have meant that natural justice was to apply to the case, unless it offended common law precedent or a statute. These three rules would have assured that no code restricted continued social improvement. It also meant the code could continue to grow as the legislature engrafted onto it new common law rules that were being continually developed.

So just what was Story willing to codify? Again the answer is tripartite. The first code would consist of those familiar rules of "the common business of life" relating to "property, personal rights and contracts." These were especially amenable to codification because they were so far established "as to admit of a scientific form and arrangement" and they were also "capable of being announced in distinct and determinate propositions." The second code was to consist of "the definition, trial, and punishment of crimes, and the incidents thereto." The third and final code was to be "the law of evidence, as applicable both to civil and criminal proceedings."[25] Agreeing to codify property, torts, contracts, crimes, and evidence was no small concession for a "conservative."

The benefits of codification were threefold. First, a code promised to increase the popular knowledge of the law. Second, it would likely reduce the number of volumes necessary for consultation by consolidating duplication. Finally, it would result in the "abridgment of professional as well as of private labor." This third benefit was especially attractive to Story. It meant that the search for "nice distinctions and differences" and "nice shades of difference" would be reduced, if not eliminated, because the code would state "the true general rule" and the lawyers could then ignore a mass of potentially confusing cases of dubious worth.[26]

The greatest branch of law to benefit would be the law of contract, "which may be affirmed to be founded in sound sense, and adapted to the ends of justice." It was only recently that commercial contracts had "attained a scientific precision," which allowed the subject to claim "an indisputable title to be treated as a fixed system of national jurisprudence." Story also noted that "the Commissioners would especially recommend as the subject of a code the following titles, viz.: the law of agency, of bailments, of guaranty, of suretyship, of bills of exchange, of promissory notes, of insurance, and of partnership."[27] Interestingly enough, some of those titles coincided with Story's own volumes of commentaries.

The codification of Massachusetts common law also provided the state with the opportunity to correct some of the existing inequities inhering in the common law itself. Story added, "This, to be sure, ought to be done with a cautious and skilful hand, and with a deep sense of the delicacy of intermeddling with established principles. If, however, no changes are attempted except such as have the sanction of experience, and the support and approbation of enlightened judges and jurists, much may be done to introduce harmony, and consistency, and simplicity into the general system."[28] Again, we see Story's bold confidence in the power of the bench and bar to reform the system from within. The legislature may have been needed to provide the democratic legitimacy, but clearly this was a formality. It was the "enlightened judges and jurists" who maintained the fundamental sense of natural justice underlying the common law system.

FELLOW LEGAL SCIENTISTS

The names of David Hoffman, James Kent, Nathan Dane, Willard Phillips, and Hugh Legaré are probably foreign to most contemporary American lawyers, but they were among the period's most promising members of the bench and bar to carry forward reform efforts like those that interested Story. Story had kind words to say about each of these men, but it is clear that his affection was more than personal. All were involved in the effort to reform, restructure, and rebuild the common law from the top down and without any disturbance or diminution to the established profession. But just because this legal scientific intervention in the common law was undertaken by intellectual elites, it was not any less radical for it.

When speaking of any of these reform-minded legal scholars, the one commonality Story noted was their appreciation of European civil law.[29] This shared characteristic appeared to have no geographical boundaries. Fellow New Englanders of Story like Dane and Phillips were on the same page as the New Yorker, Kent, as well as the southerners, Hoffman of

Baltimore, and Legaré of Charleston. Moreover, this list of civilian admirers can be greatly expanded, and as it grows it becomes even more motley in terms of geography. We could add two more South Carolinians of foreign extraction, Francis Lieber and Thomas Cooper. Although Story had nothing nice to say about Cooper, he was close to Lieber, who published several of his articles in the newly founded *Encyclopedia Americana*. Lieber, the German émigré, dedicated to Kent his 1838 *Legal and Political Hermeneutics,* a work that attempted to apply Roman law methods of interpretation to the American system. We could move northward to Virginia, where Thomas Jefferson led a life-long attack on the English style of common law then dominant in America, and where his friend St. George Tucker published an Americanized version of Blackstone, greatly influenced by European natural law thought.[30] Tucker's son, Henry St. George Tucker, professor of law at the University of Virginia, carried on his father's efforts by delivering lectures on natural law to his students in the 1840s. Story did not think very highly of any Virginian save his chief, John Marshall, but that was mostly for political, not legal reasons. His coldness towards Cooper can be similarly explained. Story's silence on Cooper's achievement in publishing the first American edition of *Justinian* was odd to say the least. Moving further northward, the chief justice of Pennsylvania, Hugh Henry Brackenridge felt the need to correct Blackstone in his *Law Miscellanies*. That state would also be the second—after Tucker's Virginia—to see a whole new edition of Blackstone, *Pennsylvania Blackstone,* authored by John Reed as a "modification" of the original *Commentaries;* on the first page Reed notes that Pennsylvania would do well to "resort to the Roman civil law," at least in part. In the northern states we have the two major writers on contract law, Daniel Chipman from Vermont and Gulian Verplanck from New York, both of whom were motivated to write after reading highly formalistic and inequitable judicial opinions on commercial contracts. And finally, back in Story's home state, Caleb Cushing, a Massachusetts Democrat, was a vocal proponent of civil law education for American law students, and in 1821 translated and published Pothier's *Treatise on Maritime Contracts,* urging a new direction in that part of the common law. It is important to note what all these new publications were not, that is, a rejection of the common law *system*. While they may have been critical of the substance of English legal practice, they never doubted for a moment that scientifically trained lawyers and judges should be the ones making the major legal decisions. Examining Story's reaction to just a few of these figures will help emphasize this intellectual wave in favor of civilian learning.

David Hoffman, the first law professor at the University of Maryland, was the first major American legal pedagogue of the nineteenth century. While St. George Tucker was prominent in Virginia during his time at William and Mary, Hoffman's publications and originality put him in a class of his own.[31] Although he continued to represent clients, Hoffman considered his professorial duties central to his legal life, whereas Tucker, who sat as a judge during his entire tenure as an academic, considered his judicial duties paramount. Hoffman's first publication was in 1817 under the title, *A Course of Legal Study*. Story reviewed the work in November of that same year for the *North American Review*. In his review, Story took the opportunity to expound upon the novel methods of legal education and training that were then cropping up in the various states. What Story most approved of in these new methods was what he called the "regular system," complete with "scientifick arrangement and harmony of principles." This new systematization complemented the progress that had been made in other areas of knowledge, like "mathematics and physical science." Story described the benefit of the new juridical science as such: "instead of sparse and scattered maxims we have regular systems built up with general symmetry of parts," which made adjudication safer in hard cases because the opinions were now "founded on inductions from rules better established and more exactly limited." Story acknowledged the fears of conservatives who preferred the old system, which "distinguished and disciplined the lawyers of the black-lettered times." But he tried to ease their worries with an analogy, which seemed unnecessarily and politically provocative. New methods of legal education, like new roads, pave over the surface and make old roads less traveled. "But who can doubt that by such means the facility of intercourse and the interchange of every thing important in the commerce of life are greatly augmented, and that publick improvements circulate with ten fold rapidity and force?"[32] Who indeed, except perhaps his political opponents in Virginia.[33]

To what was all this progress and systematization due? The answer was, "that beautiful and rational system" of the civil law. Rather than imitating the common law's "turning upon nice distinctions," the infusion of the civil law had given American law a more solid foundation, especially in the areas of equity, bailments, bills of exchange, promissory notes, and maritime law. It was in these areas that "we may remark, how much had been gained by the accessions and alluvions of the civil law." It was for these reasons that what particularly pleased Story was "the enlarged and liberal view with which Mr. Hoffman recommends the student of the common law to a full and careful study of the admiralty, maritime and civil law." Story made the point of mentioning that, "if the note on the excellence of the civil law were not too long, we should gladly insert it in this place."[34] But interestingly enough, despite the length, Hoffman's praises of the civil law were not wholly complete, for Story saw fit to make additions to the *Course*'s list of readings on this subject, including Heineccius, Mackintosh, as well as ten other works.

When Story reviewed the Reports of Court of Chancery of New York, he found similar reasons to rejoice. As he read the cases, he noted that Kent had "drawn deeply from the commercial law of foreign nations" and had "nobly extended his inquiries beyond the common and commercial law, and explored the Roman jurisprudence through its texts and commentaries, with uncommon accuracy." In Kent's opinions, "we can every where trace the happy use of that marvellous system of doctrines which Justinian collected with so much care."[35] Likewise, in Nathan Dane's eight-volume *General Abridgment and Digest of American Law*, Story tells us that "large extracts are introduced from the civil, the French, and other foreign law," which "is of great practical importance to emigrants, to merchants, and to relatives residing in distant regions." Dane recognized that "the civil law itself is an inexhaustible treasury of general principles" and that "our law of contracts rests . . . on Roman foundations." Story wondered, "Can it then be doubted, that an incorporation of such of the civil law principles, as are illustrative of the common law, into an Abridgment, is of great value to students, and especially to those, who wish to acquire philosophical views of jurisprudence, and aspire to something beyond the reach of an ordinary attorney?"[36]

Two years before Story died, he eulogized Hugh Legaré at the beginning of one of his lecture classes at Harvard in 1843. Legaré died young, and because he was no "ordinary attorney," from Story's point of view his death was all the more tragic for what he left unfinished. Story said: "I had looked to see him accomplish what he was so well fitted to do, what, I know, was the darling object of his pure ambition—to engraft the Civil Law upon the jurisprudence of this country, and thereby to expand the Common Law to greater usefulness and a wider adaptation to the progress of society."[37] Legaré had studied in Scotland and then in Paris and when he returned he "devoted himself anew to the study of the Civil Law, with a view to make it subservient to the great object of his life, the expansion of the Common Law, and the forcing into it the enlarged and liberal principles and just morality of Roman jurisprudence."[38] Perhaps Story's most remarkable claim concerned Legaré's practice before his court as attorney general, not so subtly implying that the court as a whole was open to such suggestions: "This object he seemed about to accomplish; for his arguments before the Supreme Court were crowded with the principles of Roman law wrought into the texture of the Common Law with great success. In every sentence that I heard, I was struck with this union of the two systems."[39] Legaré's learning in the civil law was obvious to anyone who read his various publications in the contemporary journals. But as one who was intimately familiar with Legaré's legal practice, Story was insistent on vouching for "his attainments in the Common Law": "he devoted himself to the Common Law with a wise perception of its defects, and a purpose to ameliorate them with the riches of the Civil Law; and I may say of him, having seen his mastery of both systems of jurisprudence—that he walked with them triumphantly, the one in one hand, and the other in the other hand, in the path of a great jurist."[40] Story's point, though perhaps dramatically stated, was that

Legaré was no mere effete scholar of European styles; rather he was a solidly practical man who used his critical skills for the good of the nation. Story hit the mark when he commented upon Legaré's desire to meld civil and common law together, as we saw in the previous chapter.

Story is often portrayed as a defender of capitalism, with all the attendant heartlessness and greed conjured up by that ideology. Yet Story was no defender of the exploitation of the down and out—his views on slavery attest to that. It is true that Story reveled in the idea of commercial power and the expansion of national wealth, but if we carefully read the context in which Story made these pronouncement, we find a far different image of capitalism than liberal self-interest.

Whenever Story discussed commerce, he characterized it as a national virtue and took the perspective of a statesman concerned with American well-being. The driving force behind commerce was "ambition and enterprise, the love of wealth, and the desire of gratifying curiosity." But these catalysts, which admittedly sound individualistic, were merely the means to the end of a rather utilitarian outlook. Promoting commerce, Story tells us, "imparts life and intelligence to the body politic, increases the comforts and enjoyments of every class of people, and gradually liberalizes and expands the mind, as well as fosters the best interests of humanity." A commercial nation could expect the benefits—both material and intellectual—of manufacture and trade to flow throughout all classes of society. Therefore, it was imperative that the laws of the nation be adapted to aid, not to impede, commercial transactions. Yet, because of "the impatience of legislative control, manifested by the mass of the people," the most likely source of legal reform was from the legal scientists.[41]

Lord Mansfield loomed large in the mind of Story. He would have agreed with Legaré that there was nothing particularly original in Mansfield's substantive doctrines. But what Story most admired about the chief justice of the King's Bench was his accomplishments as a sitting common law judge. Mansfield was Story's case-in-point that the common law was not beyond equitable considerations, and that change for the better could come about without legislation. Thus, Story said, "He broke down the narrow barrier of the common law, against the prejudices of the age, and infused into it an attractive equity, which it seemed to all his predecessors incapable of sustaining." But it was not just any equity that Mansfield had employed; it was a uniquely Roman equity. Mansfield "was an excellent civilian, and from his Scotch education was early imbued with a reverence for the civil law." With an implied rebuke of the rigidity of Blackstone's architectural metaphor, Story noted of Mansfield, "if he ever removed from the temple of English jurisprudence, a single pillar of gothic structure, it was, that he might replace it with the exquisite finish of the Corinthian order, carved in Parian marble."[42] It is again worth noting, that the sort of reform Story was advocating, and that

Mansfield had actually accomplished, kept the legal profession secure in its gothic temples. To be sure, the reform efforts aimed at more than simple interior redecorating; they amounted to some serious interior restructuring. Nevertheless, the reforming legal scientists would use the existing blueprint as their guide, hence the importance of both analogy and precedent in common law adjudication; the precedent provided the blueprint, while analogies allowed for grander accomplishments.

The point in discussing Justice Story's views on legal science has been to contextualize the less familiar, although more reform-minded, legal scientists—Verplanck, Cooper, and Legaré. Understandably, Story's hesitation to take up reform causes was due in large part to the limitations put upon him by virtue of his role as Supreme Court justice. When Story did have the opportunity to weigh in on the proposed reforms, whether through a journal article or as a codification commissioner, his reforming instincts came out in fuller force than when sitting on the bench or when writing his Harvard-contracted *Commentaries*. Story not only understood, but fully appreciated, the philosophy of codification. Likewise, it was difficult to find a more vocal proponent of the civil law than Story. His official role sometimes put him on the opposite side of the legal scientists, as when he ruled against Legaré in *Shanks v. Dupont* or when he defended *Laidlaw v. Organ* against Verplanck's criticism in his *Commentaries*. That did not stop him, however, in subsequently engaging and praising their efforts of which he could not help but take note.

NOTES

1. Joseph Story, "A Course of Legal Study," *North American Review* 6 (1817): 49; Joseph Story "A Treatise on the Law of Insurance," *North American Review* 20 (1825): 62.
2. Joseph Story, "Reports of Cases Adjudged in the Court of Chancery of New York," *North American Review* 11 (1820): 156.
3. Story, "A Course of Legal Study," 45.
4. Story, "Reports of Cases Adjudged in the Court of Chancery of New York," 140.
5. Joseph Story, "Autobiography," in ed. William W. Story, *The Miscellaneous Writings of Joseph Story* (Boston: Little & Brown, 1852; repr., Union, NJ: Lawbook Exchange, 2000), 29.
6. Story, "A Course of Legal Study," 75.
7. See M. H. Hoeflich, "John Austin and Joseph Story: Two Nineteenth Century Perspectives on the Utility of the Civil Law for the Common Lawyer" *American Journal of Legal History* 29 (1985): 36.
8. Story, "A Treatise on the Law of Insurance," 53–54.
9. Ibid., 58.
10. Ibid., 60–61.
11. Ibid., 62.
12. Ibid., 62–63.
13. Ibid. 67.
14. Story, "Reports of Cases Adjudged in the Court of Chancery of New York," 156.
15. Story, "A Treatise on the Law of Insurance," 66.
16. Ibid., 63.

17. R. Kent Newmyer, *Supreme Court Justice Joseph Story: Statesman of the Old Republic* (Chapel Hill: University of North Carolina Press, 1985), 272–81.
18. G. Blaine Baker, "Story'd Paradigms for the Nineteenth-Century Display of Anglo-American Legal Doctrine," in ed. Angela Fernandez and Markus D. Drubber, *Law Books in Action: Essays on the Anglo-American Legal Treatise* (Oxford: Hart Publishing, 2012), 86–88.
19. The other four members included: Theron Metcalf, Simon Greenleaf, Charles E. Forbes, and Luther S. Cushing.
20. Joseph Story, "Codification of the Common Law. A Report of the Commissioners, January, 1837," in *The Miscellaneous Writings of Joseph Story*, 698–702.
21. Ibid., 702–3.
22. Ibid., 703–5, 719–20.
23. Ibid., 706–8.
24. Ibid., 716–18.
25. Ibid., 715–16.
26. Ibid., 721–26.
27. Ibid., 730–31.
28. Ibid., 733.
29. M. H. Hoeflich has been arguing the influence of Roman law on Anglo-American jurisprudence for over twenty-five years, and as far as I can tell, few have seriously engaged with his work. Hoeflich is much more suggestive than he is argumentative, but his writings are very relevant to the research undertaken here. See M. H. Hoeflich, *Roman and Civil Law and the Development of Anglo-American Jurisprudence in the Nineteenth Century* (Athens: University of Georgia Press, 1997).
30. See Craig Evan Klafter, *Reason over Precedents: Origins of American Legal Thought* (Westport, CT: Greenwood Press, 1993).
31. See Bill Sleeman, "David Hoffman: A Biographical: Sketch," in ed. Sleeman, *David Hoffman: Life, Letters and Lectures at the University of Maryland, 1821–1837* (Clark, NJ: Lawbook Exchange, Ltd., 2011).
32. Story, "A Course of Legal Study," 48, 56.
33. For the politics of internal improvements, see John Lauritz Larson, *Internal Improvement: National Public Works and the Promise of Popular Government in the Early United States* (Chapel Hill: University of North Carolina Press, 2001).
34. Story, "A Course of Legal Study," 46–48, 75–76.
35. Story, "Reports of Cases Adjudged in the Court of Chancery of New York," 141.
36. Joseph Story, "A General Abridgment and Digest of American Law," *North American Review* 23 (1826): 23, 24.
37. Story, "A Course of Legal Study," 821.
38. Story, "A Course of Legal Study," 822.
39. Story, "A Course of Legal Study," 822.
40. Story, "A Course of Legal Study," 823.
41. Joseph Story, "Laws of the Sea with Reference to Maritime Commerce during Peace and War," *North American Review* 7 (1818): 324–25.
42. Ibid., 341–42.

Conclusion

Modern political debate in the United States is known for being tinged with a certain amount of religiosity that frequently claims for itself an ideological inheritance bequeathed from the founders of the American legal system. Hence, American cities, mostly southern, have placed displays of the Ten Commandments in courthouses and on other public buildings for the alleged purpose of reminding the public of the origins of US law. These passive symbols, however, seem inconsequential compared to the real work done by religious faith in the lawmaking realm. It is not uncommon to hear the commands of the Bible cited as reasons for creating public policy either through statute or judicial opinion. However, the lessons of this work have been that the intellectual founders of the American legal system—the legal scientists—strongly preferred reason to faith or instinct. Moreover, to the extent the English legal inheritance proved too unreasoned, they demanded the creation of a native legal system from first principles, whether through the piecemeal overruling of English legal precedent, the reliance on civilian rationality, or the implementation of legal codes logically deduced.

When legal scientists first began to coalesce intellectually through the medium of the printed word, they had already made the connection between law and method via the wide distribution of Blackstone in late-colonial America. Individual efforts at establishing law lectureships within the existing college structure at William and Mary, Columbia, and Transylvania in the late-eighteenth century further sowed the seed that law could be studied methodically like the other respectable fields of inquiry. Within American colleges, however, the law could also be Americanized to suit new needs. This process of Americanization, however, was most deliberately tied to rationalizing the law based upon new Enlightenment principles of utility. The promotion of democracy, markets, or political parties was subordinate to the underlying idea that the law had to promote temporal happiness to qualify as good, that is, moral, law. Yet, the promotion of legal science was not the strict province of the legal profession. The new promoters of the legal science—the law professors—could inculcate these lessons in the minds of all civically minded college youth, who, at the time, would have been the ones most assuredly leading their polities in the next generation.

The legal scientists did more than just lecture and write philosophically-based treatises. Their activities were uniformly motivated, even if they responded to local conditions in implementing the details of their legal reforms. Practicing legal scientists, like Hugh Legaré, argued on behalf of their clients emphasizing the rational consequences of their position even more so than its relation to precedent. Scholarly legal scientists critiqued the work of the courts, such as Verplanck did with *Laidlaw*. Legal scientists who held elective office or public office worked toward rationally based policy changes viewed through the lens of public utility. Legal scientists who served as judges enjoyed the freedom to craft opinions free from the precedential clutter of English common law opinions. Indeed, judges like Cooper and Verplanck could explain their rationales in a consequentialist manner, citing civil law as reason demanded.

The end of legal science has no clear date. There was no final book or lecture. No one's death can be regarded as particularly symbolic in this regard. Instead, the generational concern that motivated people like Verplanck, Cooper, Legaré, and Story simply faded for the American bar's mid-century generation of leaders. National distinction was surely less pressing to those who came of age during the height of antebellum legal reforms. We even see legal scientists' own interests shift or wane in their latter years. Thus, John Neal, who had served as one of Bentham's personal secretaries for a year in the late-1820s, initially returned to America, practiced law, began a newspaper devoted to legal theory, and edited Bentham's *Principles of Legislation*. However, he eventually gave up legal scholarship to write fiction—novels that read "as a fictionalization of ideas advanced by Jeremy Bentham."[1] Simon Greenleaf, the prominent evidence treatise writer and Harvard law professor, refused overtures in 1850 to serve as the founding professor of a proposed law school at Bowdoin College. It appears that Greenleaf had "become less sanguine that public opinion was an expression of a united wisdom" that could be nurtured to a proper understanding of the foundations of moral obligation to the law.[2]

The diminished interest in propagating institutions of legal science, whether educational institutions or media institutions, might be seen as part of a generational movement's natural senescence. On the other hand, the ideas of the legal scientists might have become so commonplace by the 1850s that specific institutional support no longer seemed necessary. What is certain, however, is that the first generation of American legal elites ensconced themselves within a movement known as legal science that was responsible for the first set of uniquely American legal ideas. These ideas are found in university lectures, normative legal treatises, and codification proposals from the 1820s and 1830s. The fact that legal education became more institutionalized and formalized, the fact that critical publications abound, and the fact that organized statute law now far eclipses common law, all seem to be testaments to the ultimate success of the original legal scientists.

NOTES

1. David J. Carlson, "'Another Declaration of Independence': John Neal's *Rachel Dyer* and the Assault on Precedent," *Early American Literature* 42, no. 3 (2007): 411.

2. Alfred S. Konefsky, "Piety and Profession: Simon Greenleaf and the Case of the Stillborn Bowdoin Law School, 1850–1861," *New England Quarterly* 85, no. 4 (2012): 717.

Bibliography

PRIMARY SOURCES

Anonymous. "Administration of Justice in New York." *Law Reporter* 2, no. 2 (1839): 33–42.

———. "Codification of the Laws of the United States of America." *Jurist, or Quarterly Journal of Jurisprudence and Legislation* 2, no. 1 (1828): 47–66.

———. "A Course of Legal Study." Review of *A Course of Legal Study*, by David Hoffman. *Biblical Repertory* 9, no. 4 (1837): 509–24.

———. "Doctrine of Contracts." Review of *An Essay on the Doctrine of Contracts*, by Gulian C. Verplanck. *United States Law Journal, and Civilian's Magazine* 2, no. 5 (1826): 72–120.

———. "Hoffman's Legal Outlines." Review of *Legal Outlines*, by David Hoffman. *American Jurist and Law Magazine* 3 (1830): 86–100.

———. "Legal Education." Review of *An Introductory Lecture, Delivered at King's College, London, November, 1, 1831*, by J. J. Park. *American Jurist and Law Magazine* 8 (1832): 247–60.

——— [V.]. Review of *An Introductory Lecture, Preparatory to a Course of Instruction on Common and Statute Law*, by Jesse Bledsoe. *Cincinnati Literary Gazette* 1, no. 9 (1824): 65–66.

———. "Sketch of the Law School at Cambridge." *American Jurist and Law Magazine* 13 (1835): 103–26.

——— [M.]. "Whether Law Is a Science?" Review of *An Introductory Lecture, Delivered to the Law Class of Transylvania University, on the 8th of November, 1832*, by Daniel Mayes. *American Jurist and Law Magazine* 9 (1833): 349–70.

Anthon, John. "An Essay on the Study of Law." In *An Analytical Abridgment of the Commentaries of Sir William Blackstone*, 2nd ed., 17–59. Philadelphia: P. H. Nicklin & T. Johnson, 1832.

Baldwin, Briscoe Gerard. *Introductory Lecture Delivered by General Briscoe G. Baldwin before His Law School, in Staunton On Monday the 3d day of October, 1831*. Staunton, VA: K. Harper, 1831. Reprinted in Bryson, *Essays on Legal Education in Nineteenth Century Virginia*, 65–75.

Barry, William T. *An Introductory Lecture on the Study of the Law, Delivered in the Chapel of Transylvania University, on Monday, October 1, 1821*. Lexington, KY: W. G. Hunt [?], 1821.

———. "Letters of William T. Barry." *William and Mary College Quarterly* 13, no. 2 (1904): 107–16.

Bentham, Jeremy. *Principles of Legislation*. Translated by John Neal from the second corrected and enlarged edition of M. Dumont. Boston: Wells & Lilly, 1830.

Bledsoe, Jesse. *Introductory Lecture on Law*. Nashville: Republican & Gazette, 1827.

———. *An Introductory Lecture on the Study of the Law, Delivered in the Chapel of Transylvania University, on Monday, November 4, 1822*. Lexington: Joseph Ficklin, 1822.

———. *An Introductory Lecture, Preparatory to a Course of Instruction on Common and Statute Law, Delivered in the Chapel of Transylvania University, on Monday, November 3d, 1823*. Lexington: William Tanner, 1823.

Brackenridge, Hugh Henry. *Law Miscellanies: Containing an Introduction to the Study of the Law; Notes on Blackstone's Commentaries, Shewing the Variations of the Law of Penn-*

sylvania from the Law of England, and What Acts of Assembly Might Require to Be Repealed or Modified; Observations on Smith's Edition of the Laws of Pennsylvania; Strictures on Decisions of the Supreme Court of the United States, and Certain Acts of Congress, with Some Law Cases, and a Variety of Other Materials, Chiefly Original. Philadelphia: P. Byrne, 1814. Reprint, New York: Arno Press, 1972.

Brockenbrough, John W. *Introductory Address to the Law Class of Lexington.* Lexington: Gazette Office, 1849.

Bryant, William Cullen. *A Discourse on the Life, Character and Writings of Gulian Crommelin Verplanck.* New York, 1870.

Bryson, W. Hamilton, ed. *Essays on Legal Education in Nineteenth Century Virginia.* Buffalo, NY: William S. Hein & Co., 1998.

Butler, Benjamin F. *Plan for the Organization of a Law Faculty and for a System of Instruction in Legal Science, in the University of the City of New-York.* New York: University Press, 1835.

Chipman, Daniel. *An Essay on the Law of Contracts, for the Payment of Specifick Articles.* Middlebury, VT: J.W. Copeland, 1822.

———. *The Life of Hon. Nathaniel Chipman, LL.D. . . . with Selections from His Miscellaneous Papers.* Boston: Charles C. Little and James Brown, 1846.

Chipman, Nathaniel. *Principles of Government: A Treatise on Free Institutions Including the Constitution of the United States.* Burlington, VT: Edward Smith, 1833. Reprint, Union, NJ: Lawbook Exchange, 2000.

Cooper, Thomas. *An Account of the Trial of Thomas Cooper, of Northumberland; on a Charge of Libel against the President of the United States.* Philadelphia: John Bioren, 1800.

———. *The Bankrupt Law of America, Compared with the Bankrupt Law of England.* Philadelphia: John Thompson, 1801. Reprint, Littleton, CO: Fred B. Rothman & Co., 1992.

———. "Bentham's Judicial Evidence." Review of *Rationale of Judicial Evidence Specially Applied to English Practice,* by Jeremy Bentham. *Southern Review* 5, no. 10 (1830): 381–426.

———, ed. *The Institutes of Justinian. With Notes by Thomas Cooper, Esq.* Philadelphia: P. Byrne, 1812.

———. *Introductory Lecture to a Course of Law.* Columbia, SC: Telescope Office, 1834.

———. *Lectures on the Elements of Political Economy.* 2nd ed. Columbia, SC: M'Morris & Wilson, 1829. Reprint, New York: Augustus M. Kelley Publishers, 1971.

———, ed. *Narrative of the Proceedings against Thomas Cooper, Esquire, President Judge of the Eighth Judiciary District of Pennsylvania, on a Charge of Official Misconduct.* Lancaster, PA: William Hamilton, 1811.

———. *The Opinion of Judge Cooper, on the Effect of a Sentence of a Foreign Court of Admiralty.* Philadelphia: Alexander James Dallas, 1810.

———. *Philosophical Writings of Thomas Cooper.* Edited by Udo Thiel. 3 vols. Bristol: Thoemmes Press, 2001.

———. *Some Information Respecting America.* Dublin, Ire.: William Porter, 1794. Reprint, New York: Augustus M. Kelley Publishers, 1969.

———, ed. *Tracts on Medical Jurisprudence.* Philadelphia: James Webster, 1819. Reprint, Clark, NJ: Lawbook Exchange, 2007.

———. *Two Essays.* Columbia, SC: D. & J. M. Faust, 1826.

Cruise, Peter. "Legal Outlines." Review of *Legal Outlines,* by David Hoffman. *North American Review* 30 (1830): 135–60.

Cushing, Caleb. "The First Part of the Institutes of the Laws of England." *North American Review* 13 (1821): 255–86.

———. "The General Laws of Massachusetts." *North American Review* 17 (1823): 69–91.

———. "On the Study of the Civil Law." *North American Review* 11 (1820): 407–12.

———. "United States Law Journal and Civilian's Magazine." *North American Review* 16 (1823): 181–83.

Dane, Nathan. *A General Abridgment and Digest of American Law.* Vol. 1. Boston: Cummings, Hilliard & Co., 1823.

Daveis, Charles Stewart. "A Dissertation on the Nature and Extent of the Jurisdiction of the Courts of the United States." *North American Review* 21 (1825): 104–41.

Du Ponceau, Peter S. "An Address Delivered at the Opening of the Law Academy of Philadelphia." *Journal of Jurisprudence* 1 (1821): 211–22.

———. *Address Delivered before the Law Academy of Philadelphia, on the Opening of the Session 1831–2*. Philadelphia: Mifflin & Parry, 1831.

———. *A Dissertation on the Nature and Extent of the Jurisdiction of the Courts of the United States*. Philadelphia: Abraham Small, 1824. Reprint, New York: Arno Press, 1972.

Duyckinck, Evert A. and George L. Duyckinck, eds. *Cyclopædia of American Literature; Embracing Personal and Critical Notices of Authors, and Selections from Their Writings. From the Earliest Period to the Present Day with Portraits, Autographs, and Other Illustrations*. 2 vols. New York: Charles Scribner, 1855.

Follen, Charles. "Law School at Cambridge." *North American Review* 36 (1833): 395–418.

Green, Nathan. *Address by Hon. Nathan Green, Judge of the Supreme Court of Tennessee, Delivered February 28th, 1849, on Entering the Duties of Professor of Law in Cumberland University, at Lebanon, Tennessee*. Lebanon: J. T. Figures, 1849.

Greenleaf, Simon. *A Discourse Pronounced at the Inauguration of the Author as Royall Professor of Law in Harvard University, August 26, 1834*. Cambridge: James Munroe and Company, 1834.

———. "Notes of Professor Greenleaf's Introductory Lecture, at the Present Term." *Law Reporter* 1, no. 8 (1838): 217–23.

Grimké, Thomas S. *An Oration, on the Practicability and Expediency of Reducing the Whole Body of the Law to the Simplicity and Order of a Code*. Charleston, SC: A. E. Miller, 1827.

———. *Reflections on the Character and Objects of All Science and Literature, and on the Relative Excellence and Value of Religious and Secular Education, and of Sacred and Classical Literature: in Two Addresses and an Oration with Additions and Improvements*. New Haven, CT: Hezekiah Howe, 1831.

Hillard, George Stillman. "A Course of Legal Study." Review of *A Course of Legal Study*, by David Hoffman. *North American Review* 46, no. 98 (1838): 72–82.

———. "Walker's Introduction to American Law." Review of *Introduction to American Law*, by Timothy Walker. *American Jurist and Law Magazine* 18 (1838): 375–90.

Hoffman, David. *A Course of Legal Study, Addressed to Students and the Profession Generally*. 2nd ed. Baltimore: Joseph Neal, 1836. Reprint, New York: Arno Press, 1972.

———. *Legal Outlines, Being the Substance of a Course of Lectures Now Delivering in the University of Maryland*. Baltimore: Edward J. Coale, 1829.

———. *Miscellaneous Thoughts on Men, Manners, and Things; by Anthony Grumbler, of Grumbleton Hall, Esquire*. Baltimore: Coale & Co., 1837.

———. *Viator; or, a Peep into My Note Book*. Baltimore: Plaskitt & Cugle, 1841.

Hopkinson, Joseph. *An Address Delivered before the Law Academy of Philadelphia, at the Opening of the Session of 1826–7*. Philadelphia: Mifflin & Perry, 1826.

———. "An Essay on the Doctrine of Contracts." Review of *An Essay on the Doctrine of Contracts*, by Gulian C. Verplanck. *American Quarterly Review* 1 (1827): 106–29.

Humphreys, Charles. *An Introductory Law Lecture*. Lexington, KY: Thomas Smith, 1826.

Kent, James. *Commentaries on American Law*. 4 vols. New York: O. Halsted, 1826–1830. Reprint, Baton Rouge: Claitor's Publishing.

———. *An Introductory Lecture to a Course of Law Lectures*. New York: Francis Childs, 1794. Reprinted as "Kent's Introductory Lecture," *Columbia Law Review* 3 (1909): 330–43.

———. *A Lecture, Introductory to a Course of Law Lectures in Columbia College*. New York: Clayton & Van Norden, 1824.

———. "An Unpublished Letter of Chancellor James Kent." *Green Bag* 9 (1897): 206–11.

Legaré, Hugh Swinton. "Bankrupt Law." *New York Review* 7, no. 14 (1840): 440–75.

———. "Codification." Review of *A History of English Law*, by George Crabb. *Southern Review* 7, no. 14 (1831): 391–412.

———. "Commentaries on American Law." Review of *Commentaries on American Law*, by James Kent. *Southern Review* 2, no. 3 (1828): 72–113.

———. "D'aguesseau." Review of *Memoir of the Life of Henry Francis D'Aguesseau, Chancellor of France*, by Charles Butler. *Southern Review* 8, no. 16 (1832): 399–443.

———. "Jeremy Bentham and the Utilitarians." Review of *Principles of Legislation*, by Jeremy Bentham. *Southern Review* 7, no. 14 (1831): 261–96.

———. "Law of Tenures." Review of *Observations on the Actual State of the English Laws of Real Property, with the outlines of a Code*, by James Humphreys. *Southern Review* 3, no. 5 (1829): 1–31.

———. "Legal Outlines." Review of *Legal Outlines*, by David Hoffman. *Southern Review* 4, no. 7 (1829): 47–69.

———. "Origin, History, and Influence of Roman Legislation." *New York Review* 5 (1839): 269–334.

Littell, William. *A Lecture, delivered at Frankfort, Ky. January 15th, 1818, by William Littell, Esq. L.L. D. On the Necessity of Establishing Law Colleges in the United States*. Frankfort, KY: Bledsoe & Farnham, 1818.

Mayes, Daniel. *An Address Delivered before the Trustees and Faculty of Transylvania University at the Opening of the Session of the Law Department, On the 7th Nov. 1831*. Lexington, KY: N. L. Finnell & J. F. Herndon, 1831.

———. *An Address to the Students of Law in Transylvania University, Delivered at the Beginning of the Session for 1835*. Lexington: J. Clarke & Co., 1835.

———. *An Introductory Lecture, Delivered to the Law Class of Transylvania University, on the 5th November, 1832*. Lexington: H. Savary & Co., 1832.

Metcalf, Theron. "A Collection of Cases Overruled, Doubted, or Limited." *North American Review* 15 (1822): 65–72.

Neal, John. "Biographical Notice of Jeremy Bentham." In Bentham, *Principles of Legislation*, 9–118.

———. *Wandering Recollections of a Somewhat Busy Life: An Autobiography*. Boston: Roberts Brothers, 1869.

Paley, William. *The Principles of Moral and Political Philosophy*. 1785. Indianapolis: Liberty Fund, 2002.

Parker, Isaac. "Inaugural Address Delivered in the Chapel of Harvard University, by the Hon. Isaac Parker, Chief Justice of Massachusetts, and Royall Professor of Law." *North American Review* 3, no. 7 (1816): 11–27.

Phillips, Willard. "Commentaries on American Law." *North American Review* 24 (1827): 345–65.

———. *A Manual of Political Economy, with Particular Reference to the Institutions, Resources, and Condition of the United States*. Boston, 1828. Reprint, New York: Augustus M. Kelley Publishers, 1968.

Porter, Jonathan. "Lectures on the Elements of Political Economy." *North American Review* 25 (1827): 408–25.

Preston, W. C. *Eulogy on Hugh Swinton Legaré*. Charleston, SC: Mayor and Aldermen of Charleston, 1843.

Priestley, Joseph. *An Essay on the First Principles of Government*. 2nd ed. 1771. In *Joseph Priestly: Political Writings*. Edited by Peter N. Miller, 1–127. Cambridge: Cambridge University Press, 1993.

Quincy, Josiah. *An Address Delivered at the Dedication of Dane Law College in Harvard University, October 23, 1832*. Cambridge, MA: E. W. Metcalf & Co., 1832.

Raymond, Daniel. *The Elements of Constitutional Law and of Political Economy*. 4th ed. Baltimore: Cushing & Brother, 1840.

———. *Thoughts on Political Economy*. Baltimore: Fielding Lucas, Jun'r, 1820.

Reed, John. *Pennsylvania Blackstone; Being a Modification of the Commentaries of Sir William Blackstone, with Numerous Alterations and Additions, Designed to Present an Elementary Exposition of the Entire Laws of Pennsylvania*. 3 vols. Carlisle, PA: George Fleming, 1831.

Rives, William C. "Sketch of the Character and Genius of Hugh S. Legare." *American Law Magazine* 2, no. 4 (1844): 259–71.
Robertson, George. *Scrap Book on Law and Politics, Men and Times*. Lexington, KY: A. W. Elder, 1855.
Sampson, William. *Sampson's Discourse, and Correspondence with Various Learned Jurists, upon the History of the Law, with the Addition of Several Essays, Tracts, and Documents, Relating to the Subject*. Washington, DC: Gales & Seaton, 1826.
Stearns, Asahel. "An Essay on the Law of Contracts for the Payment of Specific Articles." *North American Review* 17 (1823): 375–83.
Story, Joseph. "Autobiography." In W. Story, *Miscellaneous Writings*, 1–39.
———. "Codification of the Common Law. A Report of the Commissioners, January, 1837." In W. Story, *Miscellaneous Writings*, 698–734.
———. *Commentaries on Equity Jurisprudence, as Administered in England and America*. 2nd ed. 2 vols. Boston: Little & Brown, 1839.
———. "A Course of Legal Study." Review of *A Course of Legal Study*, by David Hoffman. *North American Review* 6 (1817): 45–77.
———. *A Discourse Pronounced upon the Inauguration of the Author, as Dane Professor of Law in Harvard University, on the Twenty-Fifth Day of August, 1829*. Boston: Hilliard, Gray, Little, and Wilkins, 1829.
———. "A General Abridgment and Digest of American Law." *North American Review* 23 (1826): 1–41.
———. *Joseph Story and the* Encyclopedia Americana. Clark, NJ: Lawbook Exchange, Ltd., 2006.
———. "Laws of the Sea with Reference to Maritime Commerce During Peace and War." *North American Review* 7 (1818): 323–47.
———. "Reports of Cases Adjudged in the Court of Chancery of New York." *North American Review* 11 (1820): 140–66.
———, ed. *A Treatise of the Law Relative to Merchant Ships and Seamen*, by Charles Abbott. Newburyport, MA: Edward Little & Co., 1810.
———. "A Treatise on the Law of Insurance." *North American Review* 20 (1825): 47–76.
———. "Tribute to Mr. Legaré." *Law Reporter* 6, no. 4 (1843): 188–90.
Story, William W., ed. *The Miscellaneous Writings of Joseph Story*. Boston: Little & Brown, 1852. Reprint, Lawbook Exchange, 2000.
Thompson, Lucas Powell. *Introductory Lecture Delivered by Judge Lucas P. Thompson Before His Law School in Staunton, December 3, 1839*. Staunton, VA, 1839. Reprinted in Bryson, *Essays on Legal Education in Nineteenth Century Virginia*, 117–28.
Ticknor, George. *Life, Letters, and Journals of George Ticknor*. 2 vols. Boston: Houghton Mifflin Company, 1909.
Tucker, Henry St. George. *Commentaries on the Laws of Virginia, Comprising the Substance of a Course of Lectures Delivered to the Winchester Law School*. 2 vols. Winchester, VA: Winchester Virginian, 1831.
———. *A Few Lectures on Natural Law*. Charlottesville, VA: James Alexander, 1844.
———. *Introductory Lecture Delivered by the Professor of Law in the University of Virginia, at the Opening of the Law School in September, 1841*. Charlottesville, VA: Magruder & Noel, 1841.
———. *Lectures on Government*. Charlottesville, VA: James Alexander, 1844.
Tucker, N. Beverley. "Law Lecture at William and Mary." *Southern Literary Messenger* 1, no. 4 (1834): 145–54.
———. "A Lecture, Delivered to the Law Class of William and Mary, June 17, 1839, Being the Last of a Course of Lectures on the Philosophy of Government and Constitutional Law." *Southern Literary Messenger* 5, no. 9 (1839): 587–92.
———. "Professor Beverley Tucker's Valedictory Address to His Class." *Southern Literary Messenger* 1, no. 11 (1835): 597–602.
Verplanck, Gulian C. "Address on the Fine Arts." In *Discourses and Addresses*, 121–59.
———. *The Advantages and the Dangers of the American Scholar*. New York: Wiley and Long, 1836.

———. *Discourses and Addresses on Subjects of American History, Arts, and Literature.* New York: J. & J. Harper, 1833.
———. *An Essay on the Doctrine of Contracts: Being an Inquiry How Contracts Are Affected in Law and Morals, by Concealment, Error, or Inadequate Price.* New York: G. & C. Carvill, 1825. Reprint, New York: Arno Press, 1972.
———. "The Law of Literary Property." In *Discourses and Addresses*, 215–27.
———. *A Letter to Col. William Drayton, of South-Carolina, in Assertion of the Constitutional Power of Congress to Impose Protecting Duties.* New York: E. Bliss, 1831.
———. *The Right Moral Influence and Use of Liberal Studies.* New York: J. & J. Harper, 1833.
———. *Speech When in Committee of the Whole, in the Senate of New-York, on the Several Bills and Resolutions for the Amendment of the Law and the Reform of the Judiciary System.* Albany, NY: Hoffman & White, 1839.
Walker, Timothy. *Introduction to American Law, Designed as a First Book for Students.* Philadelphia: P. H. Nicklin & T. Johnson, 1837. Reprint, New York: Da Capo Press, 1972.
———. *Introductory Lecture on the Dignity of the Law as a Profession, Delivered at the Cincinnati College, on the Fourth of November, 1837.* Cincinnati: Daily Gazette Office, 1837.
Webster, Daniel. "Reports of Cases Argued and Adjudged in the Supreme Court of the United States." *North American Review* 8 (1818): 63–71.
Wheaton, Henry. "An Essay on the Doctrine of Contracts." Review of *An Essay on the Doctrine of Contracts*, by Gulian C. Verplanck. *North American Review* 22 (1826): 253–73.
———. "A Treatise on Maritime Contracts." *North American Review* 13 (1821): 1–20.
———. "A Treatise on the Practice in the Supreme Court of New York." *North American Review* 18 (1824): 204–11.
———. "Reports of Cases Argued and Determined in the Circuit Court of the United States, for the First Circuit." *North American Review* 8 (1819): 253–76.
Wilson, James. *Collected Works of James Wilson.* Edited by Kermit L. Hall and Mark David Hall. 2 vols. Indianapolis, IN: Liberty Fund, Inc., 2007.

CASES

American Ins. Co. v. Bryan, 26 Wend. 563 (N.Y. 1841).
American Ins. Co. v. Ogden, 20 Wend. 287 (N.Y. 1838).
Davis v. Shields, 26 Wend. 341 (N.Y. 1841).
Ex Parte Dupont, 5 S.C. Eq. (Harp. Eq.) 5 (1824).
Kirkpatrick v. Stainer, 22 Wend. 244 (N.Y. 1839).
Laidlaw v. Organ, 15 U.S. 178 (1817).
Lochner v. New York, 198 U.S. 45 (1905).
McLaren v. Watson's Exec'r, 26 Wend. 425 (N.Y. 1841).
People v. White, 24 Wend. 520 (N.Y. 1840).
Powell v. Myers, 26 Wend. 591 (N.Y. 1841).
Ryckman v. Delavan, 25 Wend. 186 (N.Y. 1840).
Saltus v. Everett, 20 Wend. 267 (N.Y. 1838).
Shanks v. Dupont, 28 U.S. 242 (1830).
Swift v. Tyson, 41 U.S. 1 (1842).
Thompson v. People, 23 Wend. 537 (N.Y. 1840).
Tripp v. Cook, 26 Wend. 143 (N.Y. 1841).

SECONDARY SOURCES

Appleby, Joyce. *Inheriting the Revolution: The First Generation of Americans*. Cambridge, MA: Harvard University Press, 2000.

Ariens, Michael. "Lost and Found: David Hoffman and the History of American Legal Ethics." *Arkansas Law Review* 67 (2014): 571–625.

Baker, Elizabeth Feaster. *Henry Wheaton, 1785–1848*. Philadelphia: University of Pennsylvania Press, 1937. Reprint, New York: Da Capo Press, 1971.

Barzun, Charles L. "Common Sense and Legal Science." *Virginia Law Review* 90 (2004): 1051–92.

Bloomfield, Maxwell. *American Lawyers in a Changing Society, 1776–1876*. Cambridge, MA: Harvard University Press, 1976.

———. "David Hoffman and the Shaping of a Republican Legal Culture." *Maryland Law Review* 38 (1979): 673–88.

Blumenthal, Susana L. "Metaphysics, Moral Sense, and the Pragmatism of the Law." *Law and History Review* 26, no. 1 (2008): 177–85.

———. "The Mind of a Moral Agent: Scottish Common Sense and the Problem of Responsibility in Nineteenth-Century American Law." *Law and History Review* 26, no. 1 (2008): 99–159.

Boorstin, Daniel J. *The Americans: The National Experience*. New York: Vintage Books, 1965.

———. *The Mysterious Science of the Law: An Essay on Blackstone's Commentaries*. Cambridge, MA: Harvard University Press, 1941. Reprint, University of Chicago Press, 1996.

Brown, Elizabeth G. "The Bar on a Frontier: Wayne County, 1796–1836." *American Journal of Legal History* 14, no. 2 (1970): 136–56.

Cain, Marvin R. "Return of Republicanism: A Reappraisal of Hugh Swinton Legaré and the Tyler Presidency." *South Carolina Historical Magazine* 79, no. 1 (1978): 264–80.

Calhoun, Daniel H. *Professional Lives in America: Structure and Aspiration, 1750–1850*. Cambridge, MA: Harvard University Press, 1965.

Carlson, David J. "'Another Declaration of Independence': John Neal's *Rachel Dyer* and the Assault on Precedent." *Early American Literature* 42, no. 3 (2007): 405–34.

Carrington, Paul D. "The Revolutionary Idea of University Legal Education." *William and Mary Law Review* 31, no. 3 (1990): 527–74.

———. "Teaching Law and Virtue at Transylvania University: The George Wythe Tradition in the Antebellum Years." *Mercer Law Review* 41 (1990): 673–99.

Cawthon, Elisabeth A., and David E. Narrett, eds. *Essays on English Law and the American Experience*. College Station, TX: Texas A&M University Press, 1994.

Chroust, Anton-Hermann. *The Rise of the Legal Profession in America: The Revolution and the Post-Revolutionary Era*. Vol. 2. Norman: University of Oklahoma Press, 1965.

Cocks, Raymond. *Foundations of the Modern Bar*. London: Sweet & Maxwell, 1983.

Collier, Christopher. "Tapping Reeve, the Connecticut Common Law, and America's First Law School." *Connecticut Supreme Court History* 1 (2006): 13–25.

Cook, Charles M. *The American Codification Movement: A Study of Antebellum Legal Reform*. Westport, CT: Greenwood Press, 1981.

Davis, Richard Beale. "The Early American Lawyer and the Profession of Letters." *Huntington Library Quarterly* 12, no. 2 (1949): 191–205.

———. *Intellectual Life in Jefferson's Virginia, 1790–1830*. Chapel Hill: University of North Carolina Press, 1964. Reprint, University of Tennessee Press, 1972.

———. *Literature and Society in Early Virginia, 1608–1840*. Baton Rouge: Louisiana State University Press, 1973.

Dinwiddy, J. R. "Early-Nineteenth-Century Reactions to Benthamism." In *Radicalism and Reform in Britain, 1780–1850*, 339–61. London: Hambledon Press, 1992.

Dorfman, Joseph. "Chancellor Kent and the Developing American Economy." *Columbia Law Review* 61 (1961): 1290–317.

Dowling, William C. *Literary Federalism in the Age of Jefferson: Joseph Dennie and the Port Folio, 1801–1812*. Columbia: University of South Carolina Press, 1999.
Ellis, Joseph J. *After the Revolution: Profiles of Early American Culture*. New York: W.W. Norton & Company, 1979.
Ellis, Richard E. *The Jeffersonian Crisis: Courts and Politics in the Young Republic*. New York: Oxford University Press, 1971.
Farmer, Fannie Memory. "Legal Education in North Carolina, 1820–1860." *North Carolina Historical Review* 28, no. 3 (1951): 271–97.
Ferguson, Robert A. *Law and Letters in American Culture*. Cambridge, MA: Harvard University Press, 1984.
———. *Reading the Early Republic*. Cambridge, MA: Harvard University Press, 2004.
Fernandez, Angela and Markus D. Dubber, eds. *Law Books in Action: Essays on the Anglo-American Legal Treatise*. Oxford: Hart Publishing, 2012.
Foletta, Marshall. *Coming to Terms with Democracy: Federalist Intellectuals and the Shaping of an American Culture*. Charlottesville: University Press of Virginia, 2001.
Friedman, Lawrence M. "American Legal History: Past and Present." *Journal of Legal Education* 34 (1984): 563–76.
———. "Heart against Head: Perry Miller and the Legal Mind." *Yale Law Journal* 77 (1968): 1244–59.
Gawalt, Gerard W. *The Promise of Power: The Emergence of the Legal Profession in Massachusetts, 1760–1840*. Westport, CT: Greenwood Press, 1979.
Glick, Wendell. "Bishop Paley in America." *New England Quarterly* 27, no. 3 (1954): 347–54.
Gold, David M. *The Shaping of Nineteenth-Century Law: John Appleton and Responsible Individualism*. New York: Greenwood Press, 1990.
Gordon, Robert W. "Critical Legal Histories." *Stanford Law Review* 36 (1984): 57–125.
Graham, Jenny. "Joseph Priestly in America." In *Joseph Priestly: Scientist, Philosopher, and Theologian*. Edited by Isabel Rivers and David L. Wykes, 203–30. Oxford: Oxford University Press, 2008.
Grossberg, Michael. "Institutionalizing Masculinity: The Law as a Masculine Profession." In *Meanings for Manhood: Constructions of Masculinity in Victorian America*. Edited by Mark C. Carnes and Clyde Griffen, 133–51. Chicago: University of Chicago Press, 1990.
———. "Legal History and Social Science: Friedman's *History of American Law*, the Second Time Around." *Law & Social Inquiry* 13, no. 2 (1988): 359–83.
———. "Social History Update: 'Fighting Faiths' and the Challenges of Legal History." *Journal of Social History* 25, no. 1 (1991): 191–201.
Grossberg, Michael, and Christopher Tomlins, eds. *The Long Nineteenth Century (1789–1920)*. Vol. 2, *The Cambridge History of Law in America*. New York: Cambridge University Press, 2008.
Haber, Samuel. *The Quest for Authority and Honor in the American Professions, 1750–1900*. Chicago: University of Chicago Press, 1991.
Hadden, Sally E. and Patricia Hagler Minter, eds. *Signposts: New Directions in Southern Legal History*. Athens: University of Georgia Press, 2013.
Hall, Mark David. *The Political and Legal Philosophy of James Wilson, 1742–1798*. Columbia: University of Missouri Press, 1997.
Hamlin, Paul M. *Legal Education in Colonial New York*. New York: New York University Law Quarterly Review, 1939.
Helmholz, R. H. *Natural Law in Court: A History of Legal Theory in Practice*. Cambridge, MA: Harvard University Press, 2015.
———. "Use of the Civil Law in Post-Revolutionary American Jurisprudence." *Tulane Law Review* 66 (1992): 1649–84.
Henderson, Elizabeth K. "The Attack on the Judiciary in Pennsylvania, 1800–1810." *Pennsylvania Magazine of History and Biography* 61 (1937): 113–36.
Hoeflich, M. H. "The Americanization of British Legal Education in the Nineteenth Century." *Journal of Legal History* 8, no. 3 (1987): 244–59.

———. "*Laidlaw v. Organ*, Gulian C. Verplanck, and the Shaping of Early Nineteenth Century Contract Law: A Tale of a Case and a Commentary." *University of Illinois Law Review* 1991, no. 1 (1991): 55–66.
———. "Law & Geometry: Legal Science from Leibniz to Langdell." *American Journal of Legal History* 30 (1986): 95–121.
———. "The Lawyer as Pragmatic Reader: The History of Legal Common-Placing." *Arkansas Law Review* 55 (2002): 87–122.
———. *Legal Publishing in Antebellum America*. New York: Cambridge University Press, 2010.
———. *Roman and Civil Law and the Development of Anglo-American Jurisprudence in the Nineteenth Century*. Athens: University of Georgia Press, 1997.
———. "Roman Law and Forensic Oratory in Antebellum America." *Zeitschrift der Savigny-Stiftung für Rechtsgeschichte. Romanistische Abtheilung* 120 (2003): 189–99.
———. "Roman Law in American Legal Culture." *Tulane Law Review* 66 (1992): 1723–43.
———. "Translation and the Reception of Foreign Law in the Antebellum United States." *American Journal of Comparative Law* 50 (2002): 753–75.
Hofstadter, Richard. *The Progressive Historians: Turner, Beard, Parrington*. New York: Alfred A. Knopf, 1969.
Holmes, Oliver Wendell. *The Collected Legal Papers*. New York: Harcourt, Brace, and Co., 1920. Reprint, Mineola, NY: Dover Publications, Inc., 2007.
Honeywell, Roy J. "Nathaniel Chipman: Political Philosopher and Jurist." *New England Quarterly* 5, no. 3 (1932): 555–84.
Horwitz, Morton J. *The Transformation of American Law, 1780–1860*. Cambridge, MA: Harvard University Press, 1977.
Hulsebosch, Daniel J. *Constituting Empire: New York and the Transformation of Constitutionalism in the Atlantic World, 1664-1830*. Chapel Hill: University of North Carolina Press, 2005.
———. "Debating the Transformation of American Law: James Kent, Joseph Story, and the Legacy of the Revolution." In *Transformations in American Legal History: Essays in Honor of Professor Morton J. Horwitz*. Edited by Daniel W. Hamilton and Alfred L. Brophy, 1–27. Cambridge, MA: Harvard University Press, 2009.
———. "An Empire of Law: Chancellor Kent and the Revolution in Books in the Early Republic." *Alabama Law Review* 60, no. 2 (2009): 377–424.
Hurst, James Willard. "The Law in United States History." *Proceedings of the American Philosophical Society* 104, no. 5 (1960): 518–26.
———. "Legal History: A Research Program." *Wisconsin Law Review* (1942): 323–33.
———. "The State of Legal History." *Reviews in American History* 10, no. 4 (1982): 292–305.
Jacobstein, J. Myron, and Roy M. Mersky. *The Rejected: Sketches of the 26 Men Nominated for the Supreme Court but Not Confirmed by the Senate*. Milpitas: Toucan Valley Publications, 1993.
Johnson, Andrew J. *The Life and Constitutional Thought of Nathan Dane*. New York: Garland Publishing, 1987.
July, Robert W. *The Essential New Yorker: Gulian Crommelin Verplanck*. Durham, NC: Duke University Press, 1951.
Kelley, Maurice. *Additional Chapters on Thomas Cooper*, University of Maine Studies. Orono: University of Maine Press, 1930.
Kerr, Charles. "Transylvania University's Law Department." *Americana* 31, no. 1 (1937): 7–44.
King, Peter J. "John Neal as a Benthamite." *New England Quarterly* 39, no. 1 (1966): 47–65.
———. *Utilitarian Jurisprudence in America: The Influence of Bentham and Austin on American Legal Thought in the Nineteenth Century*. New York: Garland Publishing, 1986.

Klafter, Craig Evan. *Reason over Precedents: Origins of American Legal Thought*. Westport, CT: Greenwood Press, 1993.

———. "St. George Tucker: The First Modern American Law Professor." *Journal of the Historical Society* 6, no. 1 (2006): 133–50.

Konefsky, Alfred S. "The Legal Profession: From the Revolution to the Civil War." In Grossberg and Tomlins, *Cambridge History*, 68–105.

———. "Piety and Profession: Simon Greenleaf and the Case of the Stillborn Bowdoin Law School, 1850–1861." *New England Quarterly* 85, no. 4 (2012): 695–734.

Konkle, Burton Alva. *Joseph Hopkinson, 1770–1842: Jurist: Scholar: Inspirer of the Arts*. Philadelphia: University of Pennsylvania Press, 1931.

"Law Schools and Their Course of Study." *Western Jurist* 4 (1870): 1–12.

Lemmings, David. *Professors of the Law: Barristers and English Legal Culture in the Eighteenth Century*. Oxford: Oxford University Press, 2000.

Levy, Leonard W. *The Law of the Commonwealth and Chief Justice Shaw*. Cambridge, MA: Harvard University Press, 1957. Reprint, New York: Harper & Row, 1967.

Lieberman, David. *The Province of Legislation Determined: Legal Theory in Eighteenth-Century Britain*. Cambridge: Cambridge University Press, 1989.

Lobban, Michael. "The Age of the Federalists." Chap. 5 in *A History of the Philosophy of Law in the Common Law World, 1600–1900*. Vol. 8, *A Treatise of Legal Philosophy and General Jurisprudence*. Dordrecht: Springer, 2007.

———. *The Common Law and English Jurisprudence, 1760–1850*. Oxford: Oxford University Press, 1991.

MacGill, Hugh C., and R. Kent Newmyer. "Legal Education and Legal Thought, 1790–1920." In Grossberg and Tomlins, *Cambridge History*, 36–67.

Malone, Dumas. *The Public Life of Thomas Cooper, 1783–1839*. New Haven, CT: Yale University Press, 1926. Reprint, Columbia: University of South Carolina Press, 1961.

Manchester, A. H. *A Modern Legal History of England and Wales, 1750-1950*. London: Butterworths, 1980.

Mikhail, John. "Scottish Common Sense and Nineteenth-Century American Law: A Critical Appraisal." *Law and History Review* 26, no. 1 (2008): 167–75.

Miller, Perry. "The Common Law and Codification in Jacksonian America." *Proceedings of the American Philosophical Society* 103 (1959): 463–68.

———, ed. *The Legal Mind in America from Independence to the Civil War*. New York: Anchor Books, 1962. Reprint, Ithaca, NY: Cornell University Press, 1969.

———. *The Life of the Mind in America from the Revolution to the Civil War*. New York: Harcourt, Brace & World, Inc., 1965.

Nelson, William E. *Americanization of the Common Law: The Impact of Legal Change on Massachusetts Society, 1760–1830*. Cambridge, MA: Harvard University Press, 1975.

Newmyer, R. Kent. *Supreme Court Justice Joseph Story: Statesman of the Old Republic*. Chapel Hill: University of North Carolina Press, 1985.

Novak, William J. "Law, Capitalism, and the Liberal State: The Historical Sociology of James Willard Hurst." *Law and History Review* 18, no. 1 (2000): 97–145.

O'Brien, Michael. *A Character of Hugh Legaré*. Knoxville: University of Tennessee Press, 1985.

———. "Politics, Romanticism, and Hugh Legaré: 'The Fondness of Disappointed Love.'" In *Intellectual Life in Antebellum Charleston*. Edited by Michael O'Brien and David Moltke-Hansen, 123–51. Knoxville: University of Tennessee Press, 1986.

Oldham, James. *English Common Law in the Age of Mansfield*. Chapel Hill: University of North Carolina Press, 2004.

Parker, Kunal M. *Common Law, History, and Democracy in America, 1790–1900: Legal Thought before Modernism*. New York: Cambridge University Press, 2011.

Parrington, Vernon L. *The Romantic Revolution in America*. Vol. 2, *Main Currents in American Thought: An Interpretation of American Literature from the Beginning to 1920*. New York: Harcourt, Brace & Co., 1927.

Pearson, Ellen Holmes. *Remaking Custom: Law and Identity in the Early American Republic*. Charlottesville: University of Virginia Press, 2011.

Rhea, Linda. *Hugh Swinton Legaré: A Charleston Intellectual*. Chapel Hill: University of North Carolina Press, 1934.

Rogers, C. Paul. "Scots Law in Post-Revolutionary and Nineteenth-Century America: The Neglected Jurisprudence." *Law and History Review* 8, no. 2 (1990): 205–35.

Rorty, Richard. "The Historiography of Philosophy: Four Genres." In *Philosophy in History: Essays on the Historiography of Philosophy*. Edited by Richard Rorty, J. B. Schneewind, and Quentin Skinner, 49–75. Cambridge: Cambridge University Press, 1984.

Schofield, Philip. *Utility and Democracy: The Political Thought of Jeremy Bentham*. Oxford: Oxford University Press, 2006.

Schweber, Howard. "The 'Science' of Legal Science: The Model of the Natural Sciences in Nineteenth-Century American Legal Education." *Law and History Review* 17, no. 3 (1999): 421–66.

Seo, Sarah A., and John Fabian Witt. "The Metaphysics of Mind and the Practical Science of the Law." *Law and History Review* 26, no. 1 (2008): 161–66.

Shaffer, Thomas L. "David Hoffman on the Bible as a Law Book." *Christian Legal Society Quarterly*, Fall 1981.

———. "David Hoffman's Law School Lectures, 1822–1833." *Journal of Legal Education* 32 (1982): 127–38.

Shapiro, Barbara J. *"Beyond Reasonable Doubt" and "Probable Cause": Historical Perspectives on the Anglo-American Law of Evidence*. Berkeley: University of California Press, 1991.

———. "Law and Science in Seventeenth-Century England." *Stanford Law Review* 21 (1969): 727–66.

Sheppard, Steve. "Casebooks, Commentaries, and Curmudgeons: An Introductory History of Law in the Lecture Hall." *Iowa Law Review* 82, no. 2 (1997): 547–644.

Simpson, A. W. B. "The Rise and Fall of the Legal Treatise: Legal Principles and the Forms of Legal Literature." *University of Chicago Law Review* 48 (1981): 632–79.

Smith, Wilson. "William Paley's Theological Utilitarianism in America." *William and Mary Quarterly* 11, no. 3 (1954): 402–24.

Spann, Edward K. *Ideals and Politics: New York Intellectuals and Liberal Democracy, 1820–1880*. Albany: State University of New York Press, 1972.

Spaulding, Norman W. "The Myth of Civic Republicanism: Interrogating the Ideology of Antebellum Legal Ethics." *Fordham Law Review* 71 (2003): 1397–459.

Stein, Peter. "The Attraction of the Civil Law in Post-Revolutionary America." *Virginia Law Review* 52 (1966): 403–34.

Stevens, Robert. *Law School: Legal Education in America from the 1850s to the 1980s*. Chapel Hill: University of North Carolina Press, 1983.

Warren, Charles. *A History of the American Bar*. Boston: Little, Brown and Company, 1911. Reprint, Washington, DC: Beard Books, 1999.

Widmer, Edward L. *Young America: The Flowering of Democracy in New York City*. New York: Oxford University Press, 1999.

Wright, John D., Jr. *Transylvania: Tutor to the West*. Lexington, KY: Transylvania University, 1975.

Index

About the Author

Steven J. Macias is assistant professor of law at Southern Illinois University, Carbondale, where he has taught since 2011. Prior to that, he held visiting positions at the University of Oregon and California Western School of Law. He received graduate degrees in law and history from the University of California, Berkeley, and University College London, and he completed his undergraduate education at Stanford University. His primary interest is the history of American legal and political thought. This is his first book.

www.ingramcontent.com/pod-product-compliance
Ingram Content Group UK Ltd.
Pitfield, Milton Keynes, MK11 3LW, UK
UKHW012040150926
475560UK00001B/102

9 781498 51946